Thomas Archer

Our Sunday Book of Reading and Pictures

Thomas Archer

Our Sunday Book of Reading and Pictures

ISBN/EAN: 9783744754552

Printed in Europe, USA, Canada, Australia, Japan

Cover: Foto ©Thomas Meinert / pixelio.de

More available books at **www.hansebooks.com**

OUR SUNDAY BOOK

OF

READING AND PICTURES

Mamma's Bible Stories. First Series.
For Her Little Boys and Girls. In simple language. With Twelve Engravings. Cloth, price 2s.

Mamma's Bible Stories. Second Series.
Uniform with the First Series. Cloth, price 2s.

Mamma's Bible Stories. Third Series.
By the Daughter of Mrs. Daniel Wilson (Author of the First and Second Series), and uniform with the same. Illustrated by Stanley Berkeley. Cloth, price 2s.

THE THREE VOLUMES IN CASE, PRICE 6s.

"A favourite with every Christian mother."—*North Devon Guardian.*
"We cordially recommend this beautiful little book."—*Schoolmaster.*
"Really within the comprehension of children."—*Daily Chronicle.*
"The illustrations are excellent, the style winning and motherly."—*Western Morning News.*
"An admirable little book."—*Literary Churchman.*
"The language is simple, the type excellent, the woodcuts spirited."—*Church Times.*
"Very good, large print, short easy words."—*Saturday Review.*
"We welcome this useful little book."—*English Churchman.*

The Pattern Life;
Or, Lessons from the Life of Our Lord. By W. CHATTERTON DIX. With Eight Illustrations by P. Priolo. Cloth, price 5s.

"This is a very good book indeed, of much sounder tone than most. Valuable aid to catechetical instruction."—*Church Times.*
"An admirable work, well suited for home reading to the little ones."—*Church Review.*
"We commend it to parents and teachers as a very useful book."—*Church Bells.*

GRIFFITH FARRAN OKEDEN & WELSH
NEWBERY HOUSE
LONDON AND SYDNEY

OUR SUNDAY BOOK

OF

READING AND PICTURES

EDITED AND ARRANGED

BY

THOMAS ARCHER

AUTHOR OF "ABOUT MY FATHER'S BUSINESS" "BY FIRE AND SWORD"
"MISS GRANTLEY'S GIRLS" "STRANGE WORK" "A FOOL'S PARADISE" "VANISHING LONDON"
"WAYFE SUMMERS" "DECISIVE EVENTS IN HISTORY" ETC. ETC.

GRIFFITH FARRAN OKEDEN & WELSH
NEWBERY HOUSE
LONDON AND SYDNEY

The Rights of Translation and of Reproduction are Reserved.

Contents.

SUNDAY,
THE OLD HUNDREDTH,
ELEGY WRITTEN IN A COUNTRY CHURCHYARD,
GOTHIC ARCHITECTURE,
THE CHURCH PORCH,
SUNDAY IN THE COUNTRY AND IN LONDON,
AN OLD CHURCH SERVICE,
HYMN,
SOME MEMORIALS OF THE LATE EMPEROR FREDERICK,
THE STORY OF THE SINGING BIRD,
THE SINGERS,
THE LARGER VIEW OF LIFE,
THE OLD SONG,
REFLECTION AT SEA,
RURAL LIFE IN SWEDEN,
CONTENT,
SELF-CONTROL,
TRAVELS BY THE FIRESIDE,
SUNDAY IN A NORWAY TOWN
WEDDING RINGS,
SOCIAL DISTINCTION,
CHILDREN,
PLAY,
RECREATION,
WORK,
GRACE BEFORE MEAT,

CONTENTS.

	PAGE
BE HAPPY TO-DAY,	74
GRANDMA'S TEAM,	75
AT SCHOOL AT ETON COLLEGE,	80
SMILING,	87
A NOVEMBER WALK,	88
RURAL LIFE IN ENGLAND,	92
THE LAW OF LOVE,	98
LINES WRITTEN IN EARLY SPRING,	99
TO A WATER FOWL,	100
TO THE SKYLARK,	102
TO THE EVENING STAR,	103
CHARITY OF THOUGHT,	104
THE LANGDALE PIKES,	107
WORDSWORTH AND HIS SISTER DOROTHY,	109
EVERMORE,	112
LETTERS OF BYGONE TIMES,	115
TO THE DANDELION,	116
THE BEST AMULETS,	118
HOURS OF EXALTATION,	121
THE SPIRIT IS THE LIFE,	125
PATIENCE,	125
EASTER DAY,	126
GOD AND HEAVEN,	128
O THOU WHO DRY'ST THE MOURNER'S TEAR,	129
DEATHS OF LITTLE CHILDREN,	130
MINISTRATION OF ANGELS,	134
REST,	135
MEMORIAL VERSES,	136
THE LEGEND OF RABBI BEN LEVI,	137
SEAWEED,	141
TWILIGHT,	142
A DREAM OF THE UNIVERSE,	144
HOW TO SEE WESTMINSTER ABBEY,	148
THE REPRISAL,	149
THE PRINCE'S DREAM,	150
STRENGTH OUT OF WEAKNESS,	157
EMPLOYMENT,	158
MUSIC,	161
EDUCATION OF CHILDREN,	162
HARROW-ON-THE-HILL,	162

CONTENTS.

	PAGE
ON A DISTANT VIEW OF THE VILLAGE AND SCHOOL OF HARROW-ON-THE-HILL,	165
THE POETRY OF A ROOT CROP,	166
THE VAUDOIS TEACHER,	167
THE MUSIC OF SPEECH,	168
ON JESTING,	169
SAVED BY A HYMN,	170
THE ERUPTION OF MOUNT VESUVIUS,	172
THE WRECK OF THE HESPERUS,	177
NOBLE REVENGE,	180
BERMUDIAN "ONIONS,"	182
MAN'S BUSINESS IN LIFE,	184
IN ILLNESS,	185
LEARNING THE VERBS,	186
THOU ART, O GOD,	188
THE VILLAGE PREACHER,	189
WHOM HAVE I IN HEAVEN BUT THEE?	191
PERPETUAL FORCE,	192
THE TURF SHALL BE MY FRAGRANT SHRINE,	195
CHARACTER OF CHARLES I.,	196
ANECDOTE CONCERNING THE EXECUTION OF CHARLES I.,	198
POSIES FOR THINE OWN BED-CHAMBER,	199
FAINTING BY THE WAY,	200
ABOU BEN ADHEM,	202
A JOURNEY ACROSS THE AMERICAN PLAINS,	205
THE BIRTH OF FREEDOM,	206
RIGHT-HAND GLOVES,	207
BENNY,	208
KISSING THE BABY,	210
FLOWERS AND SNOW,	211
A REAL CHRISTMAS GIFT,	215
HIS PILGRIMAGE,	220
SIR ROGER AT CHURCH,	222
ABOVE AND BELOW,	224
NOT MANY THINGS, BUT ONE THING WELL,	228
THE DAY IS DONE,	230
THE BATTLE OF BLENHEIM,	232
THE PILGRIMS AND GIANT DESPAIR,	237
TURN THE CARPET,	240
HOME SHOULD BE FIRST,	242
CARLYLE ON A FUTURE STATE,	243

CONTENTS.

	PAGE
MY PLAYMATE,	244
UNIVERSAL BEAUTY,	246
THE EFFICACY OF PRAYER,	248
THE OLD "DISCIPLINE" FOR THE CHILD,	251
THE LIE; OR, THE SOUL'S ERRAND,	252
NEW-BORN,	255
THE ROSE,	257
MERE "DUTY,"	258
LOVE'S SUPREMACY,	260
INSTRUMENTS OR EXERCISES TO PROCURE CONTENTEDNESS,	261
THE FORSAKEN FARMHOUSE,	264
THE GREAT COLLIERY ACCIDENT AT HARTLEY, 1862,	266
TO AUTUMN,	271
THE YOUNG COUPLE,	273
HOW TO PRESERVE YOUTH,	277
THE COMIC LITERATURE OF THE JAPANESE,	278
THE WIDOW OF NAPLES,	282
EVERY MOMENT'S DUTY,	284
HOW TO KEEP CHRISTMAS,	285

List of Full-page Illustrations.

	PAGE
RAMAH, THE ABODE AND BURIAL PLACE OF SAMUEL,	11
GENERAL VON MOLTKE,	33
HAND IN HAND,	55
ETON COLLEGE,	81
THE QUADRANGLE, ETON COLLEGE,	85
A LETTER FROM AUSTRALIA,	113
MOUNT TABOR,	119
THE LATE ABBE LISZT, THE GREAT PIANIST,	159
HARROW-ON-THE-HILL,	163
THE HOUR OF PRAYER,	203
ARARAT,	225
THE BATTLE OF BLENHEIM,	235

Sunday.

O DAY most calm, most bright,
The fruit of this, the next world's bud
The indorsement of supreme delight,
Writ by a friend, and with his blood;
The couch of time; care's balm and bay;
The week were dark but for thy light,
    Thy torch doth show the way.

    .   .   .   .

    Sundays the pillars are,
On which heaven's palace archèd lies;
The other days fill up the spare
And hollow room with vanities;
They are the fruitful beds and borders
In God's rich garden: that is bare
    Which parts their ranks and orders.

    .   .   .   .   .

    The Sundays of man's life,
Threaded together on time's string,
Make bracelets to adorn the life
Of the eternal glorious King.
On Sunday, heaven's gate stands ope;
Blessings are plentiful and ripe,
    More plentiful than hope.

                      GEORGE HERBERT.

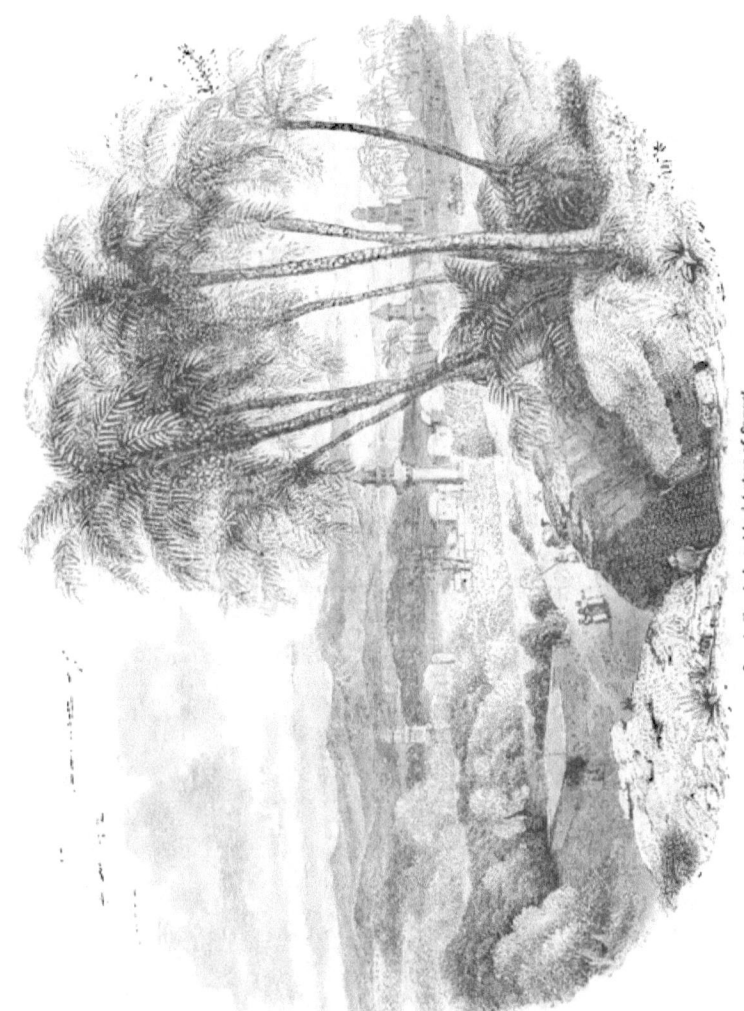

Ramah, the abode and burial place of Samuel

O TIMELY happy, timely wise,
Hearts that with rising morn arise;
Eyes that the beam celestial view,
Which evermore makes all things new!

New every morning is the love
Our wakening and uprising prove;
Through sleep and darkness safely brought,
Restored to life, and power, and thought.

New mercies, each returning day,
Hover around us while we pray;
New perils past, new sins forgiven,
New thoughts of God, new hopes of heaven.

If, on our daily course, our mind
Be set to hallow all we find,
New treasures still, of countless price,
God will provide for sacrifice.

The trivial round, the common task,
Will furnish all we need to ask;
Room to deny ourselves; a road
To bring us daily nearer God.

Only, O Lord, in Thy dear love
Fit us for perfect rest above;
And help us, this and every day,
To live more nearly as we pray.

The Old Hundredth.

THIS unique psalm-tune first appeared in John Calvin's "French Psalter," published in Geneva in 1543, as the "proper tune" to the 134th Psalm. Guilleaume Franc was musical editor of this work. He was a master in music, yet all that will be found in ordinary musical history regarding him is, that he was an "obscure musician of Strasbourg, of the sixteenth century." The Church owes him not a few of her finest melodies. A melody in Luther's Great Psalter, published from 1524 to 1560, seems to have suggested the ideas of this inimitable chorale. One of Luther's hymns of eight unequal lines, which was set to a melody of the Moravian or Waldensian early church, contains the elements of the Old Hundredth. But those were reset and remodelled by Franc, who left Strasbourg, and became "centeur," or precentor, to Theodore Beza, at Lausanne. He subsequently settled and died at Geneva, leaving as his imperishable monument the music of the "French Psalter." The music was afterwards adapted to the 100th Psalm in the first "English Psalter" ever published, edited by John Calvin, and printed for the use of the congregation of English-speaking refugees at Geneva in 1556, of which at that time John Knox was minister. The musical editor of this Psalter was Claude Goudimel, of Rome, who suffered martyrdom at Lyons, at the time of the massacre of St. Bartholomew, because he had set the English Psalms to music. This Genevan-English Psalter was reprinted in 1563–4, by "John Day, over the pump in Aldgate," and Andrew Hart, in Edinburgh, and laid the foundation of the psalmody of the Protestant Church of the world. The words of this Psalter contained thirty-seven Psalms written by Sternhold and Hopkins, the remainder being written by ten of the refugees of Geneva. William Keith, from Aberdeen, wrote the 100th Psalm. This Psalter, words and music, was for some time universally used by the Protestant Churches of England and Scotland.

When Oliver Cromwell got the Westminster General Assembly of Divines to prepare a new version of the Psalms in common metre, for the use of the churches, the Parliament sanctioned it, the English Church at once adopted it, but the Scottish people rebelled, on the ground that they had already a better Psalter of their own. Cromwell had to come to a compromise with the hardy Scots. (The only compromise he ever made in his life was with Cameron of

Lochiel, when he and his army got bewildered in the wilds of Lochaber.) This compromise was, that in Scotland a number of their favourite Psalms from the old Psalter might be published as second editions. This was done, and the music is thus called "Old"—the Old First, Old Forty-fourth, Old Hundredth, Old Hundred and Thirty-fourth, Old Hundred and Thirty-seventh, etc. These old Psalms are still sung in all Scottish churches, and the music of them (which,

with the exception of the Old Hundredth, had long fallen into disuse) has been recently revised. Dr. Mainzer, who characterized it as the finest psalmody of any age or any country, was one of the first who called attention to it, and now it is becoming the most appreciated and popular among the people. Many of the tunes will be found in the revised edition of the "Scottish Psalmody," all of them with the "old" words in Day's or Knox's old Psalters.

Elegy written in a Country Churchyard.

THE curfew tolls the knell of parting day,
  The lowing herd winds slowly o'er the lea,
The ploughman homeward plods his weary way,
  And leaves the world to darkness and to me.

Now fades the glimmering landscape on the sight,
  And all the air a solemn stillness holds,
Save where the beetle wheels his droning flight,
  And drowsy tinklings lull the distant folds;

Save that from yonder ivy-mantled tower
  The moping owl does to the moon complain
Of such as, wandering near her secret bower,
  Molest her ancient solitary reign.

Beneath those rugged elms, that yew-tree's shade,
  Where heaves the turf in many a mouldering heap,
Each in his narrow cell for ever laid,
  The rude forefathers of the hamlet sleep.

The breezy call of incense-breathing morn,
  The swallow twittering from the straw-built shed,
The cock's shrill clarion, or the echoing horn,
  No more shall rouse them from their lowly bed.

For them no more the blazing hearth shall burn,
  Or busy housewife ply her evening care:
No children run to lisp their sire's return,
  Or climb his knees the envied kiss to share.

Oft did the harvest to their sickle yield,
    Their furrow oft the stubborn glebe has broke;
How jocund did they drive their team a-field!
    How bowed the woods beneath their sturdy stroke!

Let not Ambition mock their useful toil,
    Their homely joys, and destiny obscure;
Nor Grandeur hear with a disdainful smile
    The short and simple annals of the Poor.

The boast of heraldry, the pomp of power,
    And all that beauty, all that wealth e'er gave,
Await alike the inevitable hour:—
    The paths of glory lead but to the grave.

Nor you, ye Proud, impute to these the fault
    If Memory o'er their tomb no trophies raise,
Where, through the long-drawn aisle and fretted vault,
    The pealing anthem swells the note of praise.

Can storied urn or animated bust
    Back to its mansion call the fleeting breath?
Can Honour's voice provoke the silent dust,
    Or Flattery soothe the dull cold ear of Death?

Perhaps in this neglected spot is laid
    Some heart once pregnant with celestial fire;
Hands, that the rod of empire might have swayed,
    Or waked to ecstasy the living lyre:

But Knowledge to their eyes her ample page,
    Rich with the spoils of time, did ne'er unroll;
Chill Penury repressed their noble rage,
    And froze the genial current of the soul.

Full many a gem of purest ray serene
    The dark unfathomed caves of ocean bear;
Full many a flower is born to blush unseen,
    And waste its sweetness on the desert air.

Some village Hampden that, with dauntless breast,
  The little tyrant of his fields withstood ;
Some mute inglorious Milton here may rest,
  Some Cromwell, guiltless of his country's blood.

The applause of listening senates to command,
  The threats of pain and ruin to despise,
To scatter plenty o'er a smiling land,
  And read their history in a nation's eyes,

Their lot forbade : nor circumscribed alone
  Their growing virtues, but their crimes confined ;
Forbade to wade through slaughter to a throne,
  And shut the gates of mercy on mankind ;

The struggling pangs of conscious truth to hide,
  To quench the blushes of ingenuous shame,
Or heap the shrine of Luxury and Pride
  With incense kindled at the Muse's flame.

Far from the madding crowd's ignoble strife,
  Their sober wishes never learned to stray ;
Along the cool, sequestered vale of life
  They kept the noiseless tenor of their way.

Yet e'en these bones from insult to protect
  Some frail memorial, still erected nigh,
With uncouth rhymes and shapeless sculpture decked,
  Implores the passing tribute of a sigh.

Their name, their years, spelt by the unlettered Muse,
  The place of fame and elegy supply :
And many a holy text around she strews,
  That teach the rustic moralist to die.

For who, to dumb forgetfulness a prey,
  This pleasing anxious being e'er resigned,
Left the warm precincts of the cheerful day,
  Nor cast one longing, lingering look behind !

On some fond breast the parting soul relies,
   Some pious drops the closing eye requires;
E'en from the tomb the voice of Nature cries,
   E'en in our ashes live their wonted fires.

For thee, who, mindful of the unhonoured dead,
   Dost in these lines their artless tale relate;

If chance, by lonely contemplation led,
   Some kindred spirit shall inquire thy fate,—

Haply some hoary-headed swain may say,
   Oft have we seen him at the peep of dawn
Brushing with hasty steps the dews away,
   To meet the sun upon the upland lawn:

There, at the foot of yonder nodding beech,
  That wreathes its old fantastic roots so high,
His listless length at noontide would he stretch,
  And pore upon the brook that babbles by.

Hard by yon wood, now smiling as in scorn,
  Muttering his wayward fancies, he would rove ;
Now drooping woeful-wan, like one forlorn,
  Or crazed with care, or crossed in hopeless love.

One morn I missed him on the 'customed hill,
  Along the heath, and near his favourite tree ;
Another came—nor yet beside the rill,
  Nor up the lawn, nor at the wood was he ;

The next, with dirges due, in sad array,
  Slow through the church-way path we see him borne :
Approach and read (for thou canst read) the lay
  Graved on the stone beneath yon aged thorn :—

THE EPITAPH.

Here rests his head upon the lap of Earth,
  A youth to Fortune and to Fame unknown ;
Fair Science frowned not on his humble birth,
  And Melancholy marked him for her own.

Large was his bounty, and his soul sincere ;
  Heaven did a recompense as largely send ;
He gave to Misery all he had, a tear,—
  He gained from Heaven, 'twas all he wished, a friend.

No farther seek his merits to disclose,
  Or draw his frailties from their dread abode,
There they alike in trembling hope repose,)
  The bosom of his Father and his God.

T. GRAY.

Gothic Architecture.

THERE can be no doubt that the birthplace of true Gothic Architecture was north of the Alps; it should seem on the Rhine, or in those provinces of France which then were German,—Burgundy, Lorraine, Alsace,—bordering on the Rhine. It was a splendid gift of Teutonism before Germany rose in insurrection and set itself apart from Latin Christendom. North of the Alps it attained its full perfection; there alone the Cathedral became, in its significant symbolism, the impersonation of mediæval Christianity.

The Northern climate may have had some connection with its rise and development. In Italy and the South the sun is a tyrant; breadth of shadow must mitigate his force; the wide eaves, the bold projecting cornice, must afford protection from his burning and direct rays; there would be a reluctance altogether to abandon those horizontal lines which cast a continuous and unbroken shadow; or to ascend, as it were, with the vertical up into the unslaked depths of the noonday blaze. The violent rains would be cast off more freely by a more flat and level roof at a plane of slight inclination. In the north, the precipitate ridge would cast off the heavy snow, which might have lodged and injured the edifice. So, too, within the church, the Italian had to cool and diminish, the Northern would admit and welcome the flooding light. So much, indeed, did the Gothic Architecture enlarge and multiply the apertures for light, that in order to restore the solemnity it was obliged to subdue and sheath as it were the glare, at times overpowering, by painted glass. And thus the magic of the richest colouring was added to the infinitely diversified forms of the architecture.

The Gothic cathedral was the consummation, the completion of mediæval, of hierarchical Christianity. Of that mediævalism, of that hierarchism (though Italy was the domain, and Rome the capital of the Pope), the seat was beyond the Alps. The mediæval hierarchical services did not rise to their full majesty and impressivenesss, till celebrated under a Gothic cathedral. The church might seem to expand, and lay itself out in long and narrow avenues, with the most gracefully converging perspective, in order that the worshipper might contemplate with deeper awe the more remote central ceremonial. The enormous height more than compensated for the contracted breadth. Nothing could be more finely arranged for the processional services; and the processional services became more frequent, more imposing. The music, instead of being beaten down by low broad arches, or lost within the heavier aisles, soared freely to the lofty roof, pervaded the whole building, was infinitely multiplied as it died and rose again to the fretted roof. Even the incense, curling more freely up to the immeasurable height, might give the notion of clouds of adoration finding their way to heaven.

The Gothic cathedral remains an imperishable and majestic monument of hierarchical wealth, power, devotion; it can hardly be absolutely called self-sacrifice, for if built for the honour of God and of the Redeemer, it was honour,

it was almost worship, shared in by the high ecclesiastic. That, however, has almost passed away; God, as it were, now vindicates to Himself His own. The cathedral has been described as a vast book in stone, a book which taught by symbolic language, partly plain and obvious to the simpler man, partly shrouded in not less attractive mystery. It was at once strikingly significant and inexhaustible; bewildering, feeding at once and stimulating profound meditation. Even its height, its vastness, might appear to suggest the Inconceivable, the Incomprehensible in the Godhead, to symbolize the infinity, the incalculable grandeur and majesty of the divine works; the mind felt humble under its shadow as before an awful presence. Its form and distribution was a confession of faith; it typified the creed. Everywhere was the mystic number; the Trinity was proclaimed by the nave and the aisles (multiplied sometimes, as at Bourges and elsewhere, to the other sacred number, seven), the three richly ornamented recesses of the portal, the three towers. The Rose over the west was the Unity; the whole building was a Cross. The altar, with its decorations, announced the Real Perpetual Presence. The solemn Crypt below represented the under world, the soul of man in darkness and the shadow of death, the body awaiting the resurrection.

This was the more obvious universal language. By those who sought more abstruse and recondite mysteries, they might be found in all the multifarious

details, provoking the zealous curiosity, or dimly suggestive of holy meaning. Sculpture was called into aid. All the great objective truths of religion had their fitting place. Even the Father, either in familiar symbol or in actual form, began to appear, and to assert His property in the sacred building. Already, in the Romanesque edifices, the Son, either as the babe in the lap of His Virgin Mother, on the cross, or ascending into heaven, had taken His place over the central entrance, as it were to receive and welcome the worshipper. Before long He appeared not there alone, though there in more imposing form; He was seen throughout all His wondrous history, with all His acts and miracles, down to the Resurrection, the Ascension, the return to Judgment. Everywhere was that hallowed form: in infancy, in power, on the cross, on the right hand of the Father, coming down amid the hosts of angels. The most stupendous, the most multifarious scenes were represented in reliefs, more or less bold, prominent and vigorous, or rude and harsh. The carving now aspired to more than human beauty, or it delighted in the most hideous ugliness,—majestic, gentle angels; grinning, hateful, sometimes half-comic devils. But it was not only the New and the Old Testament, it was the Golden Legend also which might be read in the unexhausted language of the cathedral. Our Lady had her own chapels for her own special votaries, and toward the east, behind the altar, the place of honour. Not only were there the twelve Apostles, the four Evangelists, the Martyrs, the four great Doctors of the Latin Church, each in his recognised form, and with his peculiar symbol,—the whole edifice swarmed with saints within and without, on the walls, on the painted windows, over the side altars. For now the mystery was so awful that it might be administered more near to the common eye, upon the altar in every succursal chapel which lined the building: it was secure in its own sanctity. There were the saints, local, national, or those especially to whom the building was dedicated; and the celestial hierarchy of the Areopagite, with its ascending orders and conventional forms, the winged seraph, the cherubic face. The whole, in its vastness and intricacy, was to the outward sense and to the imagination what Scholasticism was to the intellect, an enormous effort, a waste and prodigality of power, which confounded and bewildered rather than enlightened; at the utmost, awoke vague and indistinct emotion.

But even therein was the secret of the imperishable power of the Gothic cathedrals. Their hieroglyphic language, in its more abstruse terms, became obsolete and unintelligible; it was a purely hierarchical dialect; its meaning, confined to the hierarchy, gradually lost its signification even to them. But the cathedrals themselves retired as it were into more simple and more commanding majesty, into the solemn grandeur of their general effect. They rested only on the wonderful boldness and unity of their design, the richness of their detail. Content now to appeal to the indelible, inextinguishable kindred and affinity of the human heart to grandeur, grace, and beauty, the countless statues, from objects of adoration, became architectural ornaments. So the mediaeval churches survive in their influence on the mind and the soul of man. Their venerable antiquity comes in some sort in aid of their innate religiousness. It is that about them which was temporary and accessory, their hierarchical character, which has chiefly dropped from them and become obsolete. They are now more absolutely and exclusively churches for the worship of God. As the mediaeval pageantry has passed away, or shrunk into less imposing forms, the one object of worship, Christ, or God in Christ, has taken more full and absolute possession of the edifice. Where the service is more simple, as in our York, Durham, or Westminster, or even where the old faith prevails, in Cologne, in Antwerp, in Strasburg, in Rheims, in Bourges, in Rouen, it has become more popular, less ecclesiastical: everywhere the priest is now, according to the common sentiment, more the minister, less the half-divinised mediator. And thus all that is the higher attribute and essence of Christian architecture retains its nobler, and in the fullest sense its religious power. The Gothic cathedral can hardly be contemplated without awe, or entered without devotion.

H. H. MILMAN.

The Church Porch.

Though private prayer be a brave design,
Yet public hath more promises, more love ;
And love's a weight to hearts, to eyes a sign.
We all are but cold suitors ; let us move
   Where it is warmest. Leave thy six and seven ;
   Pray with the most, for where most pray is heaven.

When once thy foot enters the church, be bare.
God is more there than thou, for thou art there
Only by His permission. Then beware
And make thyself all reverence and fear ;
   Kneeling ne'er spoil'd silk stocking : quit thy state ;
   All equal are within the church's gate.

Resort to sermons, but to prayers most ;
Praying's the end of preaching. O be dress'd ;
Stay not for the other pin. Why, thou hast lost
A joy for it worth worlds. Thus hell doth jest
   Away thy blessings, and extremely flout thee,
   Thy clothes being fast, but thy soul loose about thee.

In time of service seal up both thine eyes,
And send them to thy heart; that spying sin
They may weep out the stains by them did rise
Those doors being shut, all by the ear comes in
   Who marks in church-time others' symmetry
   Makes all their beauty his deformity.

Let vain or busy thoughts have there no part,
Bring not thy plough, thy plots, thy pleasures thither
Christ purged His temple, so must thou thy heart;
All worldly thoughts are but thieves met together
   To cozen thee. Look to thy actions well,
   For churches either are our heaven or hell.

Judge not the preacher, for he is thy judge;
If thou mislike him, thou conceivest him not.
God calleth preaching folly. Do not grudge
To pick out treasures from an earthen pot.
   The worst speaks something good; if all want sense,
   God takes a text, and preacheth patience.

He that gets patience, and the blessing which
Preachers conclude with, hath not lost his pains;
He that by being at church escapes the ditch
Which he might fall in by companions, gains;
   He that loves God's abode, and to combine
   With saints on earth, shall one day with them shine.

GEORGE HERBERT.

SATISFYING CONSCIENTIOUS SCRUPLES.—It was at the hotel at Dumbarton. I had just got up, and rang the bell for some hot water for shaving. A waiter answered my call. "I want some hot water, if you please," I said. "And what for do you want the hot water?" "For shaving," said I. "Ye canna have hot water on the Lord's day for sic a thing as shaving," said the waiter, horror-struck at the idea. I insisted again but with the same effect. "Na, na," said he, "ye canna have it." Necessity is the mother of invention, 'tis said, and this aroused mine. I thought that if I could arrange the order in such a way that it would not affect his religious scruples, he would bring it directly. I therefore proposed that I should like some toddy, and told him to bring me the materials for making it, consisting of whisky, sugar, and boiling water. These he brought without the least demur. I gave him the whisky, which he drank, and I used the hot water.—"*The Honeymoon,*" by Count Medina Pomar.

Sunday in the Country and in London.

THOSE who are in the habit of remarking such matters must have noticed the passive quiet of an English landscape on Sunday. The clacking of the mill, the regularly recurring stroke of the flail, the din of the blacksmith's hammer, the whistling of the ploughman, the rattling of the cart, and all other sounds of rural labour are suspended. The very farm dogs bark less frequently, being less disturbed by passing travellers. At such times I have almost fancied the winds sunk into quiet, and that the sunny landscape, with its fresh green tints melting into blue haze, enjoyed the hallowed calm.

> Sweet day, so pure, so calm, so bright,
> The bridal of the earth and sky.

Well was it ordained that the day of devotion should be a day of rest. The holy repose which reigns over the face of nature has its moral influence; every restless passion is charmed down, and we feel the natural religion of the soul gently springing up within us. For my part, there are feelings that visit me in a country church, amid the beautiful serenity of nature, which I experience nowhere else; and if not a more religious, I think I am a better man on Sunday than on any other day of the seven.

But where is its sacred influence more strikingly apparent than in the very heart of that great Babel, London? On this sacred day, the gigantic monster is charmed into repose. The intolerable din and struggle of the week are at an end. The shops are shut. The fires of forges and manufactories are extinguished; and the sun, no longer obscured by murky clouds of smoke, pours down a sober, yellow radiance into the quiet streets. The few pedestrians we meet, instead of hurrying forth with anxious countenances, move leisurely along; their brows are smoothed from the wrinkles of business and care. They have put on their Sunday looks, and Sunday manners, with their Sunday clothes, and are cleansed in mind as well as in person.

And now the melodious clangour of bells from church towers summons their several flocks to the fold. Forth issues from his mansion the family of the decent tradesman, the small children in the advance; then the citizen and his comely spouse, followed by the grown-up daughters, with small morocco-bound prayer-books in the folds of their pocket-handkerchiefs. The housemaid looks after them from the window, admiring the finery of the family, and receiving, perhaps, a nod and smile from her young mistresses, at whose toilet she has assisted.

Now rumbles along the carriage of some magnate of the city, peradventure an alderman or a sheriff, and now the patter of many feet announces a procession of charity scholars, in uniforms of antique cut, and each with a prayer-book under his arm.

The ringing of bells is at an end; the rumbling of the carriage has ceased; the pattering of feet is heard no more; the flocks are folded in ancient churches, cramped up in by-lanes and corners of the crowded city, where the vigilant beadle keeps watch, like the shepherd's dog, round the threshold of the sanctuary. For a time everything is hushed; but soon is heard the deep pervading sound of the organ, rolling and vibrating through the empty lanes and courts; and the sweet chanting of the choir making them resound with melody and praise. Never have I been more sensible of the sanctifying effect of church music, than when I have heard it thus poured forth, like a river of joy, through the inmost recesses of this great metropolis, elevating it, as it were, from all the sordid pollutions of the week, and bearing the poor world-worn soul on a tide of triumphant harmony to heaven.

The morning service is at an end. The streets are again alive with the congregations returning to their homes, but soon again relapse into silence. Now comes on the Sunday dinner, which, to the city tradesman, is a meal of some importance. There is more leisure for social enjoyment at the board. Members of the family can now gather together, who are separated by the laborious occupations of the week. A school-boy may be permitted on that day to come to the paternal home; an old friend of the family takes his accustomed Sunday seat at the board, tells over his well-known stories, and rejoices young and old with his well-known jokes.

On Sunday afternoon the city pours forth its legions to breathe the fresh air and enjoy the sunshine of the parks and rural environs. Satirists may say what they please about the rural enjoyments of a London citizen on Sunday; but to me there is something delightful in beholding the poor prisoner of the crowded and dusty city, enabled thus to come forth once a week and throw himself upon the green bosom of nature. He is like a child restored to the mother's breast; and they who first spread out these noble parks and magnificent pleasure-grounds, which surround this huge metropolis, have done at least as much for its health and morality, as if they had expended the amount of cost in hospitals, prisons, and penitentiaries.

WASHINGTON IRVING.

An Old Church Service.

Miss Charlotte Yonge in her story, *Chantry House*, tells the experience of a family, who go to the old country parish church, as follows:—

"An altar draped in black like a coffin, and on the step up to the rail boys and girls eating apples and performing antics to beguile the waiting-time, while a row of white-smocked old men occupied the bench opposite to our seat conversing loud enough for us to hear them.

"My father and Clarence came in; the bells stopped; there was a sound of steps, and in the fabric in front of us there emerged a grizzled head and the back of a very dirty surplice besprinkled with iron moulds, while Chapman's back appeared above our curtain, his desk (full of dilapidated prayer-books) being wedged in between us and the reading-desk.

"The duet that then took place between him and the curate must have been heard to be credible, especially as, being so close behind the old man, we could not fail to be aware of all the remarkable shots at long words which he bawled out at the top of his voice, and I refrain from recording, lest they should haunt others as they have done me all my life. Now and then Chapman caught up a long switch, and dashed out at some obstreperous child to give an audible whack; and towards the close of the Litany he stumped out—we heard his tramp the whole length of the church, and by and by his voice issued from an unknown height, proclaiming, 'Let us sing to the praise and glory—in an anthem taken from the forty-second chapter of Genesis.'

"There was an outburst of bassoon, clarionet, and fiddle, and the performance that followed was the most marvellous we had ever heard, especially when the big butcher—fiddling all the time—declared in a mighty solo, 'I am Jo—Jo—Jo—Joseph!' and having reiterated this information four or five times, inquired with equal pertinacity, 'Doth—doth my fa-a-u-ther yet live?' Poor Emily was fairly 'convulsed;' she stuffed her handkerchief into her mouth, and grew so crimson that my mother was quite frightened, and very near putting her out at the little door of ex-communication. To our last hour we shall never forget the shock of that first anthem."

Hymn.

WHEN the angels all are singing,
All of glory ever springing,
In the ground of high heaven's graces,
Where all virtues have their places:
Oh that my poor soul were near them,
With an humble heart to hear them.

Then should faith in love's submission
Joying but in mercy's blessing,
Where that sins are in remission,
Sing the joyful soul's confessing,
Of her comforts high commending,
All in glory never ending.

But ah! wretched, sinful creatures!
How should the corrupted nature
Of this wicked heart of mine,
Think upon that love divine,
That doth time the angel's voices,
Whilst the host of heaven rejoices?

No, the song of deadly sorrow,
In the night that hath no morrow—
And their pains are never ended,
That have heavenly powers offended—
Is more fitting to the merit
Of my foul infected spirit.

Yet while mercy is removing
All the sorrows of the loving,
How can faith be full of blindness,
To despair of mercy's kindness,
Whilst the hand of heaven is giving
Comfort from the ever-living?

HYMN.

No, my soul, be no more sorry;
Look unto that life of glory,
Which the grace of faith regardeth,
And the tears of love rewardeth,
Where the soul the comfort getteth,
That the angels' music setteth.

There when thou art well conducted,
And by heavenly grace instructed,
How the faithful thoughts to fashion
Of a ravished lover's passion,
Sing with saints, to angels nighest,
Hallelujah in the highest!

NICHOLAS BRETON (1555-1624).

Some Memorials of the late Emperor Frederick.

BY COUNT VON MOLTKE.

IN 1856 the Crown Prince of Prussia paid a visit to the Queen and the Royal Princess whom two years later he was to take home as his bride. He returned to Germany by way of France, and on the road made a short stay in Paris as the guest of the Emperor Napoleon III. He was accompanied by Field-Marshal General Count (then simply General Baron) von Moltke, who acted as his personal adjutant. In a series of letters to some friend or friends, the man who is "silent in seven languages" gives his impressions of what he saw, and, viewed by the light of subsequent events, very interesting those impressions are. The first letter is dated from the "Tuileries, Pavillon Marsan, the 13th December 1856;" the tenth from the "Tuileries, the 21st December;" and the eleventh and last from "Carlsruhe, the 23rd December." A Danish translation of these letters appeared some years back, by some unknown means, in the *Dagens Nyheder*, or Copenhagen *Daily News*; but it was not till a much later date that they were published as originally written, the manuscript being sent by the Field-Marshal General himself to the editor of the *Deutsche Rundschau*.

The great German strategist preceded his then only "Royal" Highness by a day or two as far as Calais, where he found grand preparations had been made to receive the distinguished visitor, who, on at length reaching the French coast, was received by volleys of artillery thundering from the ramparts. The next morning at seven o'clock a special train, conveying the Prince and his suite, together with the officers and court officials ordered to attend upon him during his stay, moved out of the Calais station. We wonder whether, as Count von Moltke then beheld St. Denis, Montmartre, Mont Valerien, and other well-known landmarks rise in succession before him, he thought under what different circumstances he was destined one day to approach them? Here is his account of

THE RECEPTION OF THE PRUSSIAN CROWN PRINCE IN PARIS.

You pass through the *enceinte* into the magnificent *gare du Nord*. The

Prince was here received by His Highness the Prince Napoleon, whose resemblance to his famous uncle is something quite indescribable: exactly the same black hair, pallid complexion, and imperial profile. In the courtyard of the *embarcadère* two battalions were drawn up, while there were of course red carpets, imperial equipages, and an escort of *guides à cheval*. The liveries are green and gold; the harness is rich and in good taste; the horses are of extraordinary beauty, and mostly of English breed. Our road lay through the Faubourg St. Martin, to the new and fine Boulevard de Strasbourg, Montmartre, and Poissonière (past our Hôtel Rougemont), over the Boulevard des Italiens, Rue de la Paix, and the Rue de Rivoli to the Tuileries. As we drove through the triumphal arch, on the Place du Carrousel, the guard paid imperial honours. At the bottom of the grand staircase, the Prince was received by His Majesty the Emperor, who conducted him immediately to the Empress. As we knew this beforehand from the printed programme, and as there was no time to change our toilet by the way, we had all been tricked out for the last seven hours in embroidered coats and ribbons of different orders. During our drive, which took place exactly at the time when people were out walking, there was plenty of opportunity *de voir et d'être vu*.

The Emperor wore the uniform of a French Marshal and the cordon of the Order of the Black Eagle. The Empress was simply and tastefully dressed, in a high gown, dark grey and black. Immediately after the first salutation, the introduction took place, but *sans phrase*. The Emperor then conducted the Prince out of the large room in the middle pavilion (*de l'horloge*), through the long series of magnificent rooms and galleries, to his apartments on the ground floor of the Pavillon Marsan, at the corner of the Rue de Rivoli and the large open square which extends to the Arc de Triomphe. We here found Herr von Rosenberg, the two Princes Reuss, Major von Treskow, Von Romberg—in a word, the Prussians in Paris. Soon afterwards the Prince paid a visit to *oncle Jérôme* and Prince Napoleon in the Palais Royal, subsequently calling on the Princess Mathilde (Demidoff). The ex-King of Westphalia, who, despite his great age, is still very hearty, paid his return visit almost directly afterwards, and Prince Murat also was announced.

At seven o'clock dinner for the Imperial Court was served in the Galerie de Diane. Cambacérès, Rollin, Bassano, Bacciochi, Tascher, and the Princesse d'Esslingen, are all names which remind one of the *premier empire*. The ladies of honour were Madame de Marnézia, whom I conducted to table; Madame Lourmel, widow of the brave general who fell before Sebastopol; Madame de Labedoyère, who has learned German very well in Berlin; and Madame Reinwald—all very amiable and interesting. The Prince, who took the Empress in, sat between her and the Emperor; I was placed opposite. The well-known portraits of the Emperor and Empress are like, it is true; but, for all that, do not give a thoroughly correct notion of the originals. I always fancied Louis Napoleon was taller. He looks very well on horseback, but not so well on foot. I was struck by a certain immovability of his features, and by the burnt-out look, as I might almost say, of his eyes. A friendly— nay, good-natured—smile predominates on his physiognomy, which has little Napoleonic about it. He generally sits quietly, with his head slightly bent on one side; and it is precisely, perhaps, this quietude—which, as we know, does not desert him even in dangerous crises—that impresses the mobile French. Events have shown that his calm is not apathy, but the result of a reflective mind and a determined will. In a drawing-room he has not an imposing demeanour, and in conversation there is even a certain embarrassment about him. He is an *empereur*, but not a king.

The Empress Eugénie is a surprising person. She is beautiful and elegant. I was struck by the resemblance between her and Madame von B., only she is a brunette. Her neck and arms are unsurpassably beautiful; her figure is slender; her toilet choice, tasty, and rich, without being overloaded. She had on a white satin dress, of such a circumference that ladies will in future want some ells more silk than they have as yet done. The Empress wore a scarlet-red head-dress, and round her neck a double row of splendid pearls. She speaks a great deal, and with vivacity, exhibiting more animation than we are accustomed to meet in so high a position.

We dined in the Diana Gallery, which had been turned into two rooms. The workmanship of the table ornaments, in dead-silver, is exceedingly beautiful, the cooking excellent—not too many things, but choice. The servants advance with the dishes, and name the contents. This is somewhat inconvenient. You have to interrupt your conversation every moment to say whether you will have some *turbot*, or not have any *merlan*. The wine is exquisite. The regular table wine is champagne, which is handed round all dinner-time, with an accompaniment of Bordeaux, Sauterne, hock, and finally sherry and malvoisie.

It was not till dinner was cleared away that their Majesties entered into conversation with us strangers. The Empress talked with ease and great affability; she possesses the talent *de vous mettre à votre aise*. She and the Countess Hatzfeld were the only persons seated; the Emperor, the Prince, and consequently every one else, *restaient debout* till about eleven o'clock. The Grand Chamberlain took care that the gentlemen should advance singly to Her Majesty's chair. This was managed more conveniently at the English Court; at any rate, I was glad when tea was served, and when we withdrew, which we did immediately afterwards.

I have an entire suite of rooms in the Pavillon Marsan, looking out on the Rue de Rivoli, and formerly occupied by the Prince of Orléans. Heavy red damask tapestry and window curtains, magnificent candelabra fixed to the walls, boule furniture, gilt arm-chairs, immensely large glasses, fine pictures (by Poitevin), are things you can well imagine; they are pretty well the same at all Courts. But people here have not got to the real comfort, like that in my turret at Windsor. A dozen lamps with glass globes are burning, but when I want to get anything, I light a wax taper in addition. The cosiest spot is the seven-feet-deep window embrasure in which the writing-table stands, only you do not feel very warm there, though whole stacks of wood are burning in every fireplace. All through the Tuileries there is a draught of which you have no idea. The difference of temperature in the immense rooms frequently occasions a perfect hurricane among the connecting doors.

Exceedingly fatigued with the many things I had seen during the day, I quickly got into my broad and very excellent tester-bed; but it was a long time ere I found repose. At one moment, the pile of wood in a fireplace collapsed, causing a bright flame to flicker up; at another, one of the old-fashioned chimney clocks whirred out the hour, as though to remind one that under this roof times changed more rapidly than elsewhere. Even the incredible stillness in the midst of the noisy city struck one as strange, and had been obtained by the removal of the street pavement to a distance. The heavy curtains and carpets deaden every sound; and the doors turn so noiselessly upon their hinges, that I did not hear the Gentleman-of-the-Chamber enter, whom Louis XIV. had sent from the Louvre to inquire how it really was that he had been favoured with my presence in his palace. I endeavoured to prove to the Marquis out of Gervinus's History that a great many things had occurred since the *ancien régime*, and that he had nothing whatever to do in the matter. He shrugged his shoulders haughtily and left me to my own intellectual reflections, from which I did not wake till the next morning.

There is a very agreeable arrangement by which the Imperial Family do not claim the Prince till seven o'clock in the evening, so that we have the entire day at our own disposal. As early as nine a.m., when the sun had scarcely risen in Paris, we set ourselves in motion, either incognito in *voitures de place*, or officially in imperial equipages, as the case may be.

[How strangely these extracts read now that the whole aspect of the relations of Europe has changed. The Emperor of the French dead, after losing his throne in a contest with Germany, in which the Crown Prince took an active part. The Empress a widow and childless. Our Queen a widow. The Crown Prince dead almost before he came to the Imperial purple.]

The Story of the Singing Bird.

THE following story was told of Dr. Thomas Grant, first Catholic Bishop of Southwark.

Upon one occasion, when Dr. Grant was visiting a school, one of the children, with that fearless familiarity that it was his delight to foster, called out:—

"But, my lord, will it be always the same thing in heaven—always music, and light, and angels? Shan't we never get tired of it?"

Dr. Grant called the little sceptic to him, and set himself to answer her puzzle by telling her the legend of a monk to whom the same thought had once occurred, "Shall we not grow tired of heaven?"

"It was on a warm summer's day; the monk was working in a field near his monastery; the sun was hot, and he was weary of digging; his spirit flagged with his body; and he bethought himself, perhaps, after all, paradise was not worth the toil and trouble it was costing him.

"Suddenly he was roused by the singing of a bird in a tree close by. The notes were so sweet, so brilliant, so unlike any song of bird or human voice he had ever heard before, that they thrilled through his very soul.

"He dropped his spade, and walked towards the tree where the bird had perched; but as he drew near it flitted away, singing as it went; its song grew richer and more beautiful at every gush. The monk, like one drawn by a spell, followed the warbler from tree to tree, till at last the melody ceased, and he found himself in the heart of the forest, a great way from home. The sun had gone down, and he wandered about, looking in vain for the path he had come by. Emerging, after a long ramble, from the darkness of the wood, he came in sight of the monastery.

"But what had befallen it since an hour ago? The gates were crowned with ivy, and lichens and mosses were draped all over the walls. He rang; it was a strange face that answered his summons. The brother looked at him in amazement. Who was he, and whence did he come? He gave his name; but the porter grew white with fear, and, crossing himself, exclaimed,—

"'Thou art his ghost, then, for the monk who bore that name has been dead nearly a hundred years!'

"'Nearly a hundred years! Have I been gone all that time, listening for nearly a hundred years to the song of a singing-bird, and found it so sweet that it seemed to me scarce an hour?'

"And the wanderer knew that his doubt had been heard in paradise, and had been answered by the song of the singing bird."

It has been often remarked that men of great learning are frequently very fond of children. The following charming letter, addressed to one of his little five-year-old nieces, shows that Faraday was no exception to this rule:—"To Constance Deacon.—Royal Institution, 19th May, 1852.—My dear Constance, first a kiss, p—p—p—ph; next thank you for your good letter—very well written, and very pleasant; and now thanks for the letter you are going to write to me, in which you must tell me how papa and mamma do, and what you are about. I went this morning to see a fish like a great eel take his breakfast. This morning he had three frogs for breakfast; yesterday he ate nine fish in the course of the day, each as large as a sprat, and the day before fourteen. When the fish are put into the water he electrifies and kills them, and then swallows them up; and if a man happens to have his hands in the water at the same time, the fish—that is, the eel—electrifies the man too. The eel is now about twelve years old, and is heavier I think than you are. Yesterday I saw the Royal children, the Prince of Wales and the Duke of York—such nice children! They would make famous playmates for you; but I do not know whether princes do play much. I do not think they can be as happy in their play as you are. As to the 'magnic,' when you and I meet we will have a long talk about it, and make some experiments. And so, with my love to papa and mamma, and curious Constance, with kiss for each, I am your loving old uncle,—M. FARADAY."

The Singers.

God sent His singers upon earth,
With songs of sadness and of mirth,
That they might touch the hearts of men,
And bring them back to heaven again.

The first, a youth with soul of fire,
Held in his hand a golden lyre;
Through groves he wandered, and by streams,
Playing the music of our dreams.

The second, with a bearded face,
Stood singing in the market-place,
And stirred with accents deep and loud
The hearts of all the listening crowd.

A grey old man, the third and last,
Sang in cathedrals dim and vast,
While the majestic organ rolled
Contrition from its mouths of gold.

And those who heard the singers three
Disputed which the best might be;
For still their music seemed to start
Discordant echoes in each heart.

But the great Master said, "I see
No best in kind, but in degree;
I gave a various gift to each,
To charm, to strengthen, and to teach.

"These are the three great chords of might,
And he whose ear is turned aright
Will hear no discord in the three,
But the most perfect harmony."

The Larger View of Life.

THERE is something very ennobling to human character in the possession of a large *Time-view*, and its effects are visible in many cases not directly religious.

Next to having a noble future before us, it is well to have a wide and worthy past. This it is that renders the old man venerable. His actual momentary life is often poor and sad enough: the windows of sense and soul shut on the light and stir of the world without, and the avenues choked up through which the interests and passions of the hour should vibrate to his heart; but, while shaded from the dazzle of the instant, the tranquil light of half a century is spread beneath his eye. Many a gaudy bubble he has seen rise, and glitter, and burst; many a modest good take secret root and grow. Every game of hope and passion he has seen played out, and for every passage presented on the living stage, can find a parallel scene in the old drama whose curtain never drops.

The heroes and the wise of the past age, ideal to others, were real to him; his familiars are among the dead, dear yet to many hearts; and as he explores again that silent past, and climbs once more its consecrated heights, and loses himself in its sweet valleys, and rebuilds its fallen fragments, he feels something of an historic dignity, which sustains the trembling steps, and gives courage to the sorrowful decline.

And so it is with *family recollections*. To have had forefathers renowned for honourable deeds, to belong by nature to those who have bravely borne their part in life, and refreshed the world with mighty thoughts and healthy admiration, is a privilege which it were mean and self-willed to despise.

It is as a security, given for us of old, which it were false-hearted not to redeem; and in virtues bred of a noble stock, mellowed as they were by reverence, there is often a grace and ripeness wanting to self-made and brand-new excellence.

Of like value to a people are *heroic national traditions*, giving them a determined character to sustain among the tribes of men, making them familiar with images of great and strenuous life, and kindling them with faith in glorious possibilities.

No material interests, no common welfare, can so bind a community together, and make it strong of heart, as a history of rights maintained, and virtues uncorrupted, and freedom won; and one legend of conscience is worth more to a country than hidden gold and fertile plains.

It is but an extension of the same influence that we discern in the Christian theory of life; only that it opens out our time-view alike in the future and the past. It makes both our lineage and our destiny divine; proclaims us *sons* of God and *heirs*. No tie can so fasten on us as the feeling that we belong not to the present, and that we degrade our nature whenever we live for the passing moment only; that we are not our own, but the great Father, God's. Our lot is greater than ourselves, and gives to our souls a worth they would not else have dared to claim. Hence the humbleness there always is in Christian dignity. The immortal lot infinitely transcends our poor deserts. How we are to grow into the proportions of so high a life, it is wonderful to think. And yet, though it be above us always—nay, even *because* it is above us—there *is* something in it true and answering to our nature still; so that, having once lived with it, we are only half ourselves—and that the meaner half—without it. The infinite burden of duty which good hearts are constrained to bear is tolerable only to an immortal's strength. The unspeakable, imploring homage with which we look on truth and wisdom and greatness in other souls, is but sorrow and servitude except to a spirit freed with an eternal love. The Christian hope gives peace and power by restoring the broken proportions of the mind; and tranquillizes the restlessness of a spirit unconsciously "cabined, cribbed, confined." It is this truthfulness to our best and deepest nature—the power we receive from it, the quiet we find in it—that gives to the Christian estimate of life its irresistible persuasion upon the heart.

JAMES MARTINEAU.

LEIGH HUNT speaks thus of superstition: "Superstition attempts to settle everything by assertion; which never did do, and never will. And like all asserters, even well-inclined ones, it shows its feebleness in anger and threatening. It commands us to take its problems for granted, on pain of being tied up to a triangle. Then come its advocates, and assert that this mode of treatment is proper and logical, which is making bad worse. The worst of all is, that this is the way in which the finest doctrines in the world are obstructed. They are like an excellent child, making the Grand Tour with a foolish, overbearing tutor. The tutor runs a chance of spoiling the child, and makes their presence disagreeable wherever they go, except to their tradesmen. Let us hope the child has done with his tutor."

The Old Song.

THE minstrel of the classic lay
　　Of love and wine who sings,
Still found the fingers run astray
　　That touched the rebel strings.

Of Cadmus he would fain have sung,
　　Of Atreus and his line;
But all the jocund echoes rung
　　With songs of love and wine.

Ah, brother, I would fain have caught
　　Some fresher fancies' gleam:
My truant accents find, unsought,
　　The old familiar theme.

Love, love! but not the sportive child
　　With shaft and twanging bow,
Whose random arrows drove us wild
　　Some threescore years ago!

Not Eros, with his joyous laugh,
　　The urchin blind and bare;
But Love, with spectacles and staff,
　　And scanty silvered hair.

Our heads with frosted locks are white,
　　Our roofs are thatched with snow:
But red, in chilling winter's spite,
　　Our hearts and hearthstones glow.

Our old acquaintance, Time, drops in,
　And while the running sands
Their golden threads unheeded spin,
　He warms his frozen hands.

Stay, wingèd hours, too swift, too sweet,
　And waft this message o'er
To all we miss, from all we meet,
　On life's fast crumbling shore.

Say that to old affection true
　We hug the narrowing chain
That binds our heart—alas, how few
　The links that yet remain !

The fatal touch awaits them all
　That turns the rock to dust ;
From year to year they break and fall,
　They break but never rust.

Say if one note of happier strain
　This worn-out harp afford,
One throb that trembles, not in vain,
　Their memory lent its chord.

Say that when Fancy closed her wings,
　And Passion quenched his fire,
Love, love still echoed from the strings,
　As from Anacreon's lyre !

O. W. HOLMES.

REFLECTION AT SEA.

See how, beneath the moonbeam's smile,
　Yon little billow heaves its breast ;
It foams and sparkles for a while,
　And, murmuring, then subsides to rest.

So man, the sport of bliss and care,
　Rises on Time's eventful sea,
And having swelled a moment there,
　Thus melts into eternity.

THOMAS MOORE.

Rural Life in Sweden.

THERE is something patriarchal still lingering about rural life in Sweden, which renders it a fit theme for song. Almost primeval simplicity reigns over that northern land—almost primeval solitude and stillness. You pass out from the gate of the city, and, as if by magic, the scene changes to a wild woodland landscape. Around you are forests of fir. Overhead hang the long fan-like branches, trailing with moss, and heavy with red and blue cones. Underfoot is a carpet of yellow leaves, and the air is warm and balmy. On a wooden bridge you cross a little silver stream, and anon come forth into a pleasant and sunny land of farms. Wooden fences divide the adjoining fields. Across the road are gates, which are opened by troops of children. The peasants take off their hats as you pass; you sneeze, and they cry, "God bless you!" The houses in the villages and smaller towns are all built of hewn timber, and for the most part painted red. The floors of the taverns are strewed with the fragrant tips of fir-boughs. In many villages there are no taverns, and the peasants take turns in receiving travellers. The thrifty housewife shows you into the best chamber, the walls of which are hung round with rude pictures from the Bible; and brings you her heavy silver spoons—an heirloom—to dip the curdled milk from the pan. You have oaten cakes baked some months before, or bread with anise-seed and coriander in it, or perhaps a little pine bark.

Meanwhile the sturdy husband has brought his horses from the plough, and harnessed them to your carriage. Solitary travellers come and go in uncouth one-horse chaises. Most of them have pipes in their mouths, and hanging round their necks in front a leather wallet, in which they carry tobacco, and the great bank-notes of the country, as large as your two hands. You meet also groups of Dalekarlian peasant women, travelling homeward, or townward in pursuit of work. They walk barefoot, carrying in their hands their shoes, which have high heels under the hollow of the foot, and soles of birch bark.

Frequent, too, are the village churches standing by the roadsides, each in its own little garden of Gethsemane. In the parish register great events are doubtless recorded. Some old king was christened or buried in that church; and a little sexton, with a rusty key, shows you the baptismal font or the coffin. In the churchyard are a few flowers, and much green grass; and daily the shadow of the church spire, with its long tapering finger, counts the tombs, representing a dial-plate of human life, on which the hours and minutes are the graves of men. The stones are flat and large and low, and perhaps sunken, like the roofs of old houses. On some are armorial bearings; on others only the initials of the poor tenants, with a date, as on the roofs of Dutch cottages. They all sleep with their heads to the westward. Each held a lighted taper in his hand when he died; and in his coffin were placed his little heart-treasures, and a piece of money for his last journey. Babes that came lifeless into the world were carried in the arms of grey-haired old men to the only cradle they ever slept in; and in the shroud of the dead mother were laid the little garments of the child that lived and died in her bosom. And over this scene the village pastor looks from his window in the stillness of midnight, and says in his heart, "How quietly they rest, all the departed!"

Near the churchyard gate stands a poor-box, fastened to a post by iron bands, and secured by a padlock, with a sloping wooden roof to keep off the rain. If it be Sunday, the peasants sit on the church steps, and con their psalm-books. Others are coming down the road with their beloved pastor, who talks to them of holy things from beneath his broad-brimmed hat. He speaks of fields and harvests, and of the parable of the sower that went forth to sow. He leads them to the Good Shepherd, and to the pleasant pastures of the Spirit-land. He is their patriarch, and, like Melchizedek, both priest and king, though he has no other throne than the church pulpit. The women carry psalm-books in their hands, wrapped in silk handkerchiefs, and listen devoutly to the good man's words; but the young men, like Gallio, care for none of these things. They are busy counting the plaits in the kirtles of the peasant girls, their number being an indication of the wearer's wealth. It may end in a wedding.

I will endeavour to describe a village wedding in Sweden. It shall be in summer time, that there may be flowers, and in a southern province, that the bride may be fair. The early song of the lark and of chanticleer are mingling in the clear morning air, and the sun, the heavenly bridegroom with golden locks, arises in the east, just as our earthly bridegroom, with yellow hair, arises in the south. In the yard there is a sound of voices and trampling of hoofs, and horses are led forth and saddled. The steed that is to bear the bridegroom has a bunch of flowers upon his forehead, and a garland of corn-flowers around his neck. Friends from the neighbouring farms come riding in, their blue cloaks streaming to the wind; and finally the happy bridegroom, with a whip in his hand, and a monstrous nosegay in the breast of his black jacket, comes forth from his chamber; and then to horse and away towards the village, where the bride already sits and waits.

Foremost rides the spokesman, followed by some half-dozen village musicians. Next comes the bridegroom between his two groomsmen, and then forty or fifty friends and wedding guests, half of them perhaps with pistols and guns in their hands. A kind of baggage-waggon brings up the rear, laden with food and drink for these merry pilgrims. At the entrance of every village stands a triumphal arch, adorned with flowers and ribands and evergreens; and as they pass beneath it, the wedding guests fire a salute, and the whole procession stops, and straight from every pocket flies a black-jack, filled with punch or brandy. It is passed from hand to hand among the crowd; provisions are brought from the waggon, and after eating and drinking and hurrahing, the procession moves forward again, and at length draws near the house of the bride. Four heralds ride forward to announce that a knight and his attendants are in the neighbouring forest, and pray for hospitality. "How many are you?" asks the bride's father. "At least three hundred," is the answer; and to this the last replies, "Yes; were you seven times as many, you should all be welcome; and in token thereof receive this cup." Whereupon each herald receives a can of ale; and soon after, the whole jovial company comes storming into the farmer's yard, and riding round the Maypole, which stands in the centre, alight amid a grand salute and flourish of music.

In the hall sits the bride, with a crown upon her head and a tear in her eye, like the Virgin Mary in old church paintings. She is dressed in a red bodice and kirtle, with loose linen sleeves. There is a gilded belt around her waist, and around her neck strings of golden beads and a golden chain. On the crown rests a wreath of wild roses, and below it another of cypress. Loose over her shoulders falls her flaxen hair; and her blue, innocent eyes are fixed upon the ground. O thou good soul! thou hast hard hands, but a soft heart. Thou art poor. The very ornaments thou wearest are not thine. They have been hired for this great day. Yet thou art rich—rich in health, rich in hope, rich in thy first, young, fervent love. The blessing of heaven be upon thee! So thinks the parish priest, as he joins together the hands of bride and bridegroom, saying in deep solemn tones, "I give thee in marriage this damsel, to be thy wedded wife in all honour, and to share the half of thy bed, thy lock and key, and every third penny which you two may possess, or may inherit, and all the rights which Upland's laws provide, and the holy King Erik gave."

The dinner is now served, and the bride sits between the bridegroom and the priest. The spokesman delivers an oration after the ancient custom of his fathers. He interlards it well with quotations from the Bible, and invites the Saviour to be present at this marriage feast, as He was at the marriage feast of Cana of Galilee. The table is not sparingly set forth. Each makes a long arm, and the feast goes cheerily on. Punch and brandy pass round between the courses, and here and there a pipe is smoked, while waiting for the next dish. They sit long at table; but, as all things must have an end, so must a Swedish dinner. Then the dance begins. It is led off by the bride and priest, who perform a solemn minuet together. Not till after midnight comes the last dance. The girls form a ring around the bride, to keep her from the hands of the married women, who endeavour to break through the magic circle and seize their new sister. After long struggling they succeed; and the crown is taken from her head, and the jewels from her neck, and she is led off in triumph, the wedding guests following her with lighted candles in their hands. And this is a village bridal.

Nor must I forget the suddenly changing seasons of the northern clime. There is no long and lingering spring, unfolding leaf and blossom one by one; no long and lingering autumn, pompous with many-coloured leaves and the glow of Indian summers. But winter and summer are wonderful, and pass into each other. The quail has hardly ceased piping in the corn, when winter, from the folds of trailing clouds, sows broadcast over the land snow, icicles, and rattling hail. The days wane apace. Ere long the sun hardly rises above the horizon, or does not rise at all. The moon and the stars shine through the day; only, at noon, they are pale and wan, and in the southern sky a red, fiery glow, as of sunset, burns along the horizon, and then goes out. And pleasantly under the silver moon, and under the silent, solemn stars, ring the steel shoes of the skaters on the frozen sea, and voices, and the sound of bells.

And now the Northern Lights begin to burn, faintly at first, like sunbeams playing on the waters of the blue sea. Then a soft crimson glow tinges the heavens. There is a blush on the cheek of night. The colours come and go, and change from crimson to gold, from gold to crimson. The snow is stained with rosy light. Twofold from the zenith, east and west, flames a fiery sword; and a broad band passes athwart the heavens, like a summer sunset. Soft purple clouds come sailing over the sky, and through their vapoury folds the winking stars shine white as silver. With such pomp as this is merry Christmas ushered in—though only a single star heralded the first Christmas. And in memory of that day the Swedish peasants dance on straw; and the peasant girls throw straws at the timbered roof of the hall, and for every one that sticks in a crack shall a groomsman come to their wedding. Merry Christmas, indeed! For pious souls there shall be church songs and sermons, but for Swedish peasants brandy and brown ale in wooden bowls; and the great Yule-cake, crowned with a cheese, and garlanded with apples, and upholding a three-armed candlestick over the Christmas feast.

And now the glad leafy midsummer, full of blossoms and the song of nightingales, is come! Saint John has taken the flowers and festival of heathen Balder, and in every village there is a May-pole fifty feet high, with wreaths and roses and ribands streaming in the wind, and a noisy weathercock on the top, to tell the village whence the wind cometh and whither it goeth. The sun does not set till ten o'clock at night, and the children are at play in the streets an

The Aurora Borealis or Northern Lights.

hour later. The windows and doors are all open, and you may sit and read till midnight without a candle. O how beautiful is the summer night, which is not night, but a sunless yet unclouded day, descending upon earth with dews and shadows and refreshing coolness! How beautiful the long mild twilight, when morning and evening thus sit together, hand in hand, beneath the starless sky of midnight! From the church tower in the public square the bell tolls the hour with a soft musical chime ; and the watchman, whose tower is the belfry, blows a blast on his horn for each stroke of the hammer, and four times, to the four corners of the heavens, in a sonorous voice he chants,—

> "Ho! watchman, ho!
> Twelve is the clock!
> God keep our town
> From fire and brand
> And hostile hand!
> Twelve is the clock!"

From his swallow's nest in the belfry he can see the sun all night long ; and farther north the priest stands at his door in the warm midnight, and lights his pipe with a common burning-glass.

H. W. LONGFELLOW.

Content.

> Would you be free? 'Tis your chief wish, you say ;
> Come on, I'll show thee, friend, the certain way :
> If to no feasts abroad thou lov'st to go,
> While bounteous God does bread at home bestow,
> If thou the goodness of thy clothes dost prize
> By thine own use, and not by others eyes ;
> If (only safe from weathers) thou canst dwell
> In a small house, but a convenient shell ;
> If thou, without a sigh or golden wish,
> Canst look upon thy beechen bowl and dish :
> If in thy mind such power and greatness be,
> The Persian king's a slave compared with thee.

ABRAHAM COWLEY (1618-1667.)

The truth of the assertion that deep feeling has a tendency to combine with obscure ideas in preference to distinct and clear notions, may be proved by the history of fanatics and fanaticism in all ages and countries. The *odium theologicum* is ever proverbial ; and it is the common complaint of philosophers and philosophic historians that the passions of the disputants are commonly violent in proportion to the subtlety and obscurity of the questions in dispute. Nor is this fact confined to professional theologians, for whole nations have displayed the same agitations, and have sacrificed national policy to the more powerful interest of a controverted obscurity.

S. T. COLERIDGE.

Self-Control.

It seems to me that a man will best gain command over those intellectual faculties which he knows are his strongest, by cultivating the faculties that somewhat tend to counterbalance them. He in whom imagination is opulent and fervid, will regulate and discipline its exercise by forcing himself to occupations or studies that require plain common-sense.

He who feels that the bias of his judgment or tendency of his avocations is overmuch towards the positive and anti-poetic forms of life, will best guard against the narrowness of scope and feebleness of grasp which characterize the intellect that seeks common-sense only in commonplace, by warming his faculties in the glow of imaginative genius; he should not forget that where heat enters it expands. And, indeed, the rule I thus lay down, eminent men have discovered for themselves.

Men of really great capacities for practical business will generally be found to indulge in a predilection for works of fancy. The favourite reading of poets and fictionists of high order will seldom be poetry or fiction. Poetry or fiction is to them a study, not a relaxation. It is more likely that their favourite reading will be in works called abstruse or dry—antiquities, metaphysics, subtle problems of criticism, or delicate niceties of scholarship. On the other hand, the favourite reading of celebrated lawyers is generally novels.

Thus in every mind of large powers there is an unconscious struggle perpetually going on to preserve its equilibrium. The eye soon loses its justness of vision if always directed towards one object at the same distance—the soil soon exhausts its produce if you draw from it but one crop.

But it is not enough to secure counteraction for the mind in all which directs its prevailing faculties towards partial and special results; it is necessary also to acquire the powers to keep differing faculties and acquirements apart and distinct on all occasions in which it would be improper to blend them.

When the poet enters on the stage of real life as a practical man of business, he must be able to leave his poetry behind him; when the practical man of business enters into the domain of poetry, he must not remind us that he is an authority on the Stock Exchange. In a word, he who has real self-control has all his powers at his command, now to unite, and now to separate them.

SIR BULWER LYTTON.

Travels by the Fireside

THE ceaseless rain is falling fast,
    And yonder gilded vane,
Immoveable for three days past,
    Points to the misty main.

It drives me in upon myself,
    And to the fireside gleams,
To pleasant books that crowd my shelf,
    And still more pleasant dreams.

I read whatever bards have sung
    Of lands beyond the sea;
And the bright days when I was young
    Come thronging back to me.

In fancy I can hear again
    The Alpine torrents' roar,
The mule-bells on the hills of Spain
    The sea at Elsinore.

I see the convent's gleaming wall
    Rise from its groves of pine,
And towers of old cathedrals tall,
    And castles by the Rhine.

I journey on by park and spire,
    Beneath centennial trees,
Through fields with poppies all on fire,
    And gleams of distant seas.

TRAVELS BY THE FIRESIDE.

I feel no more the dust and heat,
  No more I feel fatigue,
While journeying with another's feet
  O'er many a lengthening league.

Let others traverse sea and land,
  And toil through various climes,

I turn the world round with my hand,
  Reading these poets' rhymes.

From them I learn whatever lies
  Beneath each changing zone,
And see, when looking with their eyes,
  Better than with mine own.

H. W. LONGFELLOW.

Sunday in a Norway Town.

It was Sunday, and therefore we saw Bergen in her braws; and a more orderly, douce population I never wish to come across. Not the sign of anything that was not decent, man or woman. No such thing as a rough; no such thing as a cad; no such thing as an offensive snob. But the queerest little boys I ever beheld, all in knickerbockers and little round hats. They were all exactly the same, like little round Dutchmen cut in half, with the most enormous little legs I ever saw on little boys. Had these been the days of the Danish and Hebridean wars, I should have imagined my old gillie, John M'Lean, had made a foray on Norway, and had married several of the Bergen belles; for I never saw legs anywhere else so like his own. There were a good many of the peasantry in the town that day; for they come, like the Scotch, from a great distance to attend church. Not like our good English folk, who must have their churches brought to them, and thus not have far to go to worship God. Their costume was odd, more particularly that of the young, and, I should say, unmarried women. It resembled, in shape and colour, that gown worn by the blue-coat schoolboys, with the addition of a fillet, or fold of red worsted rolled twice round their light hair. Some of the old women wore the quaintest little three-cornered white cocked hats I ever beheld. Many of the upper classes were uncommonly well got up; very neat about the head, which was real hair, and no mistake— no chignons; and as an investment, clipping the young Bergennese heads, supposing they would, for a moderate consideration, consent to it, would pay well at the beginning of the London season.

Bergen is an awfully hot place when the sun is well out, as it was during my stay; and if it was always so, I would as soon live at Cheltenham as there in summer, and that is saying a good deal. But, as I said before, it was the douce, orderly, cheerful aspect and conduct of the Bergennese on Sunday that so much pleased me; not like Scotland, as if half "the sour-featured west had set tryste to be hanged." There were no "young plants of grace that looked couthie and free." No; but honest, worthy Christian people, who, having served God in His house in spirit and truth in the morning, came forth in the afternoon to bask in the beauties of His creation. And this Sunday introduction to the Norwegian folks impressed me strongly in their favour.—"*A Trip to Norway in 1873,*" *by Sixty-one.*

Hand in hand.

Wedding Rings.

WHATEVER may have been the origin of the wedding ring, the Church took care that it should be considered a holy thing. The *Doctrine of the Masse Booke* (1554) contains a form for "the hallowing of a woman's ring at wedding," in which are the following prayers :—

"Thou maker and conserver of mankind, gever of spiritual grace and graunter of eternal salvation, Lord send thy blessing upon this ring, that she which shall weare it maye be armed wyth the vertue of heavenly defence, and that it maye profit her to eternal salvation thorowe Christ," etc.

"Halow thou, Lord, this ring which we blesse in thy holye name, that what woman soever shall weare it may stand fast in thy peace, and continue in thy wyl, and live and grow and waxe old in thy love," etc.

Holy water was then to be sprinkled upon the ring.

In the Hereford, York, and Salisbury Missals directions are given at the marriage for the ring to be put first on the thumb, after on the second finger, then on the third, and lastly on the fourth finger. The rubric still ordains the fourth finger, because it is the ring finger ; and the left hand is chosen, it is said, because the wife is in subjection to her husband, but this is doubtful. It is true that official rings are worn on the right hand, but the left hand has more usually been the favourite one for rings, probably because it is less used than the right.

In many parts of the continent wedding rings are worn by husbands as well as by wives. The wedding ring worn by Luther was a gimmal, and consisted of two perfect rings. On one hoop was set a diamond, as the emblem of power, duration, and fidelity ; and on the other a ruby, for exalted love. On the mounting of the diamond were engraved Luther's initials, and on that of the ruby his wife's ; so that when the two parts were joined the letters came close together. The motto within was, "Was Gott zusammen fugetsoll kein mensch scheiden." (What God doth join no man shall part).

Formerly widows wore their rings on the thumb as an emblem of widowhood, and we find the following trick mentioned in the *Spectator :—*

"It is common enough for a stale virgin to set up a shop in a place where she is not known, where the large thumb ring, supposed to be given her by her husband, quickly recommends her to some wealthy neighbour, who takes a liking to the jolly widow that would have overlooked the veritable spinster."

The old wedding ring usually had its motto, which was often pretty and appropriate. We will set down a few of these posies that were once common:—

"Let lyking laste."
"As God decreed so we agreed."
"Knit in one by Christ alone."
"In Christ and thee my comfort be."
"First love Christ that died for thee,
   Next to Him love none but me."
"Let us share in joy and care."
"United hearts death only parts."

"A faithful wife preserveth life."
"This and the giver are thine for ever."
"This hath alloy; my love is pure."
"The diamond is within."
"I'll win and wear you."
"I like my choice."
"Love and live happily."

Social Distinction.

THE people, you say, the people! That is you and I, beyond denial. There are not two races. The distinctions of class are illusions. I do not know whether you have remote ancestors in the *bourgeoisie*; as to myself, my maternal roots come directly from the people, and I feel them still alive at the extremity of my being. We all have them there. The first men were hunters and shepherds, then labourers and soldiers. Plunder crowned with success gave birth to its first social distinctions. There is not, perhaps, a title that was not obtained through the blood of man. One person is not above nor below another, except in point of common-sense or morality. My feeling and my reason oppose more than ever the idea of fictitious distinctions, the inequality of conditions imposed as a right acquired by some, as a forfeiture deserved by others. More than ever I feel the need of raising what is low and lifting what has fallen. While my heart exists it will be open to pity, and will take the part of the weak and calumniated. If to-day it is the down-trodden people, I will offer them my hand. If it is the oppressor and executioner, I will tell him he is cowardly and hateful. What do I care for this or that group of men, those names which have become ensigns, those expressions which have become watchwords? I make a distinction only between the wise and the foolish, the innocent and the guilty. I do not inquire where are my friends and where my enemies. They remain wherever the storm has thrown them. Those who have deserved my affection, yet cannot see with my eyes, I hold none the less dear! The inconsiderate blame of those who forsake me does not make me consider them my enemies. All friendship, unjustly withdrawn, remains intact within the heart that has not deserved such an outrage. Such a heart is above self-love; it can wait for the revival of justice and affection.

GEORGE SAND.

Children.

COME to me, O ye children!
　For I hear you are at your play,
And the questions that perplex me
　Have vanished quite away.

Ye open the eastern windows,
　That look towards the sun,
Where thoughts are singing swallows
　And the brooks of morning run.

In your hearts are the birds and the sunshine,
　In your thoughts the brooklets flow,
But in mine is the wind of Autumn,
　And the first fall of the snow.

Ah! what would the world be to us
　If the children were no more?
We should dread the desert behind us
　Worse than the dark before.

What the leaves are to the forest,
   With light and air for food,
Ere their sweet and tender juices
   Have been hardened into wood,—

That to the world are children;
   Through them it feels the glow
Of a brighter and sunnier climate
   Than reaches the trunks below.

Come to me, O ye children,
   And whisper in my ear
What the birds and the winds are singing
   In your sunny atmosphere.

For what are all our contrivings,
   And the wisdom of our books,
When compared with your caresses,
   And the gladness of your looks?

Ye are better than all the ballads
   That ever were sung or said;
For ye are living poems,
   And all the rest are dead.

Play.

THE spirit of the age says, "Move on;" but yet methinks there is a gentle spirit of the air which whispers now and then, "*Siste viator.*"

Let's go up in a balloon for a bit, and take a mental bird's-eye view of London. It is morning. See those termini, with open cavernous mouths, belching forth streams of humanity in successive jets. See them emerging from under the ground too. Hurry, hurry, hurry, every one is hurrying to his daily station to be beaten flat,—making "parts" of things "by the dozen," either literally or in a figure,—the principle of the division of labour ridden to death. A certain unwholesome cleverness forced at fever heat, but at the expense of originality of character. The whole man not developed. As a consequence, the banks of the well-defined channels which confine simple loyalty and pristine faith broken down, those clear waters overflown as in a flood, the very banks lost to sight in a swamp of careless criticism and second-hand milk-and-water convictions. Far from leading the pæan of creation, men fast losing touch even with the birds, beasts, and fishes.

There's nothing like complete contrast. Let's go right to the other extreme. Cut the ropes. Let's hover over Palestine. Flower-bestrewn, vine-entangled, cedar-shadowed Palestine! How quiet and still you lie there by the blue sea! Your coast-line looks as if you had been cut off with a blunt knife in the hurry-skurry—left behind and clean forgotten by the rest of the world.

Looking through the wrong end of the telescope, and taking in the green hills around Bethlehem, methinks I can see David seated there, a well-rounded man, a natural man. Keep quite still and listen to him as he strikes up the lyre of Gath under the twinkling stars—the stray bleating of the sheep at eventide will not hinder; they are in harmony.

"When I behold Thy heavens, the work of Thy fingers, the moon and the stars, which Thou hast ordained; what is man, that Thou art mindful of him? and the son of man, that Thou visitest him? For Thou hast made him a little lower than the angels, and hast crowned him with glory and honour. Thou madest him to have dominion over the works of Thy hands; Thou hast put all things under his feet; all sheep and oxen, yea, and the beasts of the field; the fowl of the air, and the fish of the sea, and whatsoever passeth through the paths of the sea."

Shut up the telescope. Click! Now, what's the moral? If we in England are to recover the balance of nature, which may be said to lie midway between the two extremes of England and Palestine as they are to-day,—if we are to avoid dwindling away into a fourth-rate power, and giving way, in our turn, to a nation more robust and "natural," something must be done to *counteract* the exhausting and terrible high pressure at which we live. Play, the gospel of play and hobby-horses, must be preached to our generation. "For oh! for oh! the hobby-horse is forgot." There is nothing like a hobby—something quite outside the groove in which we work—to recover the balance of nature.

Having settled that much, let's get back again. . . . Drop the grappling-irons. Here we are. Fleet Street! Can this be Fleet Street! Shutters up! There seems to have been a stampede too. Or have those bobbies locked every one up in the shops? Perhaps that's why they're now walking up and down—to see they don't get out. Will you tell us, lone policeman, what is the matter? Bank Holiday, of course! Saint Lubbock's Day! I don't indeed see thy name in the calendar, Sir John. However thou mayest, "I dinna ken, e'en sit among the saints *yet*." Thou hast given millions of flattened men a chance of rounding a bit. With thy ants, and thy bees, and thy dogs, thou hast given, too, some good hints about hobbies. Surely thou must have heard my Ariel. The young of Budgerigars, when bred in activity, in an unnatural state, are sometimes born without feathers. I think, if things had gone on much longer without these holidays, English babies would have been born into the world a few generations hence incomplete—fit *only* for a certain groove—with an inherent incapacity to take up the human part in the harmony of creation.

I have never been in Italy. She seems to me, however, to be a land of light-hearted music. It is but a law of economy that what one nation wants another should supply. Talking of holidays, we want, for one thing, light-hearted street music to bid now and again our poor look up and smile. Italy supplies that want. Thanks Italia! Thy young daughters have a freedom and a prettiness all their own.

Perambulating one summer day a poor and crowded quarter, a feeling of heaviness came over me. Grimness seemed settled down upon all. It was contagious. I felt it myself. Emerging presently into the outskirts, I came across a sight which cheered one. Outside a small roadside public-house was a little group. An old man with grey hair, and furrowed, was dancing a sort of fling with a young Italian girl as his *vis-à-vis*. He was drunk—not dead drunk, but fuddled. She, with arms a-kimbo, and a little cross nestling upon her bosom, was beautiful to a degree. She did not seem to know or care that he was fuddled. His hair was wintry, and she was trying, with wonderful grace and fascination, to make the old man merry. He had evidently spent his last farthing in the pub. As I passed, he said with choking accents—the perspiration standing on his brow, and blushing to the roots of his hair—"Do give her a penny, sir." His poor old heart was touched. She had sent a sunbeam through the closed shutters. I seemed to see the careworn features lit up with a touch of nature. "Do give her a penny, sir." Ay, that will I; a dozen pennies. If Mrs. Grundy were out of the way, I would beg, too, a kiss from thy pretty lips.

You have no Mrs. Grundy in Italy.

Now for a few straight tips—very straight tips—to working-men especially—about the *abuse* of these Bank Holidays. They were intended, as we have seen, to give too hard-worked men and women an opportunity of expanding and recovering the balance of nature. What happens, however? Bank Holiday comes round. You go out for a day's enjoyment. Of necessity you make use of the public-houses. You pour money into the landlord's pockets on that day. Ask yourself when you get home what you have got for it. Which has been bested, you or the publican? You paid him money. Did he make it his business to study your holiday wants in return? The publican is supposed to be a licensed *victualler*. Did he supply you with proper victuals? Why shouldn't you, as in a French *café*, be able to get downright good tea, coffee, and plentiful victuals as well as those monotonous "drinks"? After your holiday, instead of being refreshed and ready to return to work with a will, you are probably rendered almost incapable of work for a day or two. Too much to drink and too little to eat has done it.

How easily you are gulled! You may talk of your John Bullism, but the "foreigner," in this matter too, has more sense than you have. Any one can enter a French *café* without loss of caste, of course! It is not so with a British public-house. Why, the British publican has found by experience that all he need do to entice you into his "boozing ken"—for, alas! it is nothing else—is to stick up tinsel advertisements. "Cream gin!" for instance. Fancy "*cream* gin!" They say there's nothing in a name, but, like many other sayings, it is not quite true. There was an old lady once, who loved "that comforting word, Mesopotamia." Some poor souls, I do believe, when they take their gin, derive some sort of comfort from the innocent word "cream" attached to it. As it glides down, perhaps it calls up visions of cows and cool dairies. Why not call it "liver gin"? That, perhaps, might help to call up visions of a gin-drinker's liver. There would be this great advantage, too. Those visions would stand some chance of being realized. "Orange" gin, again. "Mountain-dew whisky." O yes, depend upon it there's something in a name.

The remedy for this unsatisfactory state of things is in great measure in your own hands. Strike a fair *bargain* with the publican, and don't let him gull you so easily.

Now for a few words with mine host. Alas! though, it is really absurd to call you "mine host." "Mine host" and his "guest" are now changed into "landlord" and "customer." Never mind. For the humour of the thing, I will say, "Mine host." There isn't a chair, by the way. Well, take a "stool," and have a chat. We don't often meet. I have been rather down on you. There's my hand now, if you're going to make it up. After all, I haven't called you very *very* bad names. What do you say to a few straight "tips"? You have *enormous* power. There is no doubt about it. You are a giant fact. Use your strength *like* a giant. There was a giant once who ground Englishmen's bones to make his bread.

"Fee, fi, fo, fum;
I smell the blood of an Englishman."

We've all heard about him. But he was a cruel ogre, quite an exceptional giant. Real, everyday giants *can* crush, but they do *not* crush. They are far more disposed to do good than harm to their fellows—to protect them, than to "grind their bones." That is why, then, I say, use your strength like a giant. Why shouldn't you be in reality "mine host"? And why shouldn't you look upon Bank Holiday makers—the millions let loose—as your "*guests*"? They are "out for a holiday," thoughtless and generous, and will, no doubt, if you will let them, go all day on nothing more substantial than a Banbury cake. Why shouldn't you provide a regular *table d' hôte* for these occasions, third class and first class; third class, say, at 6d. or 8d. a head? Don't say it wouldn't pay. Make it pay. Who that has been out camping doesn't know what wonders can be done with Irish stew, for instance, in the way of a substantial feed? You needn't go in for table linen or expensive nick-nacks. Give your "guests" all the value in solid food. Why not have flowers upon the table, too? Yes, why not? If you would only make use of them, there are many people, anxious about the great abuse of these Bank Holidays, who would be glad to present you with flowers for the occasion.

For just consider this. These people have a certain amount of money to spend,—saved up for Bank Holiday,—and spend it they will. You can, in any case, have the greater part of it too. All I say is, give them something besides drink, drink, drink, nothing but drink, for their money. You *need* not, as you very well know. Does it necessarily follow that you *will* not? The idea of attempting to enlist *you* into the ranks of philanthropy may raise a smile upon the lips of some. But why should it not be so? May I not appeal to you in the name of our common Master? Think what an awful lot you might do towards raising our country from the Slough of Despond, if you would only help the masses to spend their playtime better, in order that they might work better. These regular holidays are a singular blessing. Many people, however, say that they are a curse; and they point to you as the cause of the evil. In the name of Christ, then, will you not make a better use of the enormous power you undoubtedly possess, than to grind men's bones to make your bread? It is necessary to make this solemn appeal to high motives, because, looked at in an ordinary way, you are really but little to blame. It is a matter of simple exchange, and if the other party to the bargain is a flat, and is satisfied, you are not in strict justice to blame for that. Enter, however, into the spirit of the thing. You will know best about practical details. All I want to bring home is the principle to be worked out. It is my belief that, if loyally kept in view, it would pay handsomely as regards the rhino. It will assuredly in other ways.

Having now introduced "landlord" and "customer" to each other, I would leave them to fight it out like two schoolboys, in the good old English fashion.

REV. G. WHIT WHITE.

Recreation.

RECREATION is a second creation, when weariness hath almost annihilated one's spirits. It is the breathing of the soul, which otherwise would be stifled with continual business.

Spill not the morning (the quintessence of the day) in recreation; for sleep itself is a recreation. Add not therefore sauce to sauces; and he cannot properly have any title to be refreshed who was not first faint. Pastime, like wine, is poison in the morning. It is then good husbandry to sow the head, which hath lain fallow all night, with some serious work. Chiefly, intrench not on the Lord's day base unlawful sports; this were to spare thine own flock, and to shear God's lamb.

THOMAS FULLER (1608–1661.)

"IT was my custom in my youth," says a celebrated Persian writer, "to rise from my sleep, to watch, pray, and read the Koran. One night, as I was thus engaged, my father, a man of practised virtue, awoke. 'Behold,' said I to him, 'thy other children are lost in irreligious slumbers, while I alone wake to praise God.' 'Son of my soul,' said he, 'it is better to sleep, than to wake to remark the faults of thy brethren.'"

Work.

Down and up, and up and down,
   Over, and over, and over ;
Turn in the little seed, dry and brown ;
   Turn out the bright red clover.
Work, and the sun your work will share,
   And the rain in its time will fall ;
For Nature she worketh everywhere,
   And the grace of God through all.

With hand on the spade and heart in the sky,
   Dress the ground and till it ;
Turn in the little seed, brown and dry ;
   Turn out the golden millet.
Work, and your house shall be duly fed ;
   Work, and rest shall be won :
I hold that a man had better be dead
   Than alive, when his work is done !

Down and up, and up and down,
   On the hill top, low in the valley ;
Turn in the little seed, dry and brown ;
   Turn out the rose and lily.
Work, with a plan, or without a plan,
   And your ends they shall be shaped true ;
Work, and learn at first hand like a man—
   The best way to *know* is to *do*.

Down and up, till life shall close,
   Ceasing not your praises ;
Turn in the wild white winter snows,
   Turn out the sweet spring daisies.
Work, and the sun your work will share,
   And the rain in its time will fall ;
For Nature she worketh everywhere,
   And the grace of God through all.

ALICE CARY.

Grace Before Meat.

THE custom of saying grace at meals had, probably, its origin in the early times of the world, and the hunter-state of man, when dinners were precarious things, and a full meal was something more than a common blessing; when a belly-full was a wind-fall, and looked like a special providence. In the shouts of triumphant songs with which, after a season of sharp abstinence, a lucky booty of deer's or goat's flesh would naturally be ushered home, existed, perhaps, the germ of the modern grace. It is not otherwise easy to be understood why the blessing of food—the act of eating—should have had a particular expression of thanksgiving annexed to it, distinct from that implied and silent gratitude with which we are expected to enter upon the enjoyment of the many other various gifts and good things of existence.

I own that I am disposed to say grace upon twenty other occasions in the course of the day besides my dinner. I want a form for setting out upon a pleasant walk, for a moonlight ramble, for a friendly meeting, or a solved problem. Why have we none for books, those spiritual repasts—a grace before Milton—a grace before Shakspeare—a devotional exercise proper to be said before reading the Faerie Queen? But the received ritual having prescribed these forms to the solitary ceremony of manducation, I shall confine my observations to the experience which I have had of the grace, properly so called; commending my new scheme for extension to a niche in the grand philosophical, poetical, and perchance in part heretical liturgy, now compiling by my friend Homo Humanus, for the use of a certain snug congregation of Utopian Rabelæsian Christians, no matter where assembled.

The form, then, of the benediction before eating has its beauty at a poor man's table, or at the simple and unprovocative repast of children. It is here that the grace becomes exceedingly graceful. The indigent man, who hardly knows whether he shall have a meal the next day or not, sits down to his fare with a present sense of the blessing, which can be but feebly acted by the rich, into whose mind the conception of wanting a dinner could never, but by some extreme theory, have entered. The proper end of food—the animal sustenance

—is barely contemplated by them. The poor man's bread is his daily bread, literally his bread for the day. Their courses are perennial.

Again, the plainest diet seems the fittest to be preceded by the grace. That which is least stimulative to appetite, leaves the mind most free for foreign considerations. A man may feel thankful, heartily thankful, over a dish of plain mutton with turnips, and have leisure to reflect upon the ordinance and institution of eating; when he shall confess a perturbation of mind, inconsistent with the purposes of the grace, at the presence of venison or turtle. When I have sat (*a rarus hospes*) at rich men's tables, with the savoury soup and messes steaming up the nostrils, and moistening the lips of the guests with desire and a distracted choice, I have felt the introduction of that ceremony to be unseasonable. With the ravenous orgasm upon you, it seems impertinent to interpose a religious sentiment. It is a confusion of purpose to mutter out praises from a mouth that waters. The heats of epicurism put out the gentle flame of devotion. The incense which rises round is pagan, and the belly-god intercepts it for his own. The very excess of the provision beyond the needs, takes away all sense of proportion between the end and means. The Giver is veiled by His gifts. You are startled at the injustice of returning thanks—for what?—for having too much, while so many starve. It is to praise the gods amiss.

I have observed this awkwardness felt, scarce consciously perhaps, by the good man who says the grace. I have seen it in clergymen and others—a sort of shame—a sense of the co-presence of circumstances which unhallow the blessing. After a devotional tone put on for a few seconds, how rapidly the speaker will fall into his common voice! helping himself or his neighbour, as if to get rid of some uneasy sensation of hypocrisy. Not that the good man was a hypocrite, or was not most conscientious in the discharge of the duty; but he felt in his inmost mind the incompatibility of the scene and the viands before him, with the exercise of a calm and rational gratitude.

I hear somebody exclaim,—Would you have Christians sit down at table, like hogs to their troughs, without remembering the Giver? No—I would have them sit down as Christians, remembering the Giver, and less like hogs. Or if their appetites must run riot, and they must pamper themselves with delicacies, for which east and west are ransacked, I would have them postpone their benediction to a fitter season, when appetite is laid, when the still small voice can be heard, and the reason of the grace returns—with temperate diet and restricted dishes. Gluttony and surfeiting are no proper occasions for thanksgiving. When Jeshurun waxed fat, we read that he kicked. Virgil knew the harpy nature better, when he put into the mouth of Celæno anything but a blessing. We may be gratefully sensible of the deliciousness of some kinds of food beyond others, though that is a meaner and inferior gratitude: but the proper object of the grace is sustenance, not relishes; daily bread, not delicacies; the means of life, and not the means of pampering the carcass. With what frame or composure, I wonder, can a city chaplain pronounce his benediction at some great Hall-feast, when he knows that his last concluding pious word—and that, in all probability, the sacred name which he preaches—is but the signal for so many impatient harpies to commence their foul orgies, with as little sense of true thankfulness (which is temperance) as those Virgilian fowl! It is well if the good man himself does not feel his devotions a little clouded, those foggy sensuous steams mingling with and polluting the pure altar sacrifice.

The severest satire upon full tables and surfeits is the banquet which Satan, in the Paradise Regained, provides for a temptation in the wilderness:—

> A table richly spread in regal mode
> With dishes piled, and meats of noblest sort
> And savour; beasts of chase, or fowl of game,
> In pastry built, or from the spit, or boiled,
> Gris-amber-steamed; all fish from sea or shore,
> Freshet or purling brook, for which was drained
> Pontus, and Lucrine bay, and Afric coast.

The Tempter, I warrant you, thought these cates would go down without the recommendatory preface of a benediction. They are like to be short graces where the devil plays the host.—I am afraid the poet wants his usual decorum in this place. Was he thinking of the old Roman luxury, or of a gaudy-day at Cambridge? This was a temptation fitter for a Heliogabalus. The whole banquet is too civic and culinary, and the accompaniments altogether a profanation of that deep, abstracted, holy scene. The mighty artillery of sauces, which the cook-fiend conjures up, is out of proportion to the simple wants and plain hunger of the Guest. He that disturbed him in his dreams, from his dreams might have been taught better. To the temperate fantasies of the famished Son of God, what sort of feasts presented themselves?—He dreamed indeed.

> As appetite is wont to dream,
> Of meats and drinks, nature's refreshment sweet.

But what meats?

> Him thought, he by the brook of Cherith stood,
> And saw the ravens with their horny beaks
> Food to Elijah bringing, even and morn;
> Though ravenous, taught to abstain from what they brought:
> He saw the prophet also, how he fled
> Into the desert, and how there he slept
> Under a juniper; then how awaked
> He found his supper on the coals prepared,
> And by the angel was bid rise and eat,
> And ate the second time after repose,
> The strength whereof sufficed him forty days;
> Sometimes, that with Elijah he partook,
> Or as a guest with Daniel at his pulse.

Nothing in Milton is finelier fancied than these temperate dreams of the divine Hungerer. To which of these two visionary banquets, think you, would the introduction of what is called the grace, have been the most fitting and pertinent?

Theoretically I am no enemy to graces; but practically I own that (before meat especially) they seem to involve something awkward and unseasonable. The Quakers, who go about their business of every description with more calmness than we, have more title to the use of these benedictory prefaces. I have always admired their silent grace, and the more because I have observed their applications to the meat and drink following to be less passionate and sensual than ours. They are neither gluttons nor wine-bibbers as a people. They eat, as a horse bolts his chopped hay, with indifference, calmness, and cleanly circumstances. They neither grease nor slop themselves. When I see a citizen in his bib and tucker, I cannot imagine it a surplice.

I am no Quaker at my food. I confess I am not indifferent to the kinds of it. Those unctuous morsels of deer's flesh were not made to be received with dispassionate services. I hate a man who swallows it, affecting not to know what he is eating. I suspect his taste in higher matters. I shrink instinctively from one who professes to like minced veal. There is a physiognomical character in the tastes for food. C—— holds that a man cannot have a pure mind who refuses apple-dumplings. I am not certain but he is right. With the decay of my first innocence, I confess a less and less relish daily for those innocuous cates. The whole vegetable tribe have lost their gust with me. Only I stick to asparagus, which still seems to inspire gentle thoughts. I am impatient and querulous under culinary disappointments, as to come home at the dinner hour, for instance, expecting some savoury mess, and to find one quite tasteless and sapidless. Butter ill melted—that commonest of kitchen failures—puts me beside my tenor.—The author of the Rambler used to make inarticulate animal noises over a favourite food. Was this the music quite proper to be preceded by the grace? or would the pious man have done better to postpone his devotions to a season when the blessing might be contemplated with less perturbation? I quarrel with no man's tastes, nor would set my thin face against those excellent things, in their way, jollity and feasting. But as these exercises, however laudable, have little in them of grace or gracefulness, a man should be sure, before he ventures so to grace them, that while he is pretending his devotions otherwhere, he is not secretly kissing his hand to some great fish—his Dagon—with a special consecration of no ark but the fat tureen before him. Graces are the sweet preluding strains to the banquets of angels and children; to the roots and severer repasts of the Chartreuse; to the slender, but not slenderly acknowledged, refection of the poor and humble man: but at the heaped-up boards of the pampered and the luxurious, they become of dissonant mood, less timed and tuned to the occasion, methinks, than the noise of those better befitting organs would be which children hear tales of, at Hog's Norton. We sit too long at our meals, or are too curious in the study of them, or too disordered in our application to them, or engross too great a portion of those good things (which should be common) to our share, to be able with any grace to say grace. To be thankful for what we grasp exceeding our proportion, is to add hypocrisy to injustice. A lurking sense of this truth is what makes the performance of this duty so cold and spiritless a service at most tables. In houses where the grace is as indispensable as the napkin, who has not seen that never-settled question arise, as to *who shall say it?* while the goodman of the house and the visitor clergyman, or some other guest, belike of next authority, from years or gravity, shall be bandying about the office between them as a matter of compliment, each of them not unwilling to shift the awkward burthen of an equivocal duty from his own shoulders.

I once drank tea in company with two Methodist divines of different persuasions, whom it was my fortune to introduce to each other for the first time that evening. Before the first cup was handed round, one of these reverend gentlemen put it to the other, with all due solemnity, whether he chose to *say anything*. It seems it is the custom with some sectaries to put up a short prayer before this meal also. His reverend brother did not at first apprehend him, but upon an explanation, with little less importance he made answer that it was not a custom known in his church: in which courteous evasion the other acquiescing for good manners' sake, or in compliance with a weak brother, the supplementary or tea-grace was waived altogether. With what spirit might not Lucian have painted two priests of *his* religion playing into each other's hands the compliment of performing or omitting a sacrifice,—the hungry god meantime, doubtful of his incense, with expectant nostrils hovering over the two flamens, and (as between two stools) going away in the end without his supper!

A short form upon these occasions is felt to want reverence; a long one, I am afraid, cannot escape the charge of impertinence. I do not quite approve of the epigrammatic conciseness with which that equivocal wag (but my pleasant school-fellow) C. V. L., when importuned for a grace, used to inquire, first slyly leering down the table, "Is there no clergyman here?"—significantly adding, "Thank G—:" Nor do I think our old form at school quite pertinent, where we used to preface our bald bread-and-cheese suppers with a preamble, connecting with that humble blessing a recognition of benefits the most awful and overwhelming to the imagination which religion has to offer. *Non tunc illis erat locus.* I remember we were put to it to reconcile the phrase "good creatures," upon which the blessing rested, with the fare set before us, wilfully understanding that expression in a low and animal sense; till some one recalled a legend, which told how, in the golden days of Christ's, the young Hospitallers were wont to have smoking joints of roast meat upon their nightly beards, till some pious benefactor, commiserating the decencies, rather than the palates, of the children, commuted our flesh for garments, and gave us—*horresco referens*—trousers instead of mutton.

CHARLES LAMB.

Be Happy To-day.

How old are you? Twenty-five? Thirty? Are you happy to-day? Were you happy yesterday? Are you generally happy? If so, you have reason to judge that you will be happy by-and-by. Are you so busy that you have no time to be happy? And are you going to be happy when you are old, and you have not much to do? No; you will not. You now have a specimen of what you will be when you are old.

Look in the face of to-day. That is about the average. That will tell you what you are going to be. What you are carrying along with you is what you will have by-and-by. If you are so conducting yourself that you have peace with God, and with your fellowmen, and with your faculties; if every day you insist that duty shall make you happy, and you take as much time as is needful for the culture of your social faculties, you will not be exhausting life, and it will be continually replenished. But if you are saving everything up till you get to be an old man, habit will stand like a tyrant, and say, "You would not enjoy yourself before, and you shall not now."

How many men there are who have ground and ground to make money that they might be happy by-and-by, but who, when they have got to be fifty or sixty years old, had used up all the enjoyable nerve than was in them! During early life they carried toil, economy, and frugality to the excess of stinginess, and when the time came that they expected joy, there was no joy for them.

H. W. BEECHER.

Grandma's Team.

"It's no use; I can't find a horse anywhere, for love or money. All are either sick or kept quiet to-day for fear of being sick. I declare, I'd almost rather lose Major than disappoint mother," said Farmer Jenks, coming in on Sunday morning from a fruitless visit to his neighbours.

It was in the height of the horse distemper, and his own valuable beast stood in the stall, looking very interesting, with his legs in red flannel bandages, an old shawl round his neck, his body well covered by blankets, and a pensive expression in his fine eyes as he coughed and groaned distressfully.

You see it was particularly unfortunate to have Major give out on Sunday, for grandma had been to church, rain or shine, every Sunday for twenty years, and it was the pride of her life to be able to say this. She was quite superstitious about it, and really felt as if her wonderful health and strength were given her as a reward for her unfailing devotion.

A sincerely pious and good old lady was Grandma Jenks, and her entry into church always made a little sensation, for she was eighty-five years old, yet hale and hearty, with no affliction but lame feet. So every Sunday, all the year round, her son or grandsons drove her down to service in the wide, low chaise, got expressly for her benefit, and all the week seemed brighter and better for the quiet hour spent in the big pew.

"If the steeple should fall, folks wouldn't miss it any more than they would old Mrs. Jenks from her corner," was a saying among the people; and grandma felt as if she was not only a public character, but a public example for all to follow, for another saying in the town was,—

"Well, if old Mrs. Jenks can go to meeting, there's no excuse for our staying at home."

That pleased her, and so when the farmer came in with this bad news, she looked deeply disappointed, sat still a minute tapping her hymn-book, then took her two canes and got up, saying resolutely,—

"A merciful man is merciful to his beast, so I won't have poor Major risk his life for me; but I shall walk.'

A general outcry followed, for grandma was very lame, church a mile away, and the roads muddy after the rain.

"You can't do it, mother, and you'll be sick for the winter if you try," cried Mrs. Jenks in great trouble.

"No, dear; I guess the Lord will give me strength, since I'm going to His house," answered the old lady, walking slowly to the door.

"Blest if I wouldn't carry you myself if only I could, mother!" exclaimed the farmer, helping her down the steps with filial gentleness.

Here Ned and Charley, the boys, laughed; for grandma was very stout, and the idea of their father carrying her tickled them immensely.

"Boys, I'm ashamed of you!" said their mother, frowning at them. But grandma laughed too, and said pleasantly,—

"I won't be a burden, Moses; give me your arm, and I'll step out as well as I can, and mebby someone may come along and give me a lift."

So the door was locked, and the family set off.

But it was hard work for the old lady, and soon she said she must sit down and rest a spell. As they stood waiting for her, all looking anxious, the boys suddenly had a bright idea, and, merely saying they had forgotten something, raced up the hill again.

"I'm afraid you won't be able to do it, mother," the farmer was just saying, when the sound of an approaching carriage made them all turn to look, hoping for a lift.

Nearer and nearer drew the rattle, and round the corner came, not a horse's head, but two felt hats on two boys' heads, and Charley and Ned appeared, trotting briskly, with the chaise behind them.

"Here's your team, grandma! Jump in, and we'll get you to meeting in good time yet," cried the lads, smiling and panting as they drew up close to the stone where the old lady sat.

"Boys, boys, it's Sunday, and we can't have any jokes or nonsense now," began Mrs. Jenks, looking much scandalized.

"Well, I don't know, wife. It's a new thing, I allow, but considering the fix we are in, I'm not sure it isn't a good plan. What do *you* think, mother?" asked the farmer laughing, yet well pleased at the energy and good-will of his lads.

"If the boys behave themselves, and do it as a duty, not a frolic, and don't upset me, I reckon I'll let 'em try, for I don't believe I can get there any other way," says grandma.

"You hoped the Lord would give you strength, and so He has, in this form. Use it, mother, and thank Him for it, since the children love you so well, they would run their legs off to serve you," said the farmer soberly, as he helped the old lady in, and folded the robes round her feet.

"Steady, boys; no pranks, and stop behind the sheds. I can lend mother an arm there, and she can walk across the green. This turn-out is all very well, but we won't make a show of it."

Away went the chaise rolling gently down the hill, and the new span trotted well together, while the old lady sat calmly inside, frequently saying,—

"Don't pull too hard, Ned. I'm afraid I'm very heavy for you to draw, Charley. Take it easy, dears; there's time enough, time enough."

"You'll never hear the last of this, Moses; it will be a town joke for months to come," said Mrs. Jenks, as she and her husband walked briskly after the triumphal car.

"Don't care if I do hear on't for a considerable spell. It's nothing to be ashamed of, and I guess you'll find that folks will agree with me, even if they do laugh," answered the farmer stoutly; and he was right.

Pausing behind the sheds, grandma was handed out, and the family went into church, a little late, but quite decorously, and as if nothing funny had occurred. To be sure, Ned and Charley were very red and hot, and now and then stole looks at one another with a roguish twinkle of the eye; but a nudge from mother, or a shake of the head from father, kept them in good order, while dear old grandma couldn't do enough to show her gratitude. She passed a fan, she handed peppermints in her hymn-book, and when Ned sneezed, begged him to put her shawl over his shoulders.

After church the lads slipped away, and harnessed themselves all ready for the homeward trip. But they had to wait, for grandma met some friends and stopped to "reminiss," as she called it, and her son did not hurry her, thinking it as well to have the coast clear before his new team appeared.

It was dull and cold behind the sheds, and the boys soon got impatient. Their harness was rather intricate, and they did not want to take it off, so they stood chafing and grumbling at the delay.

"You are nearest, so just hand out that blanket and put it over me; I'm as cold as a stone," said Ned who was leader.

"I want it myself, if I've got to wait here much longer," grumbled Charley, sitting on the whiffletree, with his legs curled up.

"You're a selfish pig! I'm sure I shall have the horse-cough to-morrow if you don't cover me up."

"Now you know why father is so particular about making us cover Major when we leave him standing. You never do it if you can help it, so how do you like it yourself?"

"Whether I like it or not, I'll warm you when we get home; see if I don't, old fellow."

Up came the elders, and away went the ponies, but they had a hard tug of it this time. Grandma was not a light weight, the road pretty steep in places, and the mud made heavy going. Such a puffing and panting, heaving and hauling, was never heard or seen before. The farmer put his shoulder to the wheel, and even Mrs. Jenks tucked up her black silk skirts, and gave an occasional tug at one shaft.

Grandma bemoaned her cruelty, and begged to get out; but the lads wouldn't give up, so with frequent stoppages, some irrepressible laughter, and much persistent effort, the old lady was safely landed at the front door.

No sooner was she fairly down, than she did what I fancy might have a good effect on four-legged steeds if occasionally tried. She hugged both boys, patted and praised them, helped to pull off their harness, and wiped their hot foreheads with her own best Sunday handkerchief, then led them in and fed them well.

The lads were in high feather at the success of their exploit, and each showed it in a different way. Charley laughed and talked about it, offered to trot grandma out any day, and rejoiced in the strength of his muscles, and his soundness in wind and limb.

But Ned sat silently eating his dinner, and when some one asked him if he remembered the text of the sermon, he answered in grandma's words, "A merciful man is merciful to his beast."

"Well, I don't care, that's the only text I remember, and I got a sermon out of it, anyway," he said, when the rest laughed at him, and asked what he was thinking about.

"I seem to know now how Major feels when we keep him waiting, when I don't blanket him, and when I expect him to pull his heart out, with no time to get his breath. I'm going to beg his pardon after dinner, and tell him all about it."

Charley stopped laughing when sober Ned said that, and he saw his father and mother nod to one another, as if well pleased.

"I'll go too, and tell the old fellow that I mean to uncheck him going up hill, to scotch the wheels so he can rest, and be ever so good to him if he'll only get well."

"You might add that you mean to treat him like a horse and a brother, for you have turned pony yourself," said his father, when Charley finished his virtuous remarks.

"And don't forget to pet him a good deal, my dears, for horses like to be loved and praised and thanked, as well as boys, and we can't do too much for the noble creatures who are so faithful and useful to us," said Mrs. Jenks, quite touched by the new state of feeling.

"It's my opinion that this sickness among the horses will do a deal of good, by showing folks the great value of the beasts they abuse and neglect. Neighbour Stone is fussing over his old Whitey as if he was a child, and yet I've seen that poor brute unmercifully beaten, and kept half-starved. I told Stone that if he lost him, it would be because kind treatment came too late; and Stone never got mad, but went and poured vinegar over a hot brick under Whitey's nose, till he 'most sneezed his head off. Stone has got a lesson this time, and so have some other folks.

As the farmer spoke, he glanced at the boys, who remorsefully recalled the wrongs poor Major had suffered at their hands, not from cruelty, but thoughtlessness, and both resolved to treat him like a friend for evermore.

"Well," said grandma, looking with tender pride at the ruddy faces on either side of her, "I'm thankful to say that I've never missed a Sunday for twenty year, and I've been in all sorts of weather, and in all sorts of ways, even on an ox sled one time, when the drifts were deep, but I never went better than to-day; so in this dish of tea I'm going to drink this toast, 'Easy roads, light loads, and kind drivers to Grandma's Team.'"

LOUISA MAY ALCOTT.

A LADY, now living in California, relates the following as an incident of her early life:—

Travelling in a coach in a thinly-settled part of Alabama with her parents, she gave utterance to the enthusiasm of a young girl at the romantic scenery. Her father apologized to a fellow-passenger for her exuberance. The stranger answered, "Do not check her; enthusiasm is the gift of God;" and then he began in eloquent language to tell of the scenes he had gazed upon, and the lands he had visited, dwelling alternately on the majesty of the wilds of the West and the splendours of the highest civilisation. The girl's fancy was all aflame, and she led the stranger to speak of foreign lands, and at last of Spain; until, forgetting himself, he spoke of scenes and narrated legends in words which disclosed to her his identity. Clapping her hands, she cried, "You are Washington Irving!"

At School at Eton College.

It has been truly said, that the briefest notice of the Etonians of the eighteenth century alone would imply a biographical dictionary of half the distinguished persons in Church and State. We can scarce hope to enumerate them in a brief record of this kind. Among the Collegers we find enrolled the names of Bishops Fleetwood, Pearson, and Hare; Sir Robert Walpole, afterwards Earl of Orford, Earl Camden, Christopher Anstey (whose name figures on the oak panelling), and Sir William Draper; and, together with them, a whole host of well-known prelates, lawyers; and last, not least, Eton provosts and masters, the redoubtable Keate among the number; and Thackeray, Goodall, and Hawtrey. Foremost, of course, among the Oppidans stands Horace Walpole, who, after he had long ceased to be an Eton boy, loved to seek the hospitable shelter of the "Christopher," and thence send pleasant and gossipy letters concerning the college to his friends and whilom schoolfellows, the Montagus. Then we meet with the names of Robert Boyle and Waller the poet, of the Earl of Chatham and the two first Lord Lyttletons, of Gray, and that "miracle of talent," Sir James Macdonald, and of Charles James Fox, who while at Eton was troublesome and irregular in his habits, and much "more of a mutineer than a pupil." His father, it seems, would call for him, and take him off for a trip to Paris and Spa, to the intense chagrin of the headmaster. Charles James would presently return, overcome with foppery and French conceits; and on one occasion, it is satisfactory to be able to record, as evidence of the independent spirit ever latent in Eton's headmasters, he was soundly flogged for exhibiting his foppish airs to Dr. Barnard. At the head of the list of celebrated living Etonians stands the name of the statesman and accomplished scholar, William Ewart Gladstone.

If we pass across the college quadrangle and enter the chapel for a moment, we shall find there a memorial to one of the most elegant Latin scholars and devoted pupils whom Eton can boast. He was at the college when the life at its best was but a rough one, whether to Colleger or Oppidan; but he has transmitted to generations of Etonians the loftiest testimony of the unalloyed happiness of that life to himself. In Latin lines of exquisite beauty,

Eton College.

which he himself composed, the Marquis Wellesley has recorded over his tomb the satisfaction with which he looked forward to resting in the sacred building in which as a lad he had so often worshipped. The late Lord Derby translated these lines into verse of deep pathos, as beautiful as their original:—

> "Long lost on Fortune's wave I come to rest.
> Eton, once more, on thy maternal breast.
> On loftiest deeds to fix the aspiring gaze,
> To seek the purer lights of ancient days,
> To love the simple paths of manly truth;
> These were thy lessons to my opening youth.
> If on my later life some glory shine,
> Some honours grace my name, the meed is thine.
> My boyhood's nurse, my aged dust receive,
> And one last tear of kind remembrance give."

The Marquis's younger brother, Arthur Wellesley, the Great Duke—" a shy and retiring boy," we are told—was at Eton shortly after Richard Colley Wellesley had left it. We have little information, however, handed down to us of the Duke's career as an Eton Oppidan.

The most interesting phase of Eton existence may be said to have begun with the induction of Dr. Goodall as headmaster, in the first year of the present century. He was a man of considerable learning, an accomplished gentleman, overflowing with good-nature, and extremely popular with undermasters and pupils alike. Those were the days when George the Third was king, when young Etonians of birth held commissions as officers in His Majesty's Guards, and when the headmaster was able to report with pride that he once "had the honour of flogging a major in His Majesty's service." It was a period of considerable licence. The rod and flogging-block were in constant requisition. Scholarship, except in isolated cases, was almost unknown. The King's Scholars were more ardent in the netting of rabbits and shooting of hares on the royal demesne than painstaking in the pursuit of knowledge. Oppidans of means would drive tandem through the streets of Eton and Windsor, and revelry and punch-making at the "Christopher" too plentifully relieved the monotony of scholastic life. Rebellions were not altogether unheard of; and Eton School was degenerating into somewhat of a fashionable college of the University when Dr. Keate assumed the supreme power.

The accomplished author of "Eothen" has given a sketch of his character and person:—"He was little more, if more at all, than five feet high, and was not very great in girth, but within this space was concentrated the pluck of ten battalions." He wielded the rod with such splendid vigour that "Keate's time" remains even to this day one of the most memorable traditions of Eton. Every one knows the story of how on a certain occasion the lower Fifth Form, one of the upper classes, rebelled against a disciplinary order of the doctor's. The class comprised some eighty boys. Keate waited patiently in Upper School until each boy was tucked snugly between the sheets, and then, summoning one or two of the masters to his aid, he sent them around to each boarding-house, and had the delinquents brought to him in relays of half-a-dozen, turn and turn about. The doctor flogged the whole eighty between ten and midnight! Keate earned for himself during his headmastership the reputation of having flogged half the secretaries of state, bishops, generals, and dukes of England of the first part of the century. For all this his memory is still cherished, and, strict disciplinarian as he was, he was held in great esteem by the scholars of Eton. We unearthed a curious little volume in the British Museum Library

Upper School.

the other day giving an admirable coloured illustration of the operation of flogging as practised by Dr. Keate at Eton half a century ago. The little doctor has his robes well gathered about him, and, rod uplifted, is administering sound castigation to a victim kneeling at the flogging-block. A King's Scholar does duty as assistant executioner in arranging nice points of etiquette incident to the proceedings, and written at the foot of the picture, and set to appropriate and simple music, is the refrain—

> "Birch and green holly,
> Birch and green holly,
> If thou be'st beaten, boy,
> Thank thine own folly."

The Quadrangle Eton College.

With the advent of Dr. Hawtrey as headmaster, things changed very much for the better at Eton College, as well in matters of school discipline as of scholarship. Before his time the classical work was limited to Homer, Horace, and Virgil, the classes were unwieldy, and instruction in modern languages and other essential educational requirements were comparatively unknown. The foundation, in 1829, of the "Newcastle Scholarship"—still, we believe, the blue ribbon of Eton—inaugurated a better system of education at the school. The Collegers began to receive more individual attention in their studies, and are now looked upon as the *élite* of the school. Indeed, they can hold their own with the picked scholars of the best of our great schools, which was hardly the case a few years ago. The affiliation of King's College, Cambridge, is not now, it may be remarked, reckoned as the chief inducement to election to the foundation of Eton College, the Collegers preferring to enter into the general University competition for open scholarships, at Baliol and other colleges, in which, it is satisfactory to know, they generally manage to secure good places.—"*Everyday Life in our Public Schools.*"

Smiling.

A SMILE! Nothing on earth can smile but man! Gems may flash reflected light, but what is a diamond flash compared with an eye-flash and mirth-flash? Flowers cannot smile; this is a charm that even they cannot claim. It is the prerogative of man; it is the colour which love wears, and cheerfulness, and joy —these three. It is the light in the window of the face, by which the heart signifies to father, husband, or friend, that it is at home and waiting. A face that cannot smile is like a bud that cannot blossom, and dries up on the stalk. Laughter is day, and sobriety is night, and a smile is the twilight that hovers gently between both, more bewitching than either. But all smiles are not alike. The cheerfulness of vanity is not like the cheerfulness of love; the smile of gratified pride is not like the radiance of goodness and truth. The rains of summer fall alike upon all trees and shrubs; but when the storm passes, and every leaf hangs a-drip, each gentle puff of wind brings down the petty shower, and every drop brings with it something of the nature of the leaf or blossom on which it hung— the roadside leaf yields dust, the walnut-leaf bitterness; some flowers poison, while the grape-blossom, the rose, the sweet-briar, lend their aroma to the twinkling dew, and send them down in perfumed drops. And so it is with smiles, which every heart perfumes according to its nature—selfishness is acrid; pride, bitter; good-will, sweet and fragrant.

HENRY WARD BEECHER.

A November Walk.

THE weather is as peaceful to-day, as calm and as mild, as in early April; and perhaps an autumn afternoon and a spring morning do resemble each more in feeling, and even in appearance, than any two periods of the year. There is in both the same freshness and dewiness of the herbage; the same balmy softness in the air; and the same pure and lovely blue sky, with white fleecy clouds floating across it. The chief difference lies in the absence of flowers and the presence of leaves. But then the foliage of November is so rich and glowing and varied, that it may well supply the place of the gay blossoms of the spring; whilst all the flowers of the field or the garden could never make amends for the want of leaves,—that beautiful and graceful attire in which nature has clothed the rugged forms of trees,—the verdant drapery to which the landscape owes its loveliness and the forests their glory.

If choice must be made between two seasons, each so full of charm, it is at least no bad philosophy to prefer the present good, even whilst looking gratefully back and hopefully forward to the past and the future. And of a surety no fairer specimen of a November day could well be found than this—a day made to wander

"By yellow commons and birch-shaded hollows,
And hedgerows bordering unfrequented lanes;"

nor could a prettier country be found for our walk than this shady and yet sunny Berkshire, where the scenery, without rising into grandeur or breaking into wildness, is so peaceful, so cheerful, so varied, and so thoroughly English.

We must bend our steps towards the water side, for I have a message to leave at Farmer Riley's; and sooth to say, it is no unpleasant necessity, for the road thither is smooth and dry; retired, as one likes a country walk to be, but not too lonely; leading past the Loddon,—the bright, brimming, transparent Loddon,—a fitting mirror for this bright blue sky, and terminating at one of the prettiest and most comfortable farm-houses in the neighbourhood.

How beautiful the lane is to-day, decorated with a thousand colours! The brown road, and the rich verdure that borders it, strewed with the pale yellow leaves of the elm, just beginning to fall; hedgerows glowing with long wreaths of the bramble in every variety of purplish red; and overhead the unchanged green of the fir, contrasting with the spotted sycamore, the tawny beech, and the dry, sere leaves of the oak, which rustle as the light wind passes through them; a few common hardy yellow flowers (for yellow is the common colour of flowers, whether wild or cultivated, as blue is the rare one)—flowers of many sorts, but nearly all of one tint, still blowing in spite of the season, and ruddy berries glowing through all. How very beautiful is the lane!

And how pleasant is the hill where the road widens, with the group of cattle by the wayside, and George Hearn, the little post-boy, trundling his hoop at full speed, making all the better haste in his work because he cheats himself into thinking it play! And how beautiful, again, is this patch of common at the hill-top, with the clear pool, where Martha Pither's children,—elves of three and four and five years old,—without any distinction of sex in their sunburnt faces and tattered drapery, are dipping up water in their little homely cups, shining with cleanliness, and a small brown pitcher with the lip broken, to fill that great kettle, which, when it is filled, their united strength will never be able to lift! They are quite a group for a painter, with their rosy cheeks and chubby hands, and round, merry faces ; and the low cottage in the background, peeping out of its vine leaves and China roses, with Martha at the door, tidy and comely and smiling, preparing the potatoes for the pot, and watching the progress of dipping and filling that useful utensil, completes the picture.

But we must get on. No time for more sketches in these short days. It is getting cold too. We must proceed on our walk. Dash is showing us the way, and beating the thick double hedgerow that skirts the meadows at a rate that indicates game astir, and causes the leaves to fly as fast as an east wind after a hard frost.

Ah! a pheasant—a superb cock pheasant! Nothing is more certain than Dash's questing, whether in a hedge row or covert, for a better spaniel never went into the field ; but I fancied that it was a hare a-foot, and was almost as much startled to hear the whirring of those splendid wings, as the princely bird himself would have been at the report of a gun.

Indeed, I believe that the way in which a pheasant goes off does sometimes make young sportsmen a little nervous, until they get as it were broken in to the sound ; and then that grand and sudden burst of wing becomes as pleasant to them as it seems to be to Dash, who is beating the hedgerow with might and main, and giving tongue louder, and sending the leaves about faster than ever, very proud of finding the pheasant, and perhaps a little angry with me for not shooting it,—at least looking as if he would be angry if I were a man ; for Dash is a dog of great sagacity, and has doubtless not lived four years in the sporting world without making the discovery that although gentlemen do shoot, ladies do not.

The Loddon at last! the beautiful Loddon! and the bridge, where every one stops, as by instinct, to lean over the rails, and gaze a moment on a landscape of surpassing loveliness,—the fine grounds of the Great House, with their magnificent groups of limes and firs and poplars, grander than ever poplars were ; the green meadows opposite, studded with oaks and elms ; the clear winding river ; the mill, with its picturesque old buildings bounding the scene ; all glowing with the rich colouring of autumn, and harmonized by the soft beauty of the clear blue sky and the delicious calmness of the hour. The very peasant, whose daily path it is, cannot cross that bridge without a pause.

But the day is wearing fast, and it grows colder and colder. I really think it will be a frost. After all, spring is the pleasanter season, beautiful as this scenery is. We must get on,—down that broad, yet shadowy lane, between the park, dark with evergreens and dappled with deer, and the meadows where sheep and cows and horses are grazing under the tall elms,—that lane, where the wild bank, clothed with fern and tufted with furze, and crowned by rich-berried thorn and thick shining holly on the one side, seems to vie in beauty with the picturesque old paling, the bright laurels, and the plumy cedars on the other;—down that shady lane, until the sudden turn brings us to an opening where four roads meet, where a noble avenue turns down to the Great House, where the village church rears its modest spire from amidst its venerable yew trees, and where, embosomed in orchards and gardens, and backed by barns and ricks, and all the wealth of the farm-yard, stands the spacious and comfortable abode of good Farmer Riley,—the end and object of our walk.

And in happy time the message is said, and the answer given, for this beautiful mild day is edging off into a dense, frosty evening; the leaves of the elm and the linden in the old avenue are quivering and vibrating and fluttering in the air, and at length falling crisply on the earth, as if Dash were beating for pheasants in the tree-tops; the sun gleams dimly through the fog, giving little more of light or heat than his fair sister, the lady moon. I don't know a more disappointing person than a cold sun; and I am beginning to wrap my cloak closely around me, and to calculate the distance to my own fireside, recanting all the way my praises of November, and longing for the showery, flowery April, as much as if I were a half-chilled butterfly, or a dahlia knocked down by the frost.

Ah, dear me! what a climate this is, that one cannot keep in the same mind about it for half an hour together! I wonder, by the way, whether the fault is in the weather, which Dash does not seem to care for, or in me? If I should happen to be wet through in a shower next spring, and should catch myself longing for autumn, that would settle the question.

MISS MITFORD.

AN ANSWER.—A certain well-known Radical philosopher, and editor of a notorious review, who has no mean opinion of himself, some time ago published in his pages a clever and impartial historical *aperçu* on the subject of a much-maligned religious sect. A lady of this denomination met him at a party, and took the opportunity of thanking him for his publication. "You need not thank *me*," said the philosopher brusquely. "I thought the article good, and published it. But *I* don't believe in anything." "Indeed," said the lady mildly: "I am sorry to hear it." "No," continued the philosopher, "I don't believe in any religious rubbish. I'm an Atheist." "Indeed," again replied the lady, at a loss what to say. "Well!" exclaimed our friend, rather disappointed in his stage-effect, "you take it very calmly! Most people would have jumped up. I wonder you can bear sitting near a wicked Atheist." "Oh," said the lady, "there is no occasion for me to jump. If your Creator could bear with you for over fifty years, I suppose I can for a few minutes."

Rural Life in England.

"Oh! friendly to the best pursuits of man,
Friendly to thought, to virtue, and to peace,
Domestic life in rural pleasures passed!"—COWPER.

THE stranger who would form a correct opinion of the English character, must not confine his observations to the metropolis. He must go forth into the country; he must sojourn in villages and hamlets; he must visit castles, villas, farm-houses, cottages; he must wander through parks and gardens, along hedges and green lanes; he must loiter about country churches; attend wakes, and fairs, and other rural festivals; and cope with the people in all their conditions, and all their habits and humours.

In some countries the large cities absorb the wealth and fashion of the nation; they are the only fixed abodes of elegant and intelligent society, and the country is inhabited almost entirely by boorish peasantry. In England, on the contrary, the metropolis is a mere gathering-place, or general rendezvous of the polite classes, where they devote a small portion of the year to a hurry of gaiety and dissipation, and having indulged this kind of carnival, return again to the apparently more congenial habits of rural life. The various orders of society are therefore diffused over the whole surface of the kingdom, and the most retired neighbourhoods afford specimens of the different ranks.

The English, in fact, are strongly gifted with the rural feeling. They possess a quick sensibility to the beauties of nature, and a keen relish for the pleasures and employments of the country. This passion seems inherent in them. Even the inhabitants of cities, born and brought up among brick walls and bustling streets, enter with facility into rural habits, and evince a tact for rural occupation. The merchant has his snug retreat in the vicinity of the metropolis, where he often displays as much pride and zeal in the cultivation of his flower-garden and the maturing of his fruits, as he does in the conduct of his business and the success of a commercial enterprise. Even those less fortunate individuals, who are doomed to pass their lives in the midst of din and traffic, contrive to have something that shall remind them of the green aspect of nature. In the most dark and dingy quarters of the city, the drawing-room window resembles frequently a bank of flowers; every spot capable of vegetation has its grass-plot and flower-bed ; and every square its mimic park, laid out with picturesque taste, and gleaming with refreshing vedure.

Those who see the Englishman only in town are apt to form an unfavourable opinion of his social character. He is either absorbed in business, or

distracted by the thousand engagements that dissipate time, thought, and feeling, in this huge metropolis He has, therefore, too commonly a look of hurry and abstraction. Wherever he happens to be, he is on the point of going somewhere else ; at the moment he is talking on one subject, his mind is wandering to another ; and while paying a friendly visit, he is calculating how he shall economize time so as to pay the other visits allotted in the morning.

An immense metropolis like London is calculated to make men selfish and uninteresting. In their casual and transient meetings they can but deal briefly in commonplaces. They present but the cold superficies of character—its rich and genial qualities have no time to be warmed into a flow.

It is in the country that the Englishman gives scope to his natural feelings. He breaks loose gladly from the cold formalities and negative civilities of town, throws off his habits of shy reserve, and becomes joyous and free-hearted. He manages to collect round him all the conveniences and elegancies of polite life, and to banish its restraints. His country-seat abounds with every requisite, either for studious retirement, tasteful gratification, or rural exercise. Books, paintings, music, horses, dogs, and sporting implements of all kinds, are at hand. He puts no constraint either upon his guests or himself, but in the true spirit of hospitality provides the means of enjoyment, and leaves every one to partake according to his inclination.

The taste of the English in the cultivation of land, and in what is called landscape gardening, is unrivalled. They have studied nature intently, and discover an exquisite sense of her beautiful forms and harmonious combinations. Those charms, which in other countries she lavishes in wild solitudes, are here assembled round the haunts of domestic life. They seem to have caught her coy and furtive graces, and spread them like witchery about their rural abodes.

Nothing can be more imposing than the magnificence of English park scenery. Vast lawns that extend like sheets of vivid green, with here and there clumps of gigantic trees, heaping up rich piles of foliage: the solemn pomp of groves and woodland glades, with the deer trooping in silent herds across them; the hare, bounding away to the covert; or the pheasant, suddenly bursting upon the wing; the brook, taught to wind in natural meanderings, or expand into a glassy lake: the sequestered pool, reflecting the quivering trees, with the yellow leaf sleeping on its bosom, and the trout roaming fearlessly about its limpid waters, while some rustic temple or sylvan statue, grown green and dank with age, gives an air of classic sanctity to the seclusion.

These are but a few of the features of park scenery; but what most delights me is the creative talent with which the English decorate the unostentatious abodes of middle life. The rudest habitation, the most unpromising and scanty portion of land, in the hands of an Englishman of taste becomes a little paradise. With a nicely discriminating eye, he seizes at once upon its capabilities, and pictures in his mind the future landscape. The sterile spot grows into loveliness under his hand; and yet the operations of art which produce the effect are scarcely to be perceived. The cherishing and training of some trees; the cautious pruning of others; the nice distribution of flowers of tender and graceful foliage ; the introduction of a green slope of velvet turf ; the partial opening to a peep of blue distance, or silver gleam of water ; all these are managed with a delicate tact, a pervading yet quiet assiduity, like the magic touchings with which a painter finishes up a favourite picture.

The residence of people of fortune and refinement in the country has diffused a degree of taste and elegance in rural economy, that descends to the lowest class. The very labourer with his thatched cottage and narrow slip of ground attends to their embellishment. The trim hedge, the grass-plot before the door, the little flower-bed bordered with snug box, the woodbine trained up against the wall and hanging its blossoms about the lattice, the pots of flowers in the window, the holly providentially planted about the house, to cheat winter of its dreariness and to throw in a semblance of green summer to cheer the fireside : all these bespeak the influence of taste, flowing down from high sources, and pervading the lowest levels of the public mind. If ever Love, as poets sing, delights to visit a cottage, it must be the cottage of an English peasant.

The fondness for rural life among the higher classes of the English has had a great and salutary effect upon the national character. I do not know a finer race of men than the English gentlemen. Instead of the softness and effeminacy which characterize the men of rank in most countries, they exhibit a union of elegance and strength, a robustness of frame and freshness of complexion, which I am inclined to attribute to their living so much in the open air, and pursuing so eagerly the invigorating recreations of the country. These hardy exercises produce also a healthful tone of mind and spirits, and a manliness and simplicity of manners, which even the follies and dissipations of the town cannot easily pervert, and can never entirely destroy. In the country, too, the different orders of society seem to approach more freely, to be more disposed to blend and operate favourably upon each other. The distinctions between them do not appear to be so marked and impassable as in the cities. The manner in which property has been distributed into small estates and farms has established a regular gradation from the nobleman, through the classes of gentry, small landed proprietors, and substantial farmers, down to the labouring peasantry, and while it has thus banded the extremes of society together, has infused into each intermediate rank a spirit of independence. This, it must be confessed, is not so universally the case at present as it was formerly ; the larger estates having, in the late years of distress, absorbed the smaller, and in some parts of the country almost annihilated the sturdy race of small farmers. These, however, I believe, are but casual breaks in the general system I have mentioned.

In rural occupation there is nothing mean and debasing. It leads a man forth among scenes of natural grandeur and beauty ; it leaves him to the workings of his own mind, operated upon by the purest and most elevating of external influences. Such a man may be simple and rough, but he cannot be vulgar. The man of refinement, therefore, finds nothing revolting in an intercourse with the lower orders in rural life, as he does when he casually mingles with the lower orders of cities. He lays aside his distance and reserve, and is glad to waive the distinctions of rank, and to enter into the honest, heartfelt enjoyments of common life. Indeed, the very amusements of the country bring men more and more together, and the sound of hound and horn blend all the feelings into harmony. I believe this is one great reason why the nobility and gentry are more popular among the inferior orders in England than they are in any other country ; and why the latter have endured so many excessive pressures and extremities, without repining more generally at the unequal distribution of fortune and privilege.

To this mingling of cultivated and rustic society may also be attributed the rural feeling that runs through British literature ; the frequent use of illustrations from rural life ; those incomparable descriptions of nature that abound in the British poets, that have continued down from " The Flower and Leaf " of Chaucer, and have brought into our closets all the freshness and fragrance of the dewy landscape. The pastoral writers of other countries appear as if they had paid nature an occasional visit, and become acquainted with her general charms ; but the British poets have lived and revelled with her—they have wooed her in her most secret haunts—they have watched her minutest caprices. A spray could not tremble in the breeze—a leaf could not rustle to the ground —a diamond drop could not patter in the stream—a fragrance could not exhale from the humble violet, nor a daisy unfold its crimson tints to the morning, but it has been noticed by these impassioned and delicate observers, and wrought up into some beautiful morality.

The effect of this devotion of elegant minds to rural occupations has been wonderful on the face of the country. A great part of the island is rather level, and would be monotonous, were it not for the charms of culture ; but it is studded and gemmed, as it were, with castles and palaces, and embroidered with parks and gardens. It does not abound in grand and sublime prospects, but rather in little home scenes of rural repose and sheltered quiet. Every antique farm-house and moss-grown cottage is a picture ; and as the roads are continually winding, and the view is shut in by groves and hedges, the eye is delighted by a continual succession of small landscapes of captivating loveliness.

The great charm, however, of English scenery is the moral feeling that seems to pervade it It is associated in the mind with ideas of order, of quiet, of sober well-established principles, of hoary usage and reverend custom. Everything seems to be the growth of ages of regular and peaceful existence. The old church of remote architecture, with its low massive portal, its Gothic tower, its windows rich with tracery and painted glass, its scrupulous preservation, its stately monuments of warriors and worthies of the olden time, ancestors of the present lords of the soil; its tombstones, recording successive generations of sturdy yeomanry, whose progeny still plough the same fields and kneel at the same altar; the parsonage, a quaint, irregular pile, partly antiquated, but repaired and altered in the tastes of various ages and occupants; the stile and

footpath leading from the churchyard, across pleasant fields, and along shady hedgerows, according to an immemorial right-of-way; the neighbouring village, with its venerable cottages, its public green sheltered by trees, under which the forefathers of the present race have sported; the antique family mansion, standing apart in some little rural domain, but looking down with a protecting air on the surrounding scene; all these common features of English landscape evince a calm and settled security, and hereditary transmission of home-bred virtues and local attachments, that speak deeply and touchingly for the moral character of the nation.

It is a pleasing sight of a Sunday morning, when the bell is sending its sober melody across the quiet fields, to behold the peasantry in their best finery, with ruddy faces and modest cheerfulness, thronging tranquilly along the green lanes to church ; but it is still more pleasing to see them in the evenings, gathering about their cottage doors, and appearing to exult in the humble comforts and embellishments which their own hands have spread around them.

It is this sweet home-feeling, this settled repose of affection in the domestic scene, that is, after all, the parent of the steadiest virtues and purest enjoyments.

WASHINGTON IRVING.

The Law of Love.

Pour forth the oil, pour boldly forth,
  It will not fail until
Thou failest vessels to provide,
  Which it may freely fill.

But then, when such are found no more,
  Though flowing broad and free
Till then, and nourished from on high,
  It straightway staunched will be.

Dig channels for the streams of Love,
  Where they may broadly run ;
And Love has overflowing streams
  To fill them every one.

But if at any time thou cease
  Such channels to provide,
The very founts of Love for thee
  Will soon be parched and dried.

For we must share, if we would keep,
  That good thing from above ;
Ceasing to give, we cease to have—
  Such is the law of Love.

ARCHBISHOP TRENCH.

Lines written in Early Spring.

I HEARD a thousand blended notes
   While in a grove I sat reclined,
In that sweet mood when pleasant thoughts
   Bring sad thoughts to the mind.

To her fair works did Nature link
   The human soul that through me ran:
And much it grieved my heart to think
   What man has made of man.

Through primrose tufts, in that sweet bower,
   The periwinkle trails its wreaths;
And 'tis my faith that every flower
   Enjoys the air it breathes.

The birds around me hopped and played,—
   Their thoughts I cannot measure;
But the least motion which they made,
   It seemed a thrill of pleasure.

The budding twigs spread out their fan
   To catch the breezy air;
And I must think, do all I can,
   That there was pleasure there.

If this belief from Heaven be sent,
   If such be Nature's holy plan,
Have I not reason to lament
   What man has made of man?

                                WORDSWORTH.

To a Water Fowl.

WHITHER 'midst falling dew,
While glow the heavens with the last steps of day,
Far through their rosy depths, dost thou pursue
    Thy solitary way?

Vainly the fowler's eye,
Might mark thy distant flight to do thee wrong,
As darkly painted on the crimson sky,
    Thy figure floats along.

Seeks't thou the plashy brink
Of weedy lake, or marge of river wide?
Or where the rocky billows rise and sink
    On the chafed ocean side?

There is a Power whose care
Teaches thy way along that pathless coast,—
The desert and illimitable air—
    Love wandering, but not lost.

All day thy wings have fanned,
At that far height, the cold thin atmosphere;
Yet stoop not, weary, to the welcome land,
    Though the dark night is near.

And soon that toil shall end;
Soon shalt thou find a summer home and rest,
And scream among thy fellows; reeds shall bend
    From o'er thy sheltered nest.

TO A WATER-FOWL.

Thou'rt gone, the abyss of heaven
Hath swallowed up thy foam: yet on my heart
Deeply hath sunk the lesson thou hast given,
And shall not soon depart.

He who from zone to zone
Guides through the boundless sky thy certain flight,
In the long way that I must tread alone
Will lead my steps aright.

W. C. BRYANT.

THE GARDEN.—A garden is a beautiful book, writ by the finger of God: every flower and every leaf is a letter. You have only to learn them—and he is a poor dunce that cannot, if he will, do that—to learn them and join them, and then go on reading and reading. And you will find yourself carried away from the earth by the beautiful story you are going through. You do not know what beautiful thoughts grow out of the ground, and seem to talk to a man. And then there are some flowers that seem to me like ever-dutiful children: tend them ever so little, and they come up and flourish, and show, as I may say, their bright and happy faces to you. DOUGLAS JERROLD.

To the Skylark.

    Bird of the wilderness,
    Blithesome and cumberless,
Sweet be thy matin o'er moorland and lea!
    Emblem of happiness,
    Blest is thy dwelling-place—
Oh to abide in the desert with thee!

    Wild is thy lay and loud,
    Far in the downy cloud;
Love gives it energy, love gave it birth.
    Where on thy dewy wing,
    Where art thou journeying?
Thy lay is in heaven, thy love is on earth.

TO THE EVENING STAR.

  O'er fell and fountain sheen,
  O'er moor and mountain green,
O'er the red streamer that heralds the day,
  Over the cloudlet dim,
  Over the rainbow's rim,
Musical cherub, soar, singing, away !

  Then, when the gloaming comes,
  Low in the heather blooms,
Sweet will thy welcome and bed of love be !
  Emblem of happiness,
  Blest is thy dwelling-place—
Oh to abide in the desert with thee !

JAMES HOGG.

To the Evening Star.

Star that bringeth home the bee,
And sett'st the weary labourer free,
If any star shed peace, 'tis thou,
 That send'st it from above,
Appearing when Heaven's breath and brow
 Are sweet as hers we love.

Come to the luxuriant skies,
Whilst the landscape's odours rise,
Whilst far-off lowing herds are heard,
 And songs, when toil is done,
From cottages whose smoke unstirr'd
 Curls yellow in the sun.

Star of love's soft interviews,
Parted lovers on thee muse ;
Their remembrance in Heaven
 Of thrilling vows thou art,
Too delicious to be riven
 By absence from the heart.

CAMPBELL.

Charity of Thought.

You know how often it is difficult to be wisely charitable—to do good without multiplying the sources of evil. You know that to give alms is nothing unless you give thought also; and that, therefore, it is written, not "blessed is he that feedeth the poor," but "blessed is he that considereth the poor." And you know that a little thought and a little kindness are often worth more than a great deal of money.

Now this charity of thought is not merely to be exercised towards the poor; it is to be exercised towards all men. There is assuredly no action of our social life, however important, which by kindly thought may not be made to have a beneficial influence upon others, and it is impossible to spend the smallest sum of money, for any not absolutely necessary purpose, without a grave responsibility attaching to the manner of spending it.

The object we ourselves covet may indeed be desirable and harmless, so far as we are concerned, but the providing us with it may perhaps be a very prejudicial occupation to someone else. And then it becomes instantly a moral question whether we are to indulge ourselves or not. Whatever we wish to buy, we ought first to consider not only if the thing be fit for us, but if the manufacture of it be a wholesome and happy one, and if, on the whole, the sum we are going to spend will do as much good spent in this way as it would if spent in any other way.

It may be said that we have not time to consider all this before we make a purchase. But no time could be spent in a more important duty, and God never imposes a duty without giving the time to do it. Let us, however, only acknowledge the principle; once make up your mind to allow the consideration of the effect of your purchases to regulate the kind of your purchase, and you will soon easily find grounds enough to decide upon. The plea of ignorance will never take away our responsibilities. It is written, "If thou sayest, Behold we knew it not; doth not He that pondereth the heart consider it? and He that keepeth thy soul, doth not He know it?"

RUSKIN.

MODERATION is the silken string running through the pearl-chain of all the virtues.
THOMAS FULLER.

The Langdale Pikes.

WHILE at our pastoral banquet thus we sate,
I could not, ever and anon, forbear
To glance an upward look on two huge peaks,

That from some other vale peered into this.
"Those lusty twins," exclaimed our host, "if here
It were your lot to dwell, would soon become

Your prized companions.—Many are the notes
Which in his tuneful course the wind draws forth
From rocks, woods, caverns, heaths, and clashing shores ;
And well those lofty brethren bear their part
In the wild concert—chiefly when the storm
Rides high ; then all the upper air they fill
With roaring sound, that ceases not to flow,
Like smoke, along the level of the blast,
In mighty current ; theirs, too, is the song
Of stream and headlong flood that seldom fails ;
And, in the grim and breathless hour of noon,
Methinks that I have heard them echo back
The thunder's greeting. Nor have nature's laws
Left them ungifted with a power to yield
Music of finer tone ; a harmony,
So do I call it, though it be the hand
Of silence, though there be no voice,—the clouds,
The mists, the shadows, light of golden suns,
Motions of moonlight, all come thither—touch,
And have an answer—thither come, and shape
A language not unwelcome to sick hearts
And idle spirits ;—there the sun himself,
At the calm close of summer's longest day,
Rests his substantial orb ;—between those heights,
And on the top of either pinnacle,
More keenly than elsewhere in night's blue vault,
Sparkle the stars, as of their station proud.
Thoughts are not busier in the mind of man
Than the mute agents stirring there :—alone
Here do I sit and watch."

WORDSWORTH.

NORMAN M‘LEOD was once preaching in a district in Ayrshire, where the reading of a sermon is regarded as the greatest fault of which the minister can be guilty. When the congregation dispersed, an old woman, overflowing with enthusiasm, addressed her neighbour : " Did ye ever hear onything sae gran' ? Wasna that a sermon ? " But all her expressions of admiration being met by a stolid glance, she shouted : " Speak, woman ! Wasna that a sermon ? " " Ou ay," replied her friend sulkily ; " but he read it." " Read it ! " said the other with indignant emphasis, " I wadna care if he had whistled it."

Wordsworth and his Sister Dorothy.

THE life which the poet and his sister lived during the eight years at the Townend of Grasmere stands out with a marked individuality which it is delightful ever so often to recur to. It was as unlike the lives of most literary or other men, as the most original of his poems are unlike the ordinary run of even good poetry. Their outward life was exactly like that of the dalesmen or "statesmen"—for so the native yeomen proprietors are called—with whom they lived on the most friendly footing, and among whom they found their chief society. Outwardly their life was so, but inwardly it was cheered by imaginative visitings to which these were strangers. Sheltered as they then were from the agitations of the world, the severe frugality of the life they led ministered in more than one way to feed that poetry which introduced a new element into English thought. It kept the mind cool, and the eye clear, to feel once more that kinship between the outward world and the soul of man, to perceive that impassioned expression in the countenance of all nature, which, if felt by primeval man, ages of cultivation have long forgotten. It also made them wise to practise the same frugality in emotional enjoyment which they exercised in household economy. It has been well noted that this is one of Wordsworth's chief characteristics. It is the temptation of the poetic temperament to be prodigal of passion, to demand a life always strung to the highest pitch of emotional excitement, to be never content unless when passing from fervour to fervour. No life can long endure this strain. This is specially seen in such poets as Byron and Shelley, who speedily fell from the heights of passion to the depths of languor and despondency. The same quick using up of the power of enjoyment produces the too common product of the *blasé* man and the cynic. Wordsworth early perceived that all—even the richest—natures have but a very limited capacity of uninterrupted enjoyment, and that nothing is easier than to exhaust this capacity. Hence he set himself to husband it, to draw upon it sparingly, to employ it only on the purest, most natural, and most enduring objects, and not to speedily dismiss or throw them by and demand more, but to detain them till they had yielded him their utmost. From this in part it came that the commonest sights of earth and sky—a fine spring day, a sunset, even a chance traveller met on a moor, an ordinary sorrow of man's life—yielded to him an amount of imaginative interest inconceivable to more mundane spirits. The simple healthiness and strict frugality of his household life suited well, and must have greatly assisted, that wholesome frugality of emotion which he exercised.

But this life of theirs, retired and uneventful as it seems, was not without its own incidents. Such was the home-coming of their younger sailor-brother John, who, in the first year (1798) of their residence at Grasmere—

> "Under their cottage roof had gladly come,
> From the wild sea, a cherished visitant."

He was, what his brother calls him, "a silent poet," and had the heart and sense to feel the sterling quality of his brother's poems, and to foretell with perfect confidence their ultimate acceptance, at the time when the critic wits who ruled the hour treated them with contempt. The two brothers were congenial spirits, and William's poetry has many affecting allusions to his brother John, whose intention it was, when his last voyage was over, to settle down in "Grasmere's happy vale," and to devote the surplus of his fortune to his brother's use. On his last voyage he sailed as captain of the *Earl of Abergavenny* East Indiaman, at the opening of February 1805, and on the 5th of that month the ill-fated ship struck on the Shambles of the Bill of Portland, and the captain and most of the crew went down with her. To the brother and sister this became a permanent household sorrow. But in time they found comfort in that thought with which the poet closes a remarkable letter on his brother's loss—"So good must be better; so high must be destined to be higher."

Another lesser incident was a short tour to the Continent, in which, as the brother and sister crossed Westminster Bridge, outside the Dover coach, both witnessed that sunrise which remains fixed for ever in the famous sonnet. Another incident, and more important, was Wordsworth's marriage in October 1802, when he brought home his young wife, Mary Hutchinson, his sister's longtime friend, to their cottage at Townend. This is she whom he has sung in the lines, "She was a phantom of delight;" of whom he said in plain prose, "She has a sweetness all but angelic, simplicity the most entire, womanly self-respect and purity of heart speaking through all her looks, acts, and movements." The advent of Mrs. Wordsworth brought no change to Dorothy. She still continued to fill to her brother and his wife the same place which she had filled when her brother was alone, sharing in all the household duties and family interests, and still accompanying him in his rambles when Mrs. Wordsworth was detained at home.

WORDSWORTH AT HOME.

William had been married four years when the journey to Scotland was undertaken, and this was the home to which he brought his wife, at Grasmere Townend, as depicted by De Quincey:—

"A little semi-vestibule between two doors prefaced the entrance into what might be considered the principal room of the cottage. It was an oblong square, not above eight and a half feet high, sixteen feet long, and twelve broad; very prettily wainscoted from the floor to the ceiling with dark polished oak, slightly embellished with carving. One window there was—a perfect and unpretending cottage window—with little diamond panes, embowered at almost every season of the year with roses, and, in the summer and autumn, with a profusion of jasmine and other fragrant shrubs. From the exuberant luxuriance of the vegetation around it, this window, though tolerably large, did not furnish a very powerful light to one who entered from the open air. . . . I was ushered up a little flight of stairs, fourteen in all, to a little drawing-room, or whatever the reader chooses to call it. Wordsworth himself has described the fireplace of this room as his

'Half kitchen, and half parlour fire.'

It was not fully seven feet six inches high, and in other respects pretty nearly of the same dimensions as the rustic hall below. There was, however, in a small recess, a library of perhaps three hundred volumes, which seemed to consecrate this room as the poet's study and composing-room, and such occasionally it was.

"About four o'clock it might be when we arrived. At that hour in November the daylight soon declined, and in an hour and a half we were all collected about the tea-table.

"This with the Wordsworths, under the simple rustic system of habits which they cherished then and for twenty years after, was the most delightful meal of the day, just as dinner is in great cities, and for the same reason, because it was prolonged into a meal of leisure and conversation. That night I found myself, about eleven at night, in a pretty bedroom, about fourteen feet by twelve. Much I feared that this might turn out the best room in the house; and it illustrates the hospitality of my new friends to mention that it was.

"Next morning Miss Wordsworth I found making breakfast in the little sitting-room. No one was there, no glittering breakfast service; a kettle boiled upon the fire; and everything was in harmony with these unpretending arrangements.

"I rarely had seen so humble a *ménage;* and, contrasting the dignity of the man with this honourable poverty, and this courageous avowal of it, his utter absence of all effort to disguise the simple truth of the case, I felt my admiration increased.

"Throughout the day, which was rainy, the same style of modest hospitality prevailed. Wordsworth and his sister, myself being of the party, walked out in spite of the rain, and made the circuit of the two lakes, Grasmere and its dependency Rydal, a walk of about six miles.

"On the third morning after my arrival in Grasmere, I found the whole family, except the two children, prepared for the expedition across the mountains. I had heard of no horses, and took it for granted that we were to walk; however, at the moment of starting, a cart, the common farmer's cart of the country, made its appearance, and the driver was a bonny young woman of the vale. Accordingly we were all carted along to the little town of Ambleside, three and a half miles distant. Our style of travelling occasioned no astonishment; on the contrary, we met a smiling salutation wherever we appeared; Miss Wordsworth being, as I observed, the person most familiarly known of our party, and the one who took upon herself the whole expenses of the flying colloquies exchanged with stragglers on the road."

Evermore.

Our noisy years seem moments in the being
Of the Eternal Silence, truths that wake
    To perish never ;
Which neither listlessness nor mad endeavours,
    Nor man nor boy,
Nor all that is at enmity with joy,
Can utterly abolish or destroy !
    Hence in a season of calm weather,
    Though inland far we be,
Our souls have sight of that immortal sea
  Which brought us hither,
  Can in a moment travel thither,
And see the children sport upon the shore,
And hear the mighty waters rolling evermore.

WORDSWORTH.

A letter from Australia.

Letters of Bygone Times.

LANGUAGE which now would be sneered at as only fit for a sentimental novel, was the common style of our ancestors. They were not ashamed of their feelings, and uttered what they felt in the nearest words that sprang to their lips. And what letters were theirs! Modern usages have not only made letter-writing a thing of the past, but a thing to ridicule; and a long letter is received with a profession of horror, and commenced with a yawn at the expense of the writer. But in the olden time, a gentleman would indite an epistle of from four to ten folio pages to his family and his friends, filled with precisely the same matter he would have uttered by word of mouth; and, so far from this being deemed an infliction, it was a dearly-loved right to give and receive. "Out of sight," *could not* have been "out of mind" then. On the contrary, during the whole time of writing and reading these letters, the absent was the one subject of thought; and thus our fathers bequeathed to us an ever-living individuality, a presence yet here to those who seek it, that we can never leave to our descendants. The whole history of past England, its deep religion, its mighty valour, its noble wisdom, all the poetry of its life, are yet existent in the letters of the dead. But the history of the present will be that of an abstract theme, of a vast crowd of unknown strangers who have lived in England. Biographies may be multiplied to infinity, telling what the public at large said; but the individual will not speak of us—will be in person unknown.—"*The Life of Thomas Wentworth, Earl of Stafford*," *by Elizabeth Cooper.*

To the Dandelion.

Dear common flower, that grow'st beside the way,
   Fringing the dusty road with harmless gold,
First pledge of blithesome May,
   Which children pluck, and full of pride uphold ;
High-hearted buccaneers, o'erjoyed that they
An El Dorado in the grass have found,
Which not the rich earth's ample round
May match in wealth—thou art more dear to me
Than all the prouder summer-blooms may be.

Gold such as thine ne'er drew the Spanish prow
   Through the primeval hush of Indian seas,
Nor wrinkled the lean brow
   Of age, to rob the lover's heart of ease ;
'Tis the Spring's largess, which she scatters now
To rich and poor alike with lavish hand,
Though most hearts never understand
To take it at God's value, but pass by
The offered wealth with unrewarded eye.

Thou art my tropics and mine Italy ;
   To look at thee unlocks a warmer clime ;
The eyes thou givest me
   Are in the heart, and heed not space or time ;
Not in mid June the golden-cuirassed bee
Feels a more summer-like, warm ravishment
In the white lily's breezy tent—
His conquered Sybaris—than I when first
From the dark green thy yellow circles burst.

TO THE DANDELION.

Then I think of deep shadows on the grass;
   Of the meadows where in sun the cattle graze—
Where, as the breezes pass,
   The gleaming rushes lean a thousand ways;
Of leaves that clumber in a cloudy mass,
Or whiten in the wind; of waters blue,
That from the distance sparkle through
Some woodland gap; and of a sky above,
Where one white cloud like a stray lamb doth move.

My childhood's earliest thoughts are linked with thee;
   The sight of thee brings back the robin's song,
Who, from the dark old tree
   Beside the door, sang clearly all day long;
And I, secure in childish piety,
Listened as if I heard an angel sing
With news from heaven, which he did bring
Fresh every day to my untainted ears,
When birds and flowers and I were happy peers.

How like a prodigal doth Nature seem,
   When thou, for all thy gold, so common art!
Thou teachest me to deem
   More sacredly of every human heart,
Since each reflects in joy its scanty gleam
Of heaven, and could some wondrous secret show,
Did we but pay the love we owe,
And, with a child's undoubting wisdom, look
On all these living pages of God's book.

JAMES RUSSELL LOWELL.

"PRAY, Mr. Betterton," asked the good Archbishop Sancroft of the celebrated actor, "can you inform me what is the reason you actors on the stage, speaking of things imaginary, affect your audience as if they were real, while we in church speak of things real, which our congregations receive only as if they were imaginary?" "Well, really, my lord," answered Betterton, "I don't know, unless we actors speak of things imaginary as if they were real, while you in the pulpit speak of things real as if they were imaginary." It was a clever answer, and is as applicable now as when the Archbishop put the question.

The Best Amulets.

SUPERSTITIOUS persons carry amulets externally upon their breasts: carry you a select store of holy texts within, and you will be much more effectively armed against the powers of evil than any most absolute monarch behind a bristling bodyguard. Such texts you may find occurring in many places, from the Kalidasas and Sakyamunis of the East, to Pythagoras, Plato, Aristotle, and Epictetus, in the West; but if you are wise, and above the seduction of showy and pretentious novelties, you will store your memory early in youth with the golden texts of the Old and New Testaments; and, as the Bible is a big book— not so much a book, indeed, as a great literature in small bulk—perhaps I could not do better in this place than indicate for you a few books or chapters which you will find it of inestimable value to graft into your soul deeply before you come much into contact with those persons of coarse moral fibre, low aspirations, and lukewarm temperament, commonly called men of the world. First, of course, there is the Sermon on the Mount; then the 13th chapter of the 1st Epistle to the Corinthians; then the Gospel of John; then the General Epistle of James; the two Epistles to Timothy; the 8th chapter of the Romans; the 5th and 6th chapters of the Ephesians; and the same chapters of the Galatians.

In the Old Testament, every day's experience will reveal to you more clearly the profound wisdom of the Book of Proverbs. As a guide through life, it is not possible to find a better directory than this book; and I remember the late Principal Lee, who knew Scotland well, saying with emphasis that our country owed no small part of the practical sagacity for which it is so famed, to an early familiarity with this body of practical wisdom, which in old times used to be printed separately, and found in every man's pocket.

For seasons of devout meditation, of course, the Psalms of the great minstrel monarch are more to be commended; and among them I should recommend specially, as calculated to infuse a spirit of deep and catholic piety into the souls of the young, Psalms i., viii., xix., xxiv., xxxii., xxxvii., xlix., li., liii., lxxiii., xc., ciii., civ., cvii., cxxi., cxxxi., cxxxiii. And these Psalms ought not only to be frequently read, till they make rich the blood of the soul with a genial and generous piety, but they ought to be sung to their proper music till they create round us a habitual atmosphere of pure and elevated sentiment, which we breathe as the breath of our higher life.

PROFESSOR BLACKIE.

Hours of Exaltation.

ALTHOUGH we have usually a general and common use of all the senses, yet, in persons of certain temperaments, some single sense has its moods of predominance, and all the others subside and accompany it, as a low and pleasant harmony in music. We have compared it to the habit of a band, in which the French horn seems to rise at times above all others, and to float upon the harmony like a yacht upon the sea; then subsiding, the clarionets emerge and shout above all other instruments, but only for a moment, and then, mingling with their companions, they send forth the bugle or other instrument. Some such change as this is going on in everyone who carries all his senses into nature for the enjoyment of her melodies and harmonies.

Some days seem to be characterised by some single sense. There are head-days, heart-days, there are eye-days and ear-days, and promiscuous days in which delicious sensations of pleasure at life in general predominate. These last are transcendent. It would seem as if each faculty, every sense, and all the nerves had come to an agreement, and were sensitively submissive to all the effects of nature and society. In such transfigurations it scarcely matters what happens. Nothing can be amiss—all sounds, all colours, all movements, all conditions of cloud, air, temperature; all things—grass, rock, or wood, are not only satisfying, but blissful. We seem to hang like a harp in the air, and all things reach forth to touch the strings for joy.

And the sense of perfect rejoicing is so unconnected with any apparent cause, or else so far beyond their ordinary effects, that the mind is in a gentle wondering all the time as to what can be the cause of such satisfaction. Thus it is that consciousness is reversed; and whereas commonly we feel that happiness is an effect *within* us, that its seat is in our own mind, upon these rare days of ubiquitous and general gladness it seems as if the happiness lay *without* us, and we were voyagers sailing through it, and it lapped and murmured upon us from without, as waves and ripples do upon the summer sides of tranquil ships.

The air seems made up of happiness—the clouds, the trees, the grass, the pathless woods, land and water, all seem to pulsate happiness, to emit it, to breathe it forth upon us; and it falls upon us as dew upon flowers, as serenades rising into the moonlit air seem to rain down on every roof and every casement through the whole town. It is a rare and gracious treat, when in these moods, nature, like some magnificent Handel, seems to rest from her graver labours and exercises, and to run her fingers, in wild caprices of fancy and joy, over the keys of her organ, exercising herself upon every stop, and filling the whole air and world with delights innumerable!

We are filled with the very affluence of peacefulness and joy. There is neither sorrow, nor want, nor madness, nor trouble in the wide world! The glory of the Lord, that at other times hangs upon the horizon, like embattled clouds, full gorgeous with the sun, on such days as we have described, descends and fills the whole earth. The impassioned language of the Psalmist and prophets, which on other days is lifted up so high above our imagination that we can scarcely hear it, now comes down and sounds all its grandeur in our ears. The mountains praise the Lord. The trees clap their hands. The clouds are His chariot, and bear Him through the air, leaving brightness and joy along the path. The birds know their King. The flowers lift up their heads, and with the silent tongue of perfume praise God with choice of odours! The whole earth doth praise Thee!

In these transcendent moods each sense radiates a glory upon whatever it perceives. Sounds are magical. That which we usually notice with no favour becomes sweet. Even discordant sounds are smoothed and softened. The eye detects new lines, new symmetries, more beautiful forms, more exquisite colours, than it is wont to do. The memories that come up from the past bring joys even greater for the moment than the reality. Friends and friendships are glorified. And over against the past stands the future, full of dim joys that hourly increase. These joys of the past and of the future may be likened to that hour, at certain conjunctions of the sun and moon, when one has just left the horizon, but suffuses it yet with his trail of light, while the other, dim in the east, is advancing every moment with growing brightness to rule the hour.

But such days have no art to perpetuate themselves. To-morrow will sweep you to the opposite pole. Yet they are of great use. They exalt an ideal of life. Subjects held up in their light will never be as low and ignoble as they may have been before. And the light in which duty, love, and labour shine in these lucid days will give us exaltation for many days after.

The roots of nature are in the human mind. The life and meaning of the outward world is not in itself, but in us. And when we have taken in all that the eye can gather, the ear, the hand, and the other senses, we have but the *body*; we do not yet read and know the spirit and truth which cannot be received by the senses, but by the soul. And nature comprises in herself all the effects which she causes upon the *senses*, and all that she causes upon the *mind*. He will see the most without who has the most within; and he who only sees with his bodily organs sees but the surface. He who paints or describes with the senses alone is but a surface artist. This superficial reading of nature is as if one had been taught, like Milton's daughters, to read the Greek language fluently without understanding any part of its meaning. The sound is sweet, the reading is fluent; but all the life and contents are wanting. And he that reads nature reads God's language. He only pronounces the words without the meanings who sees the natural world by his senses only, and not also by his feelings. The bell from yonder steeple sounds out suddenly through the storm-washed air. What does that sound mean? To the bell, rattling. To the mechanical philosopher it means the vibration produced upon the ear. To the watchmaker it means twelve o'clock—noon. To the labourer it means rest and food. To the schoolboy it means release from a living tomb. To the nurse it is the hour for appointed medicine. To the impatient bridegroom is is the hour of wedding. It is the funeral hour also, and the sexton cracks his whip. It means separation and heart-pangs to those aboard the cars. That bell-stroke means all that it can make a man feel and think. It bears back the thought on its waves, and stands us upon the shores of childhood. It opens the door of tears or of smiles, of joyful remembrance or of sadness. It reaches towards the feelings. These pulsations beat upon the gate of eternity. Lying upon the warm and fragrant grass, flecked all over with the golden-spotted shadow of an elm, that deep, solitary, single stroke of the bell, lifted high above the ground, that does not sound out one note and cease, as a trumpet does, but moves and warbles; that pulses again and again, going and coming as if it were beckoning and soliciting us to follow; upon that sound we do ride bravely heavenward, and in its dying cadences hear a hundred voices speaking things to the feeling unutterable in human language. And that single sound *is* all that it can *do*. It is a cause that includes in itself all the effects it is capable of producing.

Nature likewise implants her spirit in the human soul. Her shape is without us. Her meaning is within us.

This great mountain behind me is not simply granite lifted up against the eastern sky as a bulwark against the morning sun, which it hinders from my windows a full morning hour. It is a silent prophet of God, that reveals both ways, past and future, backward and forward; and all that I think when I gaze upon it, and all that I feel, and all that airy middle experience of deliquescing thought resolving itself into emotion, tenuous and misty, and all that it suggests by association, all belong to it.

What a man sees in nature will therefore depend upon what he has to see with. Deprived of four senses, a man would perceive only sounds; deprived of but three senses, he would perceive only sounds and sights. If he have all his physical senses and nothing more, he will see the rind and husk of nature. If he bring reason along, he will perceive the connections and homogeneities of natural objects, their relations to each other and to us. If he add imagination, he will yet find deeper insight; if feeling, deeper yet; if religious feeling, more profoundly; and if he hold all these up against the background of the Infinite, then, indeed, to his unspeakable satisfaction, the heavens declare the *glory of God*, and the firmament showeth His handiwork. Then day unto day uttereth speech, and night unto night showeth knowledge.

In this view is revealed the difference between one man and another in the enjoyment of nature. One man communes with natural objects by many more faculties than another. One artist represents nature seen with the *eyes* simply; another, as seen with the *soul*. And though we cannot by form and colour represent all or the chief part of that which the mind perceives, yet what we do picture will be very different if seen only superficially or likewise with feeling.

The augmentations of pleasure in this way are wonderful. The least things and the most obscure become ministers of rare delight. The hands of a giant upon the keys of an organ make no more music than the hands of a common man, for the sound is in the instrument, not in the hand that touches it. And the fingers of nature, touching the faculties of the human soul, produce effects, not by the magnitude of the thing acting, but by the music within the instrument touched.

Nevertheless, there is a great difference between one thing and another in nature. All things are not just alike, and the seeming difference of outward things is not altogether in us. It is not to obliterate or confuse a well-known truth that we write, but to make plainer a truth not so well known—that is, it requires foresight, an object to project its image, and an eye to receive it; so on a larger sphere, an outward world is required to produce an effect and an inward nature to receive it; and both of these working together are required before either of them is clearly developed.

H. W. BEECHER.

OBEDIENCE is peace. To recognise a great will that is sovereign, and to bow myself to it, not because it is sovereign, but because it is sweet, and sweet because I love it, and love him whose it is—that is peace. And then, whatever may be outward circumstances, there shall be "peace subsisting at the heart of endless agitation;" and deep in my soul I may be tranquil, though all about me may be the hurly-burly of the storm.

The Spirit is the Life.

It may have struck some of you that Jesus Christ never said anything about political abuses. Concerning slavery, we never detect any speech that has fallen from His lips. He never protested against absolute government, and the abominations by which men in His day, and in ours, have been trodden down. And why so? Because He put down this great truth: Change the spirit, and the thing will go. All ghosts get themselves away when the morning star arises. His doctrine was the morning star. "I am the light of the world." Get the light of the world, and the ghosts and hideous spectres must vanish away. Get the spirit of a man right, and you rectify everything in the man. Hence the sublime doctrine of the Scriptures, when they speak of converting the inner life of a man. Change that, and all is changed. Teach the soul of a man, and all the outward circumstances, doing everything, thinking, speaking, dressing, all will change. Hence comes in the sublime scriptural doctrine that a man is born over again, starts life afresh with a new soul. And what matters it quibbling that the body is the same, if in that body a new spirit, a new soul, a new man, hath gotten? This is the philosophy taught as the true Christian reform: Earnestly labour to convert the people; to alter their way of looking at life; change the soul of the people by incessant teaching of the upright, noble, and true; by incessant education; and remember that it is a noble people that makes a noble government, and not a noble government that makes a noble people.

GEORGE DAWSON.

Patience.

PATIENCE! why, 'tis the soul of peace.
Of all the virtues, 'tis nearest kin to heaven;
It makes men look like gods. The best of men
That e'er wore earth about Him was a sufferer;
A soft, meek, patient, humble, tranquil spirit:
The first true gentleman that ever breathed.

THOMAS DEKKER.

Easter Day.

"And as they were afraid, and bowed down their faces to the earth, they said unto them, Why seek ye the living among the dead? He is not here, but is risen."—St. Luke xxiv. 5, 6.

O day of days! shall hearts set free
No "minstrel rapture" find for thee?
Thou art the Sun of other days,
They shine by giving back thy rays:

Enthronèd in thy sovereign sphere,
Thou shedd'st thy light on all the year;
Sundays by thee more glorious break,
An Easter Day in every week:

And week days, following in their train,
The fulness of thy blessing gain,
Till all, both resting and employ,
Be one Lord's day of holy joy.

Then wake, my soul, to high desires,
And earlier light thine altar fires:
The World some hours is on her way,
Nor thinks on thee, thou blessèd day;

Or, if she think, it is in scorn:
The vernal light of Easter morn
To her dark gaze no brighter seems
Than Reason's or the Law's pale beams.

"Where is your Lord?" she scornful asks;
"Where is His hire? we know His tasks:
Sons of a king ye boast to be;
Let us your crowns and treasures see."

We in the words of Truth reply,
(An angel brought them from the sky.)
"Our crown, our treasure is not here,
'Tis stor'd above the highest sphere:

EASTER DAY.

"Methinks your wisdom guides amiss,
To seek on earth a Christian's bliss:
We watch not now the lifeless stone;
Our only Lord is risen and gone."

Yet e'en the lifeless stone is dear
For thoughts of Him who late lay here;
And the base world, now Christ hath died,
Ennobled is and glorified.

No more a charnel-house, to fence
The relics of lost innocence,
A vault of ruin and decay;
Th' imprisoning stone is roll'd away:

'Tis now a cell where angels use
To come and go with heavenly news,
And in the ears of mourners say,
"Come, see the place where Jesus lay:"

'Tis now a fane, where Love can find
Christ everywhere embalm'd and shrin'd;
Aye gathering up memorials sweet,
Where'er she sets her duteous feet.

Oh! joy to Mary first allow'd,
When rous'd from weeping o'er His shroud,
By His own calm, soul-soothing tone,
Breathing her name, as still His own!

Joy to the faithful Three renew'd,
As their glad errand they pursued!
Happy, who so Christ's word convey,
That He may meet them on their way!

So is it still: to holy tears,
In lonely hours, Christ risen appears;
In social hours, who Christ would see
Must turn all tasks to Charity.   KEBLE.

God and Heaven.

THE silver cord in twain is snapped,
  The golden bowl is broken,
The mortal mould in darkness wrapped,
  The words funereal spoken;

The tomb is built, or the rock is cleft,
  Or delved is the grassy clod
And what for mourning man is left?
  O what is left—but God!

The tears are shed that mourned the dead,
    The flowers they wore are faded;
The twilight dun hath veiled the sun,
    And hope's sweet dreamings shaded:
And the thoughts of joy that were planted deep
    From our heart of hearts are riven;
And what is left us when we weep?
    O what is left—but Heaven!

BOWRING.

O Thou who dry'st the Mourner's Tear.

Air—Haydn.

"He healeth the broken in heart, and bindeth up their wounds."—PSALM cxlvii. 3.

O THOU who dry'st the mourner's tear,
    How dark this world would be,
If, when deceived and wounded here,
    We could not fly to Thee!
The friends who in our sunshine live,
    When winter comes, are flown;
And he who has but tears to give,
    Must weep those tears alone.
But Thou wilt heal that broken heart,
    Which, like the plants that throw
Their fragrance from the wounded part,
    Breathes sweetness out of woe.

When joy no longer soothes or cheers,
    And even the hope that threw
A moment's sparkle o'er our tears
    Is dimm'd and vanish'd too,
Oh, who would bear life's stormy doom,
    Did not Thy wing of love
Come, brightly wafting through the gloom
    Our Peace-branch from above!
Then sorrow, touch'd by Thee, grows bright
    With more than rapture's ray:
As darkness shows us worlds of light
    We never saw by day!

MOORE.

Deaths of Little Children.

A GRECIAN philosopher being asked why he wept for the death of his son, since the sorrow was in vain, replied, "I weep on that account." And his answer became his wisdom. It is only for sophists to contend that we, whose eyes contain the fountains of tears, need never give way to them. It would be unwise not to do so on some occasions. Sorrow unlocks them in her balmy moods. The first bursts may be bitter and overwhelming; but the soil on which they pour would be worse without them. They refresh the fever of the soul—the dry misery which parches the countenance into furrows, and renders us liable to our most terrible "flesh-quakes."

There are sorrows, it is true, so great, that to give them some of the ordinary vents is to run a hazard of being overthrown. There we must rather strengthen ourselves to resist, or bow quietly and drily down, in order to let them pass over us, as the traveller does the wind of the desert. But where we feel that tears would relieve us, it is false philosophy to deny ourselves at least that first refreshment, and it is always false consolation to tell people that, because they cannot help a thing, they are not to mind it. The true way is, to let them grapple with the unavoidable sorrow, and try to win it into gentleness by a reasonable yielding. There are griefs so gentle in their very nature, that it would be worse than false heroism to refuse them a tear. Of this kind are the deaths of infants.

Particular circumstances may render it more or less advisable to indulge in grief for the loss of a little child; but, in general, parents should be no more advised to repress their first tears on such an occasion, than to repress their smiles towards a child surviving, or to indulge in any other sympathy. It is an appeal to the same gentle tenderness; and such appeals are never made in vain. The end of them is an acquittal from the harsher bonds of affliction—from the tying down of the spirit to one melancholy idea.

It is the nature of tears of this kind, however strongly they may gush forth, to run into quiet waters at last. We cannot easily, for the whole course of our lives, think with pain of any good and kind person whom we have lost. It is the divine nature of their qualities to conquer pain and death itself; to turn the memory of them into pleasure; to survive with a placid aspect in our imaginations. We are writing at this moment just opposite a spot which contains the grave of one inexpressibly dear to us. We see from our window the trees about it, and the church spire. The green fields lie around. The clouds are travelling overhead, alternately taking away the sunshine and restoring it. The vernal winds, piping of the flowery summer-time, are nevertheless calling to mind the far-distant and dangerous ocean, which the heart that lies in that grave had many reasons to think of. And yet the sight of this spot does not give us pain. So far from it, it is the existence of that grave which doubles every charm of the spot; which links the pleasures of our childhood and manhood together; which puts a hushing tenderness on the winds; and a patient joy upon the

landscape; which seems to unite heaven and earth, mortality and immortality, the grass of the tomb and the grass of the green field; and gives a more maternal aspect to the whole kindness of nature. It does not hinder gaiety itself. Happiness was what its tenant, through all her troubles, would have diffused. To diffuse happiness and to enjoy it, is not only carrying on her wishes, but realising her hopes; and gaiety, freed from its only pollutions, malignity and want of sympathy, is but a child playing about the knees of its mother. The remembered innocence and endearments of a child stand us instead of virtues that have died older. Children have not exercised the voluntary offices of friendship; they have not chosen to be kind and good to us; nor stood by us, from conscious will, in the hour of adversity. But they have shared their pleasures and pains with us as well as they could; the interchange of good offices between us has, of necessity, been less mingled with the troubles of the world; the sorrow arising from their death is the only one which we can associate with their memories. These are happy thoughts that cannot die. Our loss may always render them pensive; but they will not always be painful. It is a part of the benignity of nature that pain does not survive like pleasure, at any time, much less where the cause of it is an innocent one. The smile will remain reflected by memory, as the moon reflects the light upon us when the sun has gone into heaven.

When writers like ourselves quarrel with earthly pain (we mean writers of the same intentions, without implying, of course, anything about abilities or otherwise), they are misunderstood if they are supposed to quarrel with pains of every sort. This would be idle and effeminate. They do not pretend, indeed, that humanity might not wish, if it could, to be entirely free from pain; for it endeavours, at all times, to turn pain into pleasure: or at least to set off the one with the other, to make the former a zest and the latter a refreshment. The most unaffected dignity of suffering does this, and, if wise, acknowledges it. The greatest benevolence towards others, the most unselfish relish of their pleasures, even at its own expense, does but look to increasing the general stock of happiness, though content, if it could, to have its identity swallowed up in that splendid contemplation. We are far from meaning that this is to be called selfishness. We are far, indeed, from thinking so, or of so confounding words. But neither is it to be called pain when most unselfish, if disinterestedness be truly understood. The pain that is in it softens into pleasure, as the darker hue of the rainbow melts into the brighter. Yet even if a harsher line is to be drawn between the pain and pleasure of the most unselfish mind (and ill-health, for instance, may draw it), we should not quarrel with it if it contributed to the general mass of comfort, and were of a nature which general kindliness could not avoid. Made as we are, there are certain pains without which it would be difficult to conceive certain great and overbalancing pleasures. We may conceive it possible for beings to be made entirely happy, but in our composition something of pain seems to be a necessary ingredient, in order that the materials may turn to as fine account as possible, though our clay, in the course of ages and experience, may be refined more and more. We may get rid of the worst earth, though not of earth itself.

Now the liability to the loss of children—or rather what renders us sensible of it, the occasional loss itself—seems to be one of these necessary bitters thrown into the cup of humanity. We do not mean that every one must lose one of his children in order to enjoy the rest, or that every individual loss afflicts us in the same proportion. We allude to the deaths of infants in general. These might be as few as we could render them. But if none at all ever took place, we should regard every little child as a man or woman secured; and it will be easily conceived what a world of endearing cares and hopes this security would endanger. The very idea of infancy would lose its continuity with us. Girls and boys would be future men and women, not present children. They would have attained their full growth in our imaginations, and might as well have been men and women at once. On the other hand, those who have lost an infant, are never, as it were, without an infant child. They are the only persons who, in one sense, retain it always, and they furnish their neighbours with the same idea. The other children grow up to manhood and womanhood, and suffer all the changes of mortality. This one alone is rendered an immortal child. Death has arrested it with his kindly harshness, and blessed it into an eternal image of youth and innocence.

Of such as these are the pleasantest shapes that visit our fancy and our hopes. They are the ever-smiling emblems of joy; the prettiest pages that wait upon imagination. Lastly, "Of these are the kingdom of heaven." Wherever there is a province of that benevolent and all-accessible empire, whether on earth or elsewhere, such are the gentle spirits that must inhabit it. To such simplicity, or the resemblance of it, must they come. Such must be the ready confidence of their hearts, and creativeness of their fancy. And so ignorant must they be of the "knowledge of good and evil," losing their discernment of that self-created trouble, by enjoying the garden before them, and not being ashamed of what is kindly and innocent.

LEIGH HUNT.

CARLYLE'S PLAIN SPEAKING.—Although the writings of Carlyle are distinguished by such a strange distortion of the English tongue, his conversation was remarkably simple and straightforward. He talked right to the point. His hatred of sham was fearlessly expressed. On one occasion, when a lady of distinction—at whose house the Scotch philosopher was a guest—bewailed the wickedness of the Jews in not receiving Jesus as their Saviour, she finished her diatribe against them by saying:

"How different would have been His reception had He appeared in our own time! How delighted we should all be to throw our doors open to Him, and listen to His divine precepts! Don't you think so, Mr. Carlyle?"

The plain-spoken philosopher, thus appealed to, said, in his broadest Scotch accent:

"No, madam, I don't. I think, had He come with plenty of money, and good recommendations, and fashionably dressed, and preached doctrines palatable to the higher orders, I might have had the honour to receive from your ladyship a card of invitation, on the back of which would be written, 'To meet our Saviour;' but if He had come denouncing those aristocrats, the Pharisees, and associating with the Publicans and Radicals of the day, we should have treated Him now very much as the Jews did then, and cried out, '*Take Him to Newgate and hang Him!*'"

Ministration of Angels.

AND is there care in heaven? And is there love
   In heavenly spirits to these creatures base,
That may compassion of their evils move?
   There is: else much more wretched were the case

Of men than beasts. But O! th' exceeding grace
   Of highest God, that loves His creatures so;
And all His works with mercy doth embrace,
   That blessèd angels He sends to and fro,
To serve to wicked man—to serve his wicked foe!

How oft do they their silver bowers leave
  To come to succour us that succour want !
How oft do they with golden pinions cleave
  The flitting skies, like flying pursuivant,
    Against foul fiends to aid us militant !
  They for us fight, they watch and duly ward,
And their bright squadrons round about us plant ;
  And all for love and nothing for reward :
  O, why should heavenly God to men have such regard ?

EDMUND SPENSER (1553-1598).

Rest.

TRUE knowledge is true rest. In whatever world it is into which we penetrate and inquire, to know is to rest. Even in our sorrows, when the worst is over and is known, we begin to rest, even if it be only in the irrevocable despair ; so to solve a problem is to rest ; or to be assured of an affection is to rest ; or to reach home after the long toil is to rest. How deep that peace is when we are relieved from the heartache and the agony ! Rest ! It is, I believe, the deepest instinct in man, and when you touch it, you also, I believe, touch the highest instinct.

There is the *labourer's* rest, when the burden and the heat of the day are over, and the door opens to receive the wearied, careworn man.

There is the *child's* rest, when peace folds her soft wings over her pillow "before the evil days come."

There is the rest in *sickness*, the soft, sweet sleep when the fever is over, and we bless the pitying God ; we step softly across the room and turn aside the curtains, and look in and shed the tear over that pitiful yet smiling face, so tranquil now. There is the rest—the rest we shall all know, when the sickness, and the nausea, and the pitiless pain have ceased with the maddening of "the fever called *living*," when the lashes have fallen for the last time over the eyes, and we touch the cold, cruel lips that will never, never, *never* speak to us or smile on us again, and over brow and bosom are spread *that* rest.

E. PAXTON HOOD.

Memorial Verses.

I.—From Dryden.

As precious gums are not for lasting fire,
They but perfume the temple, and expire:
So was she soon exhal'd, and vanish'd hence;
A short sweet odour, of a vast expense.
She vanish'd, we can scarcely say she died;
For but a *now* did heaven and earth divide.
As gentle dreams our waking thoughts pursue;
Or, one dream pass'd, we slide into a new;
So close they follow, such wild order keep,
We think ourselves awake and are asleep:
So softly death succeeded life in her:
She did but dream of heav'n, and she was there.
No pains she suffer'd, nor expir'd with noise:
Her soul was whisper'd out with God's still voice;
As an old friend is beckon'd to a feast,
And treated like a long-familiar guest,
He took her as He found, but found her so,
As one in hourly readiness to go.

II.—From Andrew Marvell.

Enough; and leave the rest to fame;
'Tis to commend her, but to name
Courtship, which, living, she declin'd,
When dead, to offer were unkind.
Where never any could speak ill,
Who would officious praises still?
Nor can the truest wit, or friend,
Without detracting, her commend;
To say she liv'd a virgin chaste
In this age loose and all unlaced;
Nor was, when vice is so allowed,
Of virtue or ashamed or proud;
That her soul was on heaven so bent,
No minute but it came and went,
That, ready her last debt to pay,
She summ'd her life up every day;
Modest as morn, as mid-day bright,
Gentle as evening, cool as night,
'Tis true, but all too-weakly said;
'Tis more significant—she's dead.

The Legend of Rabbi Ben Levi.

RABBI BEN LEVI, on the Sabbath, read
A volume of the law, in which it said,
"No man shall look upon My face and live."
And as he read, he prayed that God would give
His faithful servant grace, with mortal eye
To look upon His face and yet not die.
Then fell a sudden shadow on the page,
And, lifting up his eyes, grown dim with age,
He saw the Angel of Death before him stand,
Holding a naked sword in his right hand.
Rabbi Ben Levi was a righteous man,
Yet through his veins a chill of terror ran,
With trembling voice he said, "What wilt thou here?"
The Angel answered, "The time draws near
When thou must die; yet first, by God's decree,
Whate'er thou askest shall be granted thee."
Replied the Rabbi, "Let these living eyes
First look upon my place in Paradise."
Then said the Angel, "Come with me and look."
Rabbi Ben Levi closed the sacred book,
And rising, and uplifting his gray head,
"Give me thy sword," he to the Angel said,
"Lest thou shouldst fall upon me by the way."
The Angel smiled, and hastened to obey,
Then led him forth to the Celestial Town,
And sat him on the wall, whence, gazing down,
Rabbi Ben Levi with his living eyes,
Might look upon his place in Paradise.
Then straight into the City of the Lord
The Rabbi leaped with the Death-Angel's sword,
And through the streets there swept a sudden breath
Of something there unknown, which men call Death.

Meanwhile the Angel stayed without, and cried,
"Come back!" To which the Rabbi's voice replied,
"No! in the name of God, whom I adore,
I swear that hence I will depart no more!"

Then all the Angels cried, "O holy One,
See what the son of Levi here has done!
The kingdom of heaven he takes by violence,
And in Thy name refuses to go hence!"
The Lord replied, "My Angels, be not wroth:
Did e'er the son of Levi break his oath?
Let him remain; for he with mortal eye
Shall look upon My face and yet not die."

Beyond the outer wall the Angel of Death
Heard the great voice, and said, with panting breath,
"Give back the sword, and let me go my way."
Whereat the Rabbi paused, and answered, "Nay!
Anguish enough already hath it caused
Among the sons of men." And while he paused,
He heard the awful mandate of the Lord
Resounding through the air, "Give back the sword!"

The Rabbi bowed his head in silent prayer;
Then said he to the dreadful Angel, "Swear
No human eye shall look on it again;
But when thou takest away the souls of men,
Thyself unseen, and with an unseen sword,
Thou wilt perform the bidding of the Lord."

The Angel took the sword again, and swore,
And walks on earth unseen for evermore.

LONGFELLOW.

HE that would pass the latter part of his life with honour and decency, must, when he is young, consider that he shall one day be old; and remember when he is old that he has once been young. In youth he must lay up knowledge for his support when his powers of action shall forsake him; and in age forbear to animadvert with rigour on faults which experince only can correct.

Seaweed.

WHEN descends on the Atlantic
    The gigantic
Storm-wind of the equinox,
Landward in his wrath he scourges
    The toiling surges,
Laden with seaweed from the rocks:

From Bermuda's reefs; from edges
    Of sunken ledges,
In some far-off, bright Azore:
From Bahama, and the dashing
    Silver-flashing
Surges of San Salvador;

From the tumbling surf, that buries
    The Orkneyan skerries,
Answering the hoarse Hebrides;
And from wrecks of ships, and drifting
    Spars uplifting
On the desolate, rainy seas;—

Ever drifting, drifting, drifting
    On the shifting
Currents of the restless main;
Till in sheltered coves and reaches
    Of sandy beaches,
All have found repose again.

So when storms of wild emotion
    Strike the ocean
Of the poet's soul, ere long
From each cave and rocky fastness,
    In its vastness,
Floats some fragment of a song;

OUR SUNDAY BOOK.

From the far-off isles enchanted,
    Heaven has planted
With the golden fruit of Truth;
From the flashing surf, whose vision
    Gleams Elysian
In the tropic clime of Youth;

From the strong Will, and the Endeavour
    That for ever
Wrestles with the tides of Fate;
From the wreck of Hopes far-scattered,
    Tempest-shattered,
Floating waste and desolate;—

Ever drifting, drifting, drifting
    On the shifting
Currents of the restless heart:
Till at length in books recorded,
    They, like hoarded
Household words, no more depart.

                                LONGFELLOW.

Twilight.

THE twilight is sad and cloudy,
    The wind blows wild and free,
And like the wings of sea-birds
    Flash the white caps of the sea.

But in the fisherman's cottage,
    There shines a ruddier light,
And a little face at the window
    Peers out into the night.

TWILIGHT.

Close, close it is pressed to the window,
    As if those childish eyes
Were looking into the darkness,
    To see some form arise.

And a woman's waving shadow
    Is passing to and fro,
Now rising to the ceiling,
    Now bowing and bending low.

What tale do the roaring ocean,
    And the night-wind, bleak and wild,
As they beat at the crazy casement,
    Tell to that little child?

And why do the roaring ocean,
    And the night-wind, wild and bleak,
As they beat at the heart of the mother,
    Drive the colour from her cheek?

A Dream of the Universe.

I HAD been reading an excellent dissertation upon the vulgar old error which regards the space from one earth and sun to another as empty. Our sun, together with all its planets, fills only the 31,419,460,000,000,000th part of the whole space between itself and the next solar body. Gracious Heavens! thought I, in what an unfathomable abyss of emptiness were this universe swallowed up and lost, if all were void and utter vacuity except the few shining points of dust which we call a planetary system! According to Herschel, the most remote of the galaxies which the telescope discovers lie at such a distance from us, that their light which reaches us at this day must have set out on its journey two millions of years ago; and thus, by optical laws, it is possible that whole squadrons of the starry hosts may be now reaching us with their beams, which have themselves perished ages ago. Upon this scale of computation for the dimensions of the world, what heights and depths and breadths must there be in this universe—in comparison of which the positive universe would be itself a nihility, were it crossed, pierced, and belted about by so illimitable a wilderness of nothing! But is it possible that any man can for a moment overlook those vast forces which must pervade these imaginary deserts with eternal surges of flux and reflux, to make the very paths to those distant starry coasts voyageable to our eyes? Can you lock up in a sun or in its planets their reciprocal forces of attraction? Does not the light stream through the immeasurable spaces between our earth and the nebula which is farthest removed from us? And in this stream of light there is as ample an existence of the positive, and as much a home for the abode of a spiritual world, as there is a dwelling-place for thy own spirit in the substance of the brain. To these and similar reflections succeeded the following dream:

Methought my body sank down in ruins, and my inner form stepped out apparelled in light, and by my side there stood another Form which resembled my own, except that it did not shine like mine, but lightened unceasingly.

"Two thoughts," said the Form, "are the wings with which I move: the thought of *Here* and the thought of *There*. And behold! I am yonder," pointing to a distant world. "Come, then, and wait on me with thy thoughts and with thy flight, that I may show to thee the universe under a veil."

And I flew along with the Form.

In a moment our earth fell back behind our consuming flight into an abyss of distance; a faint gleam only was reflected from the summits of the Cordilleras, and a few moments more reduced the sun to a little star; and soon there remained nothing visible of our system except a comet, which was travelling from our sun with angelic speed in the direction of Sirius.

Our flight now carried us so rapidly through the flocks of the solar bodies—flocks past counting, unless to their Heavenly Shepherd—that scarcely could they expand themselves before us into the magnitude of moons before they sank behind us into pale nebular gleams, and their planetary earths could not reveal themselves for a moment to the transcendent rapidity of our course. At length Sirius and all the brotherhood of our constellations and the galaxy of our heavens stood far below our feet as a little nebula among other yet more distant nebulæ. Thus we flew on through the starry wildernesses: one heaven after another unfurled its immeasurable banners before us, and then rolled up behind us; galaxy behind galaxy towered up into solemn altitudes before which the spirit shuddered; and they stood in long array, through which the Infinite Being might pass into progress. Sometimes the Form that lightened would outfly my weary thoughts; and then it would be seen far off before me like a coruscation amongst the stars—till suddenly I thought again to myself the thought of *There*, and then I was at its side.

But as we were thus swallowed up by one abyss of stars after another, and the heavens above our heads were not emptier, neither were the heavens below them fuller; and as suns without intermission fell into the solar ocean like waterspouts of a storm which fall into the ocean of waters; then, at length, the human heart within me was over-burdened and weary, and yearned after some narrow cell or quiet oratory in this metropolitan cathedral of the universe. And I said to the Form at my side,—

"Oh, spirit, has, then, this universe no end?"

And the Form answered and said,—

" Lo, it has no beginning!"

Suddenly, however, the heavens above us appeared to be emptied, and not a star was seen to twinkle in the mighty abyss, no gleam of light to break the unity of the infinite darkness. The starry hosts behind us had all contracted into an obscure nebula, and at length that also had vanished. And I thought to myself, "At last the universe has ended," and I trembled at the thought of the illimitable dungeon of pure, pure darkness which here began to imprison the creation; I shuddered at the dead sea of nothing, in whose unfathomable zone of blackness the jewel of the glittering universe seemed to be set and buried for ever; and through the night in which we moved I saw the Form, which still lightened as before, but left all around it unilluminated. Then the Form said to me in my anguish,—

"Oh, creature of little faith, look up; the most ancient light is coming!"

I looked; and in a moment came a twilight, in the twinkling of an eye a galaxy, and then with a choral burst rushed in all the company of stars. For centuries grey with age, for millennia hoary with antiquity, had the starry light been on its road to us; and at length, out of heights inaccessible to thought, it had reached us. Now, then, as through some renovated century, we flew through new cycles of heavens. At length again came a starless interval, and far longer it endured before the beams of a starry host again had reached us.

As we thus advanced for ever through an interchange of nights and solar heavens, and as the interval grew still longer and longer before the last heaven we had quitted contracted to a point, and at once we issued suddenly from the middle of thickest night into an aurora borealis, the herald of an expiring world, we found throughout this cycle of solar systems that a day of judgment had indeed arrived: the suns had sickened, and the planets were heaving, rocking, yawning in convulsions, the subterraneous waters of the great deeps were breaking up, and lightnings that were ten diameters of a world in length ran along from east to west, from zenith to nadir; and here and there, where a sun should have been, we saw instead through the misty vapour a gloomy, ashy leaden corpse of a solar body, that sucked in flames from the perishing world, but gave out neither light nor heat; and as I saw, through a vista which had no end, mountain towering above mountain, and piled up with what seemed glittering snow from the conflict of solar and planetary bodies, then my spirit bent under the load of the universe, and I said to the Form,—

"Rest, rest, and lead me no further: I am too solitary in the creation itself, and in its deserts yet more so; the full world is great, but the empty world is greater, and with the universe increase its Saharas."

Then the Form touched me like the flowing of a breath, and spoke more gently than before,—

"In the presence of God there is no emptiness: above, below, between and round about the stars, in the darkness and in the light, dwelleth the true and very Universe, the sum and fountain of all that is. But thy spirit can bear only earthly images of the unearthly; now, then, I cleanse thy sight with euphrasy; look forth, and behold the images."

Immediately my eyes were opened; and I looked, and I saw as it were an interminable sea of light—sea immeasurable, sea unfathomable, sea without a shore. All spaces between all heavens were filled with happiest light, and there was a thundering of floods, and there were seas above the seas, and seas below the seas, and I saw all the trackless regions that we had voyaged over; and my eye comprehended the farthest and the nearest, and darkness had become light and the light darkness; for the deserts and wastes of the creation were now filled with the sea of light, and in this sea the suns floated like ash-grey blossoms, and the planets like black grains of seed. Then my heart comprehended that immortality dwelled in the spaces between the worlds, and death only amongst the worlds. Upon all the suns there walked upright shadows in the form of men, but they were glorified when they quitted these perishable worlds, and when they sank into the sea of light; and the murky planets, I perceived, were but cradles for the infant spirits of the universe of light. In the Saharas of the creation I saw—I heard—I felt—the glittering, the echoing, the breathing of life and creative power. The suns were but as spinning-wheels, the planets no more than weavers' shuttles, in relation to the infinite web which composes the veil of Isis, which veil is hung over the whole creation, and lengthens as any finite being attempts to raise it. And in sight of this immeasurability of life no sadness could endure, but only joy that knew no limit, and happy prayers.

But in the midst of this great vision of the universe the Form that lightened eternally had become invisible, or had vanished to its home in the unseen world of spirits. I was left alone in the centre of a universe of life, and I yearned after some sympathising being. Suddenly from the starry deeps there came floating through the ocean of light a planetary body, and upon it there stood a woman whose face was as the face of a Madonna, and by her side there stood a child, whose countenance varied not, neither was it magnified as he drew nearer. This child was a king, for I saw that he had a crown upon his head; but the crown was a crown of thorns. Then, also, I perceived that the planetary body was our unhappy earth, and as the earth drew near, this child, who had come forth from the starry deeps to comfort me, threw upon me a look of gentlest pity and of unutterable love, so that in my heart I had a sudden rapture of joy such as passes all understanding, and I awoke in the tumult of my happiness.

I awoke, but my happiness survived my dream, and I exclaimed,—"Oh, how beautiful is death! seeing that we die in a world of life and of creation without end;" and I blessed God for my life upon earth, but much more for the life in those unseen depths of the universe which are emptied of all but the supreme reality, and where no earthly life nor perishable hope can enter.

DE QUINCEY.
(FROM THE GERMAN OF JEAN PAUL RICHTER.)

How to see Westminster Abbey.

No one can understand Westminster Abbey, and few can realize its beauties in a single visit. Too many tombs will produce the same satiety as too many pictures. There can be no advantage, and there will be less pleasure, in filling

the brain with a hopeless jumble, in which kings and statesmen, warriors, ecclesiastics, and poets are tossing about together. Even those who give the shortest time to their London sight-seeing, should not pay less than three visits to the Abbey. On the first, unwearied by detail, let them have the luxury of enjoying the architectural beauties of the place, with the general view of the interior, the chapter-house, cloisters, and their monastic surroundings. On the second, let them study the glorious chapels which surround the choir, and which contain nearly all the tombs of antiquarian or artistic interest. On the third, let them labour as far as they can through the mass of monuments which crowd the transepts and nave, which are often mere cenotaphs, and which almost always derive their only interest from those they commemorate. These three visits may enable visitors to *see* Westminster Abbey, but it will require many more to *know* it—visits at all hours of the day, to drink in the glories of the light and shadow in the one great church of England which retains its beautiful ancient colouring, undestroyed by so-called "restoration"—visits employed in learning the way by which the minster has grown, arch upon arch, and monument upon monument; and other visits given to studying the epitaphs on the tombs, and considering the reminiscences they awaken.—"*Walks in London.*"

The Reprisal.

I HAVE consider'd it, and find
   There is no dealing with thy mighty passion;
For, though I die for thee, I am behind;
   My sins deserve the condemnation.

Oh, make me innocent, that I
   May give a disentangled state and free;
And yet thy wounds still my attempts defy,
   For by thy death I die for thee.

Ah! was it not enough that thou,
   By thy eternal glory, didst outgo me?
Couldst thou not grief's sad conquests me allow,
   But in all victories overthrow me?

Yet by confession will I come
   Into the conquest. Though I can do nought
Against thee, in thee I will overcome
   The man who once against thee fought.

GEORGE HERBERT.

The Prince's Dream.

IF we may credit the fable, there is a tower in the midst of a great Asiatic plain wherein is confined a prince who was placed there in his earliest infancy, with many slaves and attendants, and all the luxuries that are compatible with imprisonment.

Whether he was brought there from some motive of state, whether to conceal him from enemies, or to deprive him of rights, has not transpired; but it is certain that up to the date of this little history, he had never set his foot outside the walls of that high tower, and that of the vast world without he knew only the green plains which surrounded it: the flocks and the birds of that region were all his experience of living creatures, and all the men he saw outside were shepherds.

And yet he was not utterly deprived of change, for sometimes one of his attendants would be ordered away, and his place would be supplied by a new one. This fresh companion the prince would never weary of questioning, and letting him talk of cities, of ships, of forests, of merchandise, of kings; but though in turns they all tried to satisfy his curiosity, they could not succeed in conveying very distinct notions to his mind; partly because there was nothing in the tower to which they could compare the external world, partly because, having chiefly lived lives of seclusion and indolence in Eastern palaces, they knew it only by hearsay themselves.

At length, one day, a venerable man of a noble presence was brought to the tower, with soldiers to guard him and slaves to attend him. The prince was glad of his presence, though at first he seldom opened his lips, and it was manifest that confinement made him miserable. With restless feet he would wander from window to window of the stone tower, and mount from storey to storey; but mount as high as he would, there was still nothing to be seen but the vast unvarying plain, clothed with scanty grass, and flooded with the glaring sunshine; flocks and herds and shepherds moved across it sometimes, but nothing else, not even a shadow, for there was no cloud in the sky to cast one. The old man, however, always treated the prince with respect, and answered his questions with a great deal of patience, till at length he found a pleasure in satisfying his curiosity, which so much pleased the poor young prisoner, that, as a great condescension, he invited him to come out on the roof of the tower and drink sherbet with him in the cool of the evening, and tell him of the country beyond the desert, and what seas are like, and mountains, and towns.

"I have learnt much from my attendants, and know this world pretty well by hearsay," said the prince, as they reclined on the rich carpet which was spread on the roof.

The old man smiled, but did not answer; perhaps because he did not care to undeceive his young companion, perhaps because so many slaves were present, some of whom were serving them with fruit, and others burning rich odours on a little chafing-dish that stood between them.

"But there are some words that I never could attach any particular meaning to," proceeded the prince, as the slaves began to retire, "and three in particular that my attendants cannot satisfy me upon, or are reluctant to do so."

"What words are those, my prince?" asked the old man. The prince turned on his elbow to be sure that the last slave had descended the tower stairs, then replied,—

"O man of much knowledge, the words are these—Labour, and Liberty, and Gold."

"Prince," said the old man, "I do not wonder that it has been hard to make thee understand the first, the nature of it, and the cause why most men are born to it; as for the second, it would be treason for thee and me to do more than whisper it here, and sigh for it when none are listening; but the third need hardly puzzle thee, thy hookah is bright with it; all thy jewels are set in it; gold is inlaid in the ivory of thy bath; thy cup and thy dish are of gold, and golden threads are wrought into thy raiment."

"That is true," replied the prince, "and if I had not seen and handled this gold, perhaps I might not find its merits so hard to understand; but I possess it in abundance, and it does not feed me, nor make music for me, nor fan me when the sun is hot, nor cause me to sleep when I am weary; therefore, when my slaves have told me how merchants go out and brave the perilous wind and sea, and live in the unstable ships, and run risks from shipwreck and pirates, and when, having asked them why they have done this, they have answered, 'For gold,' I have found it hard to believe them; and when they have told me how men have lied and robbed and deceived, how they have murdered one another, and leagued together to depose kings, to oppress provinces, and all for gold, then I have said to myself, either my slaves have combined to make me believe that which is not, or this gold must be very different from the yellow stuff that this coin is made of, this coin which is of no use but to have a hole pierced through it and hang to my girdle, that it may tinkle when I walk."

"Notwithstanding," said the old man, "nothing can be done without gold; for look you, prince, it is better than bread and fruit and music, for it can buy them all, since all men love it, and have agreed to exchange it for whatever they may need."

"How so?" asked the prince.

"If a man has many loaves, he cannot eat them all," answered the old man; "therefore he goes to his neighbour, and says, 'I have bread and thou hast a coin of gold, let us change;' so he receives the gold, and goes to another man, saying, 'Thou hast two houses and I have none, lend me one of thy houses to live in, and I will give thee my gold;' thus again they change; and he that has the gold says, 'I have food enough and goods enough, but I want a wife; I will go to the merchant and get a marriage gift for her father, and for it I will give him this gold.'"

"It is well," said the prince; "but in time of drought, if there is no bread in a city, can they make it of gold?"

"Not so," answered the old man, "but they must send their gold to a city where there is food, and bring that back instead of it."

"But if there was a famine all over the world," asked the prince, "what would they do then?"

"Why, then, and only then," said the old man, "they must starve, and the gold would be nought, for it can only be changed for that which *is*; it cannot make that which is not."

"And where do they get gold?" asked the prince; "is it the precious fruit of some rare tree, or have they whereby they can draw it down from the sky at sunset?"

"Some of it," said the old man, "they dig out of the ground."

Then he told the prince of ancient rivers running through terrible deserts, whose sands glitter with golden grains, and are yellow in the fierce heat of the sun, and of dreary mines where the Indian slaves work in gangs tied together, never seeing the light of day; and lastly (for he was a man of much knowledge, and had travelled far), he told him of the valley of the Sacramento in the New World, and of those mountains where the people of Europe send their criminals, and where now their free men pour forth to gather gold, and dig for it as hard as if for life, sitting up by it at night lest any should take it from them; giving up houses and country, and wife and children, for the sake of a few feet of mud, whence they dig clay that glitters as they wash it; and how they sift it and rock it as patiently as if it were their own children in the cradle, and afterwards carry it in their bosoms, and forego on account of it safety and rest.

"But, prince," he proceeded, observing that the young man was absorbed in his narrative, "if you would pass your word to me never to betray me, I would procure for you a sight of the external world, and in a trance you should see those places where gold is dug, and traverse those regions forbidden to your mortal footsteps."

Upon this the prince threw himself at the old man's feet, and promised heartily to observe the secrecy required, and entreated that, for however short a time, he might be suffered to see this wonderful world.

Then, if we may credit the story, the old man drew nearer to the chafing-dish which stood between them, and, having fanned the dying embers in it, cast upon them a certain powder and some herbs, from whence, as they burned, a peculiar smoke arose. As their vapours spread, he desired the prince to draw near and inhale them, and then (says the fable) when he should sleep he should find himself, in his dream, at whatever place he might desire, with this strange advantage, that he should see things in their truth and reality, as well as in their outward shows.

So the prince, not without some fear, prepared to obey; but first he drank his sherbet, and handed over the golden cup to the old man by way of recompense; then he reclined beside the chafing-dish, and inhaled the heavy perfume till he became overpowered with sleep, and sank down upon the carpet in a dream.

The prince knew not where he was, but a green country was floating before him, and he found himself standing in a marshy valley, where a few wretched cottages were scattered here and there with no means of communication. There was a river, but it had overflowed its banks and made the central land impassable; the fences had been broken down by it, and the fields of corn laid low; a few wretched peasants were wandering about there; they looked half clad and half starved. "A miserable valley, indeed!" exclaimed the prince; but as he said it a man came down from the hills with a great bag of gold in his hand.

"This valley is mine," said he to the people; "I have bought it for gold. Now, make banks that the river may not overflow, and I will give you gold; also make fences and plant fields, and cover in the roofs of your houses, and buy yourselves richer clothing." So the people did so, and as the gold got lower in the bag, the valley grew fairer and greener, till the prince exclaimed, "O gold, I see your value now! O wonderful, beneficent gold!"

But presently the valley melted away like a mist, and the prince saw an army besieging a city; he heard a general haranguing his soldiers to urge them on, and the soldiers shouting and battering the walls; but shortly, when the city was well-nigh taken, he saw some men secretly throwing gold among the soldiers, so much of it that they threw down their arms to pick it up, and said that the walls were so strong that they could not throw them down. "O powerful gold!" thought the prince; "thou art stronger than the city walls!"

After that it seemed to himself that he was walking about in a desert country, and in his dream he thought, "Now I know what labour is, for I have

The Prince's Dream.

seen it, and its benefits; and I know what liberty is, for I have tasted it; I can wander where I will, and no man questions me; but gold is more strange to me than ever, for I have seen it buy both liberty and labour." Shortly after this, he saw a great crowd digging upon a barren hill, and when he drew near he understood that he had reached the summit of his wishes, and that he was to see the place where the gold came from.

He came up, and stood a long time watching the people as they toiled ready to faint in the sun, so great was the labour of digging up the gold.

He saw who had much, and could not trust any one to help them to carry it, binding it in bundles over their shoulders, and bending and groaning under its weight; he saw others hide it in the ground, and watch the place clothed in rags, that none might suspect that they were rich; but some, on the contrary, who had dug up an unusual quantity, he saw dancing and singing, and vaunting their success, till robbers waylaid them when they slept, and rifled their bundles and carried their golden sand away.

"All these men are mad," thought the prince, "and this pernicious gold has made them so."

After this, as he wandered here and there, he saw groups of people smelting the gold under the shadow of the trees, and he observed that a dancing, quivering vapour rose up from it, which dazzled their eyes, and distorted everything that they looked at; arraying it also in different colours from the true one. He observed that this vapour from the gold caused all things to rock and reel before the eyes of those who looked through it, and also, by some strange affinity, it drew their hearts towards those who carried much gold on their persons, so that they called them good and beautiful; it also caused them to see darkness and dulness in the faces of those who carried none. "This," thought the prince, "is very strange;" but not being able to explain it, he went still further, and there he saw more people. Each of these had adorned himself with a broad golden girdle, and was sitting in the shade, while other men waited on them.

"What ails these people?" he inquired of one who was looking on, for he observed a peculiar air of weariness and dulness in their faces. He was answered that the girdles were very tight and heavy, and, being bound over the regions of the heart, were supposed to impede its action, and prevent it from beating high, and also to chill the wearer, as, being of opaque material, the warm sunshine of the earth could not get through to warm him.

"Why, then, do they not break them asunder," exclaimed the prince, "and fling them away?"

"Break them asunder!" cried the man; "why, what a madman you must be; they are made of the purest gold!"

"Forgive my ignorance," replied the prince; "I am a stranger."

So he walked on, for feelings of delicacy prevented him from gazing any longer at the men with the golden girdles; but as he went he pondered on the misery he had seen, and thought to himself that this golden sand did more mischief than all the poisons of the apothecary: for it dazzled the eyes of some, it strained the hearts of others, it bowed down the heads of many to the earth with its weight; it was a sore labour to gather it, and when it was gathered, the robber might carry it away; it would be a good thing, he thought, if there were none of it.

After this he came to a place where were sitting some aged widows and some orphan children of the gold-diggers, who were helpless and destitute; they were weeping and bemoaning themselves, but stopped at the approach of a man, whose appearance attracted the prince, for he had a very great bundle of gold on his back, and yet it did not bow him down at all; his apparel was rich, but he had no girdle on, and his face was anything but sad.

"Sir," said the prince to him, "you have a great burden; you are fortunate to be able to stand under it."

"I could not do so," he replied, "only that as I go on I keep lightening it;" and as he passed each of the widows, he threw gold to her, and, stooping down, hid pieces of it in the bosoms of the children.

"You have no girdle," said the prince.

"I once had one," answered the gold gatherer; "but it was so tight over my breast that my very heart grew cold under it, and almost ceased to beat. Having a great quantity of gold on my back, I felt almost at the last gasp; so I threw off my girdle, and, being on the bank of a river, which I knew not how to cross, I was about to fling it in, I was so vexed! 'But no,' thought I, 'there are many people waiting here to cross besides myself. I will make my girdle into a bridge, and we will cross over on it.'"

"Turn your girdle into a bridge!" exclaimed the prince doubtfully, for he did not quite understand.

The man explained himself.

"And then, sir, after that," he continued, "I turned one half of my burden into bread, and gave it to these poor people. Since then I have not been oppressed by its weight, however heavy it may have been; for few men have a heavier one. In fact, I gather more from day to day."

As the man kept speaking, he scattered his gold right and left with a cheerful countenance, and the prince was about to reply, when suddenly a great trembling under his feet made him fall to the ground. The refining fires of the gold gatherers sprang up into flames, and then went out; night fell over everything on the earth, and nothing was visible in the sky but the stars of the southern cross, which were glittering above him.

"It is past midnight," thought the prince, "for the stars of the cross begin to bend."

He raised himself upon his elbow, and tried to pierce the darkness, but could not. At length a slender blue flame darted out, as from ashes in a chafing-dish, and by the light of it he saw the strange pattern of his carpet and the cushions lying about. He did not recognise them at first, but presently he knew that he was lying in his usual place, at the top of his tower.

"Wake up, prince," said the old man.

The prince sat up and sighed, and the old man inquired what he had seen.

"O man of much learning!" answered the prince, "I have seen that this is a wonderful world; I have seen the value of labour, and I know the uses of it; I have tasted the sweetness of liberty, and am grateful, though it was but in a dream; but as for that other word that was so great a mystery to me, I only know this, that it must remain a mystery for ever, since I am fain to believe that all men are bent on getting it; though, once gotten, it causeth them endless disquietude, only second to their discomfort that are without it. I am fain to believe that they can procure with it whatever they most desire, and yet that it cankers their hearts and dazzles their eyes; that it is their nature and their duty to gather it; and yet that, when once gathered, the best thing they can do is to scatter it!"

Alas! the prince visited this wonderful world no more; for the next morning, when he awoke, the old man was gone. He had taken with him the golden cup which the prince had given him. And the sentinel was also gone, none knew whither. Perhaps the old man had turned his golden cup into a golden key.

JEAN INGELOW.

Strength out of Weakness.

EVERY man in his lifetime needs to thank his faults. As no man thoroughly understands a truth until first he has contended against it, so no man has a thorough acquaintance with the hindrances or talents of men until he has suffered from the one and seen the triumph of the other over his own want of the same. Has he a defect of temper that unfits him to live in society? Thereby he is driven to entertain himself alone and acquire habits of self-help; and thus, like the wounded oyster, he mends his shell with pearl. Our strength grows out of our weakness. Not until we are pricked and stung and sorely shot at awakens this indignation which arms itself with secret forces. The wise man always throws himself on the side of his assailants. It is more his interest than it is theirs to find his weak point. The wound citatrizes and falls off from him like a dead skin, and when they would triumph, lo! he has passed on invulnerable.

EMERSON.

Employment.

If as a flower doth spread and die,
Thou wouldst extend me to some good,
Before I were by frost's extremity
                    Nipt in the bud.

The sweetness and the praise were Thine:
But the extension and the room,
Which in Thy garland I should fill, were mine
                    At Thy great doom.

For as Thou dost impart Thy grace,
The greater shall our glory be:
The measure of our joys is in this place,
                    The stuff with Thee.

Let me not languish, then, and spend
A life as barren to Thy praise
As is the dust, to which that life doth tend,
                    But with delays.

All things are busy; only I
Neither bring honey with the bees,
Nor flowers to make that, nor the husbandry
                    To water these.

I am no link of Thy great chain,
But all my company is a weed.
Lord, place me in Thy consort, give one strain
                    To my poor reed.

                            GEORGE HERBERT.

The late Abbé Listz—the great pianist.

Music.

The meaning of song goes deep. Who is there that in logical words can express the effect music has on us? A kind of inarticulate, unfathomable speech, which leads us to the edge of the Infinite, and lets us for moments gaze into that!—CARLYLE.

SUCH was the bard, whose heavenly strains of old
Appeased the fiend of melancholy Saul;
Such was, if old and heathen fame say true,
The man who bade the Theban domes ascend,
And tamed the savage nations with his song;
And such the Thracian, whose harmonious lyre,
Tuned to soft woe, made all the mountains weep,
Soothed even th' inexorable powers of hell,
And half redeem'd his lost Eurydice.
Music exalts each joy, allays each grief,
Expels diseases, softens every pain,
Subdues the rage of poison, and the plague;
And hence the wise of ancient days adored
One power of physic, melody, and song.

ARMSTRONG.

A MINERALOGIST'S LABOUR LOST.—There is one science the value of which it is very difficult to make a Highlander comprehend, and that is mineralogy. He connects botany with the art of healing; astronomy with guidance from the stars, or navigation; chemistry with dyeing, brewing, etc.; but "chopping bits of the rocks," as he calls it—this has always been a mystery.

A shepherd, while smoking his cutty at a small Highland inn, was communicating to another in Gaelic his experiences of "mad Englishmen," as he called them.

"There was one," said the narrator, "who once gave me his bag to carry to the inn by a short cut across the hills, while he walked by another road. I was wondering myself why it was so dreadfully heavy, and when I got out of his sight I was determined to see what was in it. I opened it, and what do you think it was? But I need not ask you to guess, for you would never find out. It was stones!"

"Stones!" exclaimed his companion, opening his eyes; "stones! Well, well, that beats all I ever knew or heard of them. And did you carry it?"

"Carry it! Do you think I was as mad as himself? No; I emptied them all out, but I filled the bag again from the cairn near the house, and gave him good measure for his money."—*Dr. M'Leod's "Annals of a Highland Parish."*

Education of Children

BRING thy children up in learning and obedience, yet without outward austerity. Praise them openly, reprehend them secretly. Give them good countenance and convenient maintenance according to thy ability, otherwise thy life will seem their bondage; and what portion thou shalt leave them at thy death, they will thank death for it, and not thee. And I am persuaded that the foolish cockering of some parents, and the over-stern carriage of others, causeth more men and women to take ill courses, than their own vicious inclinations. Marry thy daughters in time, lest they marry themselves. And suffer not thy sons to pass the Alps; for they shall learn nothing there but pride, blasphemy, and atheism. And if by travel they get a few broken languages, that shall profit them nothing more than to have one meal served in divers dishes. Neither by any counsel shalt thou train them up in wars; for he that sets up his rest to live by that profession can hardly be an honest man or a good Christian. Besides, it is a science no longer in request than use: for soldiers in peace are like chimneys in summer.

SIR PHILIP SIDNEY (1575).

Harrow-on-the-Hill.

REGARDED only for its picturesque situation, Harrow would probably be a famous spot, but its great reputation is derived from its having for three centuries possessed one of the eight great public schools of England. Here many men, who became famous in the history, the arts, and the literature of the country, were educated; and the place has been especially associated with the memory of Byron, whose lines of farewell to Harrow are usually quoted in connection with it.

The tombstone on the steep brow of the churchyard, where as a youth the poet reclined and meditated as he looked forth at the glorious prospect, is a prominent object of attraction to visitors. The view towards the east is bounded by London; ten miles distant is Hyde Park and the Marble Arch. Southward is the Crystal Palace and the range of the Surrey Hills. The view south-east extends from Knockholt Beeches, Hayes Common, etc., to Shooter's Hill, and across the Thames to the Langdon Hills, on the Essex side. The prospect west and south-west is extensive and exceedingly beautiful, including Windsor Castle, and a great part of the counties of Berkshire and Buckinghamshire; while on the north are Hampstead, Hendon, and Barnet.

Harrow-on-the-Hill.

On a distant View of the Village and School of Harrow-on-the-Hill.

Oh! mihi præteritos referat si Jupiter annos.—VIRGIL.

YE scenes of my childhood, whose loved recollection
Embitters the present compared with the past,
Where science first dawn'd on the powers of reflection,
And friendships were form'd too romantic to last;

Where fancy yet joys to trace the resemblance
Of comrades in friendship and mischief allied;
How welcome to me your ne'er-fading remembrance,
Which rests in the bosom, though hope is denied!

Again I revisit the hills where we sported,
The streams where we swam, and the fields where we fought;
The school where, loud warn'd by the bell, we resorted
To pore o'er the precepts by pedagogues taught.

Again I behold, where for hours I have ponder'd,
As reclining at eve, on yon tombstone I lay;
Or round the steep brow of the churchyard I wander'd,
To catch the last gleam of the sun's setting ray.

I once more view the room, with spectators surrounded,
Where as Zanga, I trod on Alonzo o'erthrown;
While to swell my young pride, such applauses resounded,
I fancied that Mossop himself was outshone.

Or, as Lear, I pour'd forth the deep imprecation,
By my daughters of kingdom and reason deprived;
Till, fired by loud plaudits and self-adulation,
I regarded myself as a Garrick revived.

Ye dreams of my boyhood, how much I regret you!
Unfaded your memory dwells in my breast;
Though sad and deserted, I ne'er can forget you;
Your pleasures may still be in fancy possest.

To Ida full oft may remembrance restore me,
While fate shall the shades of the future unroll;
Since darkness o'ershadows the prospect before me,
More dear is the beam of the past to my soul.

But if, through the course of the years which await me,
Some new scene of pleasure would open to view,
I will say, while with rapture the thought shall elate me,
"Oh, such were the days which my infancy knew!"

BYRON.

The Poetry of a Root Crop.

[Written by Charles Kingsley in the early days of his incumbency at Eversley.]

UNDERNEATH their cider robe,
Russet swede and golden globe,
Feathered carrot, burrowing deep,
Stedfast wait in charmèd sleep;
Treasure-houses, wherein lie,
Locked by angels' alchemy,
Milk, and hair, and blood, and bone,
Children of the barren stone;
Children of the flaming air,
With his blue eye keen and bare,
Spirit-peopled smiling down
On frozen field and toiling town—
Toiling town that will not heed
God His voice for rage and greed;
Frozen fields that surpliced lie,
Gazing patient at the sky;
Like some marble carven nun,
With folded hands when work is done,
Who mute upon her tomb doth pray
Till the Resurrection Day.

The Vaudois Teacher.

[The manner in which the Waldenses disseminated their principles among the Catholics, was by carrying with them a box of trinkets or articles of dress. Having entered the houses of the gentry, and disposed of some of their goods, they intimated that they had inestimable jewels, and would then present their purchasers with a Bible or Testament.]

Oh, lady fair, these silks of mine are beautiful and rare—
The richest web of the Indian loom, which beauty's queen might wear;
And my pearls are as pure as thine own fair neck, with whose radiant light they vie,
I have brought them with me a weary way,—will my gentle lady buy?

And the lady smiled on the worn old man, through the dark and clustering curls,
Which veiled her brow, as she bent to view his silks and glittering pearls;
And she placed their price in the old man's hand, and lightly turn'd away,
But she paused at the wanderer's earnest call—"My gentle lady, stay!"

"Oh, lady fair, I have yet a gem, which a purer lustre flings,
Than the diamond flash of the jewelled crown on the lofty brow of kings—
A wonderful pearl, of exceeding price, whose virtue shall not decay,
Whose light shall be as a spell to thee, and a blessing on thy way!"

The lady glanced at the mirroring steel, where her form of grace was seen,
Where her eye shone clear, and her dark locks waved their clasping pearls between:
"Bring forth the pearl of exceeding worth, thou traveller grey and old;
And name the price of thy precious gem, and my page shall count the gold."

The cloud went off from the pilgrim's brow, as a small and meagre book,
Unchased with gold or gem of cost, from his folding-robe he took.
"Here, lady fair, is the pearl of price, may it prove as such to thee!
Nay—keep thy gold—I ask it not; the Word of God is free!"

The hoary traveller went his way, but the gift he left behind
Hath had its pure and perfect work on that high-born maiden's mind
And she hath turned from the pride of sin to the lowliness of truth,
And given her human heart to God in its beautiful hour of youth!

And she hath left the gray old halls, where an evil faith had power,
The courtly knights of her father's train, and the maidens of her bower;
And she hath gone to the Vaudois vales, by lordly feet untrod,
Where the poor and needy of earth are rich in the perfect love of God.

JOHN G. WHITTIER.

The Music of Speech.

MUSIC—how much lies in that! A musical thought is one spoken by a mind that has penetrated to the inmost heart of the thing, detected the inmost mystery of it—namely, the melody that lies hidden in it, the inward harmony of coherence which is its soul, whereby it exists and has a right to be here in this world. All inmost things, we may say, are melodious, naturally utter themselves in song. The meaning of song goes deep. Who is there that in logical words can express the effect music has on us? A kind of inarticulate, unfathomable speech which leads us to the edge of the Infinite, and lets us for moments gaze into that! Nay, all speech, even the commonest speech, has something of song in it. Not a parish in the world but has its parish accent—the rhythm or tune to which the people there sing what they have to say! Accent is a kind of chanting; all men have accent of their own, though they only notice that of others.

Observe, too, how passionate language does of itself become musical—with a finer music than the mere accent; the speech of a man in zealous anger becomes a chant, a song. All deep things are song. It seems, somehow, the very central essence of us—song; as if all the rest were but wrappages and hulls. The primal element of us and of all things. The Greeks fabled of sphere-harmonies—it was the feeling they had of the inner structure of Nature; that the soul of all her voices and utterances was perfect music.

Poetry, therefore, we will call musical thought. The poet is he who thinks in that manner. At bottom it turns still on power of intellect; it is a man's sincerity and depth of vision that make him a poet. See deep enough and you see musically, the heart of nature being everywhere music—if you can only reach it.

CARLYLE.

On Jesting.

HARMLESS mirth is the best remedy against the consumption of the spirits; therefore jesting is not unlawful if it trespasseth not in quantity, quality, or reason.

It is good to make a jest, but not to make a trade of jesting.

The Earl of Leicester, knowing that Queen Elizabeth was much delighted to see a gentleman dance well, brought the master of a dancing-school to dance before the Queen.

"Pshaw!" said the Queen, "it is his profession; I will not see him." She liked it not where it was the master-quality, but where it attended on other accomplishment. The same we may say of jesting.

Jest not with the two-edged sword of God's Word. Will nothing please thee to wash thy hands in but the font; or to drink healths in but the church-chalice? And remember, the whole art is learnt at the first admission, and profane jest will come without calling. It is most dangerous to wit wantonly with the majesty of God. Wherefore, if even without thine intention, and against thy will, thou chancest to hit Scripture in ordinary discourse, yet fly to the city of refuge, and pray to God to forgive thee.

Sinful jests make fools laugh and wise men frown. Seeing we are civilised Englishmen, let us not be naked savages in our talk.

Scoff not at the natural defects of any, which are not in their power to amend. Oh, it is cruelty to beat a cripple with his own crutches! Neither flout any for his profession, if honest, though it be poor and painful. Mock not a cobbler for his black thumbs.

He that relates another man's wicked jest with delight, adopts it for his own. Purge them therefore from this poison. If the profaneness can be scoured from the wit, it is like a lamprey—take out the back, it may make good meat. But if the very staple of the jest be profaneness, then it is a viper, all poison—meddle not with it.

FULLER.

LIFE has such hard conditions that every dear and precious gift, every rare virtue, every pleasant faculty, every genial endowment, love, hope, joy, wit, sprightliness, benevolence, must sometimes be put into the crucible to distil the one elixir—patience.

Saved by a Hymn.

ABOUT the year 1754, when war was raging between the French and English in Canada, and when the Indians took the part of the French, it happened one day that a party of Indians surrounded the house of a poor family from Germany, at a time when the mother and one of the sons were absent. The father, however, was at home, as were also the eldest son and two little girls, named Barbara and Regina. The savages burst into the house, killed the men, and carried off the little girls, together with many other children of their own age, leading them by forced marches, and through trackless woods, in order to escape pursuit. Arrived at the Indian encampment, the little captives were divided amongst their captors. At this time Barbara was ten years old, and Regina nine. What became of Barbara was never known, but Regina was given to an old widow, who was very harsh and cruel to the little captive. Here she remained till she was about nineteen years old. But she did not forget her early home training. She said her prayers night and morning, often repeated the verses from the Bible, and sang the little hymns which she had learned at home. Especially would she often sing,—

"Alone, yet not alone am I,
Though in this solitude so drear."

It was her one hope and constant prayer that our dear Lord would in His own time restore her to her friends. In the year 1764 the long-deferred hope was at last realized. An English colonel discovered the Indian encampment, attacked and took it by storm. Peace was made with the Indians, on condition that they should give up all their prisoners, when no less than four hundred captives were brought in by the Indians and handed over to the English. Many of them had quite forgotten their native tongue, and most of them were so strangely altered that their own mothers could not recognise them. After being fed and clothed, they were taken to a town named Carlisle, and it was published in the newspapers that all parents who had had children carried off by the Indians might come there and reclaim them. Amongst others, there came to Carlisle poor Regina's sorrowing mother. She searched up and down the ranks of the recovered captives, but nowhere could she discover her daughters. So great and bitter was her disappointment, that she burst into tears. The bystanders endeavoured to console her. The colonel asked her, 'Do you remember nothing by which your children might be discovered?' She answered, that she only remembered a hymn which she used to sing to them when babies. The colonel told her to sing this hymn, which she did as follows:—

"Alone, yet not alone am I,
   Though in this solitude so drear;
I feel my Saviour always nigh,
   He comes the weary hours to cheer.
I am with Him, and He with me;
   Even here, alone I cannot be."

Scarcely had she begun to sing when Regina rushed from the crowd, began to sing it also, and threw herself into her mother's arms. Thus the early training in religious things had brought about this meeting and recognition.

The Eruption of Mount Vesuvius.

THE cloud which had scattered so deep a murkiness over the day had now settled into a solid and impenetrable mass. It resembled less even the thickest gloom of a night in the open air than the close and blind darkness of some narrow room. But in proportion as the blackness gathered, did the lightnings around Vesuvius increase in their vivid and scorching glare. Nor was their horrible beauty confined to the usual hues of fire; no rainbow ever rivalled their varying and prodigal dyes. Now brightly blue as the most azure depth of a southern sky,—now of a livid and snake-like green, darting restlessly to and fro as the folds of an enormous serpent,—now of a lurid and intolerable crimson, gushing forth through the columns of smoke, far and wide, and lighting up the whole city from arch to arch,—then suddenly dying into a sickly paleness, like the ghost of their own life!

In the pauses of the showers you heard the rumbling of the earth beneath, and the groaning waves of the tortured sea; or, lower still, and audible but to the watch of intensest fear, the grinding and hissing murmur of the escaping gases through the chasms of the distant mountain. Sometimes the cloud appeared to break from its solid mass, and, by the lightning, to assume quaint and vast mimicries of human or of monster shapes, striding across the gloom, hurtling one upon the other, and vanishing swiftly into the turbulent abyss of shade; so that, to the eyes and fancies of the affrighted wanderers, the unsubstantial vapours were as the bodily forms of gigantic foes—the agents of terror and of death.

The ashes in many places were already knee-deep; and the boiling showers which came from the steaming breath of the volcano forced their way into the houses, bearing with them a strong and suffocating vapour. In some places, immense fragments of rock, hurled upon the house-roofs, bore down along the streets masses of confused ruin, which yet more and more, with every hour, obstructed the way; and as the day advanced, the motion of the earth was more sensibly felt—the footing seemed to slide and creep—nor could chariot or litter be kept steady even on the most level ground.

Sometimes the huger stones, striking against each other as they fell, broke into countless fragments, emitting sparks of fire, which caught whatever was combustible within their reach; and along the plains beyond the city the darkness was now terribly relieved, for several houses and even vineyards had been set on flames, and at various intervals the fire rose sullenly and fiercely against the solid gloom. To add to this partial relief of the darkness, the citizens had, here and there, in the more public places, such as the porticos of temples and the entrances to the forum, endeavoured to place rows of torches; but these rarely continued long; the showers and the winds extinguished them, and the sudden darkness into which their sudden birth was converted had something in it doubly terrible and doubly impressing on the impotence of human hopes, the lesson of despair.

Frequently, by the momentary light of these torches, parties of fugitives encountered each other, some hurrying towards the sea, others flying from the sea back to the land; for the ocean had retreated rapidly from the shore—an utter darkness lay over it, and upon its groaning and tossing waves the storm of cinders and rock fell without the protection which the streets and roofs afforded to the land. Wild—haggard—ghastly with supernatural fears, these groups encountered each other, but without the leisure to speak, to consult, to advise; for the showers fell now frequently, though not continuously, extinguishing the lights which showed to each band the death-like faces of the other, and hurrying all to seek refuge beneath the nearest shelter. The whole elements of civilisation were broken up. Ever and anon, by the flickering lights, you saw the thief hastening by the most solemn authorities of the law, laden with the produce of his sudden gains. If, in the darkness, wife was separated from husband, or parent from child, vain was the hope of reunion. Each hurried blindly and confusedly on. Nothing in all the various and complicated machinery of social life was left save the primal law of self-preservation.

Through this awful scene did Glaucus wade his way, accompanied by Ione (I-ō-nē) and the blind girl. Suddenly, a rush of hundreds, in their path to the sea, swept by them. Nydia was torn from the side of Glaucus, who with Ione was borne rapidly onward; and when the crowd (whose forms they saw not, so thick was the gloom) were gone, Nydia was still separated from their side. Glaucus shouted her name. No answer came. They retraced their steps—in vain: they could not discover her,—it was evident she had been swept along some opposite direction by the human current. Their friend, their preserver was lost! And hitherto Nydia had been their guide. *Her blindness rendered the scene familiar to her alone.* Accustomed, through a perpetual night, to thread the windings of the city, she had led them unerringly towards the seashore, by which they had resolved to hazard an escape. Now, which way could they wend? All was rayless to them—a maze without a clue. Wearied, despondent, bewildered, they, however, passed along, the ashes falling upon their heads, the fragmentary stones dashing up in sparkles before their feet.

Advancing, as men grope for escape in a dungeon, they continued their uncertain way. At the moments when the volcanic lightnings lingered over the streets, they were enabled, by that awful light, to steer and guide their progress: yet little did the view it presented to them cheer or encourage their path. In parts, where the ashes lay dry and uncommixed with the boiling torrents, cast upward from the mountain at capricious intervals, the surface of the earth presented a leprous and ghastly white. In other places, cinder and rock lay matted in heaps, from beneath which emerged the half-hid limbs of some crushed and mangled fugitive. The groans of the dying were broken by wild shrieks of women's terror—now near, now distant—which, when heard in the utter darkness, were rendered doubly appalling by the crushing sense of helplessness and the uncertainty of the perils around; and clear and distinct through all were the mighty and various noises from the Fatal Mountain; its rushing winds; its whirling torrents; and, from time to time, the burst and roar of some more fiery and fierce explosion.

Suddenly the place became lighted with an intense and lurid glow. Bright and gigantic through the darkness, which closed around it like the walls of hell, the mountain shone—a pile of fire! Its summit seemed riven in two; or rather, above its surface there seemed to rise two monster shapes, each confronting each, as Demons contending for a World. These were of one deep blood-red hue of fire, which lighted up the whole atmosphere far and wide; but *below*, the nether part of the mountain was still dark and shrouded, save in three places, adown which flowed, serpentine and irregular, rivers of the molten lava. Darkly red through the profound gloom of their banks, they flowed slowly on, as towards the devoted city. Over the broadest there seemed to spring a cragged and stupendous arch, from which, as from the jaws of hell, gushed the sources of the stupendous Phlegethon. And through the stilled air was heard the rattling of the fragments of rock, hurling one upon another as they were borne down the fiery cataracts—darkening, for one instant, the spot where they fell, and suffused the next in the burnished hues of the flood along which they floated!

Glaucus turned in awe, caught Ione in his arms, and fled along the street, that was now intensely luminous. But suddenly a duller shade fell over the air. Instinctively he turned to the mountain, and behold! one of the two gigantic crests, into which the summit had been divided, rocked and wavered to and fro; and then, with a sound, the mightiness of which no language can describe, it fell from its burning base, and rushed, an avalanche of fire, down the sides of the mountain! At the same instant gushed forth a volume of blackest smoke—rolling on, over air, sea, and earth.

Another—and another—and another shower of ashes, far more profuse than before, scattered fresh desolation along the streets. Darkness once more wrapped them as a veil; and Glaucus, his bold heart at last quelled and despairing, sank beneath the cover of an arch, and, clasping Ione to his heart, resigned himself to die.

Meanwhile Nydia, when separated by the throng from Glaucus and Ione, had in vain endeavoured to regain them. In vain she raised that plaintive cry so peculiar to the blind; it was lost amidst a thousand shrieks of more selfish terror. Again and again she returned to the spot where they had been divided —to find her companions gone, to seize every fugitive—to inquire of Glaucus— to be dashed aside in the impatience of distraction. Who in that hour spared one thought to his neighbour! Perhaps in scenes of universal horror, nothing is more horrid than the unnatural selfishness they engender. At length it occurred to Nydia, that as it had been resolved to seek the seashore for escape, her most probable chance of rejoining her companions would be to persevere in that direction. Guiding her steps, then, by the staff which she always carried, she continued, with incredible dexterity, to avoid the masses of ruin that encumbered the path—to thread the streets—and unerringly (so blessed now was that accustomed darkness, so afflicting in ordinary life!) to take the nearest direction to the seaside.

Poor girl! her courage was beautiful to behold!—and Fate seemed to favour one so helpless! The boiling torrents touched her not, save by the general rain which accompanied them; the huge fragments of scoria shivered the pavement before and beside her, but spared that frail form: and when the lesser ashes fell over her, she shook them away with a slight tremor, and dauntlessly resumed her course.

She had gone some distance towards the seashore, when she chanced to hear from one of the fugitives that Glaucus was resting beneath the arch of the forum. She at once turned her back on the sea and retraced her steps to the city. She gained the forum—the arch; she stooped down—she felt around— she called on the name of Glaucus.

A weak voice answered—"Who calls on me? Is it the voice of the Shades? Lo! I am prepared!"

"Arise! follow me! Take my hand! Glaucus, thou shalt be saved!"

In wonder and sudden hope, Glaucus arose—"Nydia still! Ah! thou, then, art safe!"

The tender joy of his voice pierced the heart of the poor Thessalian, and she blessed him for his thought of her.

Half leading, half carrying Ione, Glaucus followed his guide.

After many pauses and incredible perseverance, they gained the sea, and joined a group, who, bolder than the rest, resolved to hazard any peril rather than continue in such a scene. In darkness they put forth to sea; but, as they cleared the land and caught new aspects of the mountain, its channels of molten fire threw a partial redness over the waves.

Utterly exhausted and worn out, Ione slept on the breast of Glaucus, and Nydia lay at his feet. Meanwhile the showers of dust and ashes, still borne aloft, fell into the wave, and scattered their snows over the deck. Far and wide, borne by the winds, those showers descended upon the remotest climes, startling even the swarthy African; and whirled along the antique soil of Syria and Egypt.

And meekly, softly, beautifully dawned at last the light over the trembling deep!—the winds were sinking into rest—the foam died from the glowing azure of that delicious sea. Around the east, their mists caught gradually the rosy hues that heralded the morning; light was about to resume her reign. Yet, still, dark and massive in the distance lay the broken fragments of the destroying cloud, from which red streaks, burning more and more dimly, betrayed the yet rolling fires of the mountain of the "Scorched Fields." The white walls and gleaming columns that had adorned the lovely coasts were no more. Sullen and dull were the shores so lately crested by the cities of Herculaneum and Pompeii. The darlings of the Deep were snatched from her embrace! Century after century shall the mighty Mother stretch forth her azure arms, and know them not—moaning round the sepulchres of the Lost!

SIR E. BULWER LYTTON.

"I THINK WE MIGHT FINISH OUR PLAY NOO."—Dr. Macleod gives a story he heard from Anderson in his own schooldays. Two girls were one day playing, and one of them started the question whether it was right for children to play. She said her minister had told them the day before that Christ was nowhere described in the Bible as having laughed once: He was the Man of Sorrows. The other girl stopped her game straightway, but instantly she added, "I dinna ken, Maggie, but I think the minister was surely saying mair than he had any richt to say. We read that Jesus went to a marriage at Cana in Galilee. The marriage folks would likely, like other marriage folks, be happy and laughing. D'ye think the Lord would sit glooming at them without even a smile on His face? No, no, Maggie. I would not like to say 'laughing,' but I am quite sure if He went to a wedding He would be happy like the rest while He was there. I think we might finish our play noo."—*Life of the Rev. William Anderson, L.L.D., by George Gilfillan.*

The Wreck of the Hesperus.

It was the schooner Hesperus,
  That sailed the wintry sea;
And the skipper had taken his little daughter
  To bear him company.

Blue were her eyes as the fairy-flax,
  Her cheeks like the dawn of day,
And her bosom white as the hawthorn buds,
  That ope in the month of May.

The skipper he stood beside the helm,
  His pipe was in his mouth,
And he watched how the veering flaw did blow
  The smoke now West, now South.

Then up and spake an old sailor,
  Had sailed the Spanish Main,
" I pray thee, put in to yonder port,
  For I fear a hurricane.

" Last night the moon had a golden ring,
  And to-night no moon we see!"
The skipper he blew a whiff from his pipe,
  And a scornful laugh laughed he.

Colder and louder blew the wind,
  A gale from the North-east :
The snow fell hissing in the brine,
  And the billows frothed like yeast.

Down came the storm, and smote amain
 The vessel in its strength;
She shuddered and paused, like a frighted steed,
 Then leaped her cable's length.

"Come hither! come hither! my little daughter,
 And do not tremble so;
For I can weather the roughest gale
 That ever wind did blow."

He wrapped her warm in his seaman's coat,
 Against the stinging blast;
He cut a rope from a broken spar,
 And bound her to the mast.

"O father! I hear the church-bells ring;
 Oh, say, what may it be?"
"'Tis a fog-bell on a rock-bound coast "—
 And he steered for the open sea.

"O father! I hear the sound of guns;
  Oh, say, what may it be?"
"Some ship in distress, that cannot live
  In such an angry sea!"

"O father, I see a gleaming light;
  Oh, say, what may it be?"
But the father answered never a word,
  A frozen corpse was he.

Lashed to the helm, all stiff and stark,
  With his face turned to the skies,
The lantern gleamed through the gleamings now,
  On his fixed and glassy eyes.

Then the maiden clasped her hands, and prayed
  That saved she might be;
And she thought of Christ, who stilled the wave
  On the Lake of Galilee.

And fast through the midnight dark and drear,
  Through the whistling sleet and snow,
Like a sheeted ghost, the vessel swept
  Towards the reef of Norman's Woe.

And ever the fitful gusts between,
  A sound came from the land;
It was the sound of the trampling surf
  On the rocks and the hard sea-sand.

The breakers were right beneath her bows,
  She drifted a dreary wreck,
And a whooping billow swept the crew
  Like icicles from her deck.

She struck where the white and fleecy waves
  Looked soft as carded wool;
But the cruel rocks, they gored her side,
  Like the horns of an angry bull.

Her rattling shrouds, all sheathed in ice,
  With the masts went by the board ;
Like a vessel of glass, she stove and sank,
  Ho! ho! the breakers roared!

At daybreak, on the bleak sea-beach,
  A fisherman stood aghast,
To see the form of a maiden fair
  Lashed close to a drifting mast.

The salt sea was frozen on her breast,
  The salt tears in her eyes ;
And he saw her hair, like the brown seaweed,
  On the billows fall and rise.

Such was the wreck of the Hesperus,
  In the midnight and the snow!
Christ save us all from a death like this,
  On the reef of Norman's Woe!

LONGFELLOW.

Noble Revenge.

A YOUNG officer (in what army no matter) had so far forgotten himself, in a moment of irritation, as to strike a private soldier, full of personal dignity (as sometimes happens in all ranks), and distinguished for his courage. The inexorable laws of military discipline forbade to the injured soldier any practical redress. He could look for no retaliation by acts. Words only were at his command ; and in a tumult of indignation, as he turned away, the soldier said to his officer that he would "make him repent of it."

This, wearing the shape of a menace, naturally rekindled the officer's anger, and intercepted any disposition which might be rising within him towards a sentiment of remorse ; and thus the irritation between the two young men grew hotter than before.

Some weeks after this a partial action took place with the enemy. Suppose yourself a spectator, and looking down into a valley occupied by two armies.

They are facing each other, you see, in martial array. But it is no more than a skirmish which is going on; in the course of which, however, an occasion suddenly arises for a desperate service. A redoubt, which has fallen into the enemy's hands, must be recaptured at any price, and under circumstances of all but hopeless difficulty. A strong party has volunteered for the service; there is a cry for somebody to head them; you see a soldier step out from the ranks to assume this dangerous leadership; the party moves rapidly forward; in a few minutes it is swallowed up in clouds of smoke; for one half-hour from behind those clouds you receive hieroglyphic reports of bloody strife—fierce repeating signals, flashes from the guns, rolling musketry, and exulting hurrahs, advancing or receding, slackening or redoubling.

At length all is over; the redoubt has been recovered; that which was lost is found again; the jewel which had been made captive is ransomed with blood. Crimsoned with glorious gore, the wreck of the conquering party is relieved, and at liberty to return. From the hill you see it ascending. The plume-crested officer in command rushes forward, with his left hand raising his hat in homage to the blackened fragments of what once was a flag; whilst with his right hand he seizes that of the leader, though no more than a private from the ranks.

That perplexes you not; mystery you see none in that. For distinctions of order perish, ranks are confounded, "high and low" are words without a meaning, and to wreck goes every notion of feeling that divides the noble from the noble, or the brave man from the brave. But wherefore is it that now, when suddenly they wheel into mutual recognition, suddenly they pause? This soldier, this officer—who are they? O reader! once before they had stood face to face—the soldier it is that was struck; the officer it is that struck him. Once again they are meeting; and the gaze of armies is upon them. If for a moment a doubt divides them, in a moment the doubt has perished. One glance exchanged between them publishes the forgiveness that is sealed for ever. As one who recovers a brother whom he had accounted dead, the officer sprang forward, threw his arms around the neck of the soldier, and kissed him, as if he were some martyr glorified by the shadow of death from which he was returning: whilst on his part, the soldier, stepping back, and carrying his open hand through the beautiful motions of the military salute to a superior, makes this immortal answer—that answer which shut up for ever the memory of the indignity offered to him, even whilst for the last time alluding to it,—

"Sir," he said, "I told you before that I would make you repent."

DE QUINCEY.

OCCASIONS do not make a man frail, but they do show what he is.

THOMAS A KEMPIS.

Bermudian "Onions."

So the Reverend and I had at last arrived at Hamilton, the principal town in the Bermuda Islands. A wonderfully white town, white as snow itself. White as marble; white as flour. Yet looking like none of these exactly. Never mind, we said; we shall hit upon a figure by-and-bye that will describe this peculiar white. It was a town that was compacted together upon the sides and tops of a cluster of small hills. Its outlying borders fringed off and thinned away among the cedar forests, and there was no woody distance of curving coast, or leafy islet sleeping upon the dimpled, painted sea, but was flecked with shining white points—half-concealed houses peeping out of the foliage. The architecture of the town was mainly Spanish, inherited from the colonists of two hundred and fifty years ago. Some ragged-topped cocoa-palms, glimpsed here and there, gave the land a tropical aspect.

There was an ample pier of heavy masonry; upon this, under shelter, were some thousands of barrels containing that product which has carried the fame of Bermuda to many lands, the potato. With here and there an onion. That last sentence is facetious; for they grow at least two onions in Bermuda to one potato. The onion is the pride and joy of Bermuda. It is her jewel, her gem of gems. In her conversation, her pulpit, her literature, it is her most frequent and eloquent figure. In Bermudian metaphor it stands for perfection—perfection absolute.

The Bermudian weeping over the departed exhausts praise when he says, "He was an onion!" The Bermudian extolling the living hero bankrupts applause when he says, "He is an onion!" The Bermudian setting his son upon the stage of life to dare and do for himself, climaxes all counsel, supplication, admonition, comprehends all ambition, when he says, "Be an onion!"

When parallel with the pier, and ten or fifteen steps outside it, we anchored. It was Sunday, bright and sunny. The groups upon the pier—men, youths, and boys—were whites and blacks in about equal proportion. All were well and neatly dressed, many of them nattily, a few of them very stylishly. One would have to travel far before he would find another town of twelve thousand inhabitants that could represent itself so respectably, in the matter of clothes, on a freight-pier, without premeditation or effort. The women and young girls black and white, who occasionally passed by, were nicely clad, and many were elegantly and fashionably so. The men did not affect summer clothing much but the girls and women did, and their white garments were good to look at, after so many months of familiarity with sombre colours.

Around one isolated potato barrel stood four young gentlemen, two black, two white, becomingly dressed, each with the head of a slender cane pressed against his teeth, and each with a foot propped up on the barrel. Another young gentleman came up, looked longingly at the barrel, but saw no rest for his foot there, and turned pensively away to seek another barrel. He wandered here and there, but without result. Nobody sat upon a barrel, as is the custom of the idle in other lands, yet all the isolated barrels were humanly occupied. Whosoever had a foot to spare put it on a barrel, if all the places on it were not already taken. The habits of all peoples are determined by their circumstances. The Bermudians lean upon barrels because of the scarcity of lamp-posts.

Many citizens came on board and spoke eagerly to the officers—inquiring about the Turco-Russian war news, I supposed. However, by listening judiciously, I found that this was not so. They said, "What is the price of onions?" or, "How's onions?" Naturally enough this was their first interest; but they dropped into the war the moment it was satisfied.

We went ashore, and found a novelty of a pleasant nature. There were no hackmen, hacks, or omnibuses on the pier or about it anywhere, and nobody offered his services to us, or molested us in any way. I said it was like being in heaven. The Reverend rebukingly, and rather pointedly, advised me to make the best of it, then. We knew of a boarding-house, and what we needed now was somebody to pilot us to it. Presently a little barefooted coloured boy came along, whose raggedness was conspicuously un-Bermudian. His rear was so marvellously bepatched with coloured squares and triangles, that one was half-persuaded he had got it out of an atlas. When the sun struck him right, he was as good to follow as a lightning-bug. We hired him and dropped into his wake. He piloted us through one picturesque street after another, and in due course deposited us where we belonged. He charged nothing for his map, and but a trifle for his services; so the Reverend doubled it. The little chap received the money with a beaming applause in his eye which plainly said, "This man's an onion!"

MARK TWAIN.

GUESSES AT TRUTH.—Were we merely the creatures of outward impulses, what would faces of joy be but so many glaciers, on which the seeming smile of happiness at sunrise is only a flinging back of the rays they appear to be greeting, from frozen and impassive heads?

Man's Business in Life.

MAN's proper business in this world falls mainly into three divisions:—

First: To know themselves and the existing state of the things they have to do with. Secondly: To be happy in themselves and in the existing state of things. Thirdly: To mend themselves and the existing state of things, as far as either are marred and mendable.

These, I say, are the three plain divisions of proper human business on this earth. For these three the following are usually substituted and adopted by human creatures:—

First: To be totally ignorant of themselves and the existing state of things. Secondly: To be miserable in themselves and the existing state of things. Thirdly: To let themselves and the existing state of things alone—at least in the way of correction.

The dispositions which induce us to manage thus wisely the affairs of this life seem to be:—

First: A fear of disagreeable facts, and conscious shrinking from clearness of light, which keep us from examining ourselves, and increase gradually into a species of instinctive terror at all truth, and love of glosses, veils, and decorative lies of every sort. Secondly: A general readiness to take delight in everything past, future, far off, or somewhere else, rather than in things now, near, and here; leading us gradually to place our pleasure principally in the exercise of the imagination, and to build all our satisfaction on things as they are not.

Which power being one not accorded to the lower animals, and having, indeed, when disciplined, a very noble use, we pride ourselves upon it whether disciplined or not, and pass our lives complacently in substantial discontent and visionary satisfaction.

RUSKIN.

THE men of real power are always men of one idea, who send all the force of their being along one line; and it is possible for any of us to win a true success in life if we will early choose one sphere and persistently labour in it. The cause of so many life failures may be put into these few words: "The men had not really anything to live for."

In Illness.

How glorious the summer,
   Out in the field and street!
The few who love me bring it
   In odours fresh and sweet—

Bring it in dainty blossoms
   Of rosebud and of rose;
Breathe it in soft carressing,
   Bear it about their clothes.

The new-mown hay has kissed them,
  Though poor the raiment be,
And God has sent His blessings
  To my bedside and me.

Lie there, sweet buds of beauty,
  Unsunned,—by winds unblown ;
Live, for my fond love, longer
  Than life of flowers alone.
And keep, ah ! keep your freshness
  For one who sighs and pines
For joys that summer heightens,
  Although her life declines ;
Keep the bright blush that, gathered,
  Deadens to sicklier hue ;
Keep life for her who gazes
  On life and hope in you.

M. J. S.

Learning the Verbs.

"TO BE," "TO DO," OR "TO SUFFER."

"To be?" Well I followed the track,
  That gave me a chance of existence ;
But I honestly own, looking back,
  That it's prettiest viewed from a distance.
Just now it seems easy and bright,
  But I haven't forgotten my scrambles
Over horrible rocks, or the night
  That I spent in the midst of the brambles.
  At times from the path I might stray,
    And thus make the journeying rougher ;
  But still I was learning the way,
    "To Be, or to Do, or to Suffer !"

LEARNING THE VERBS.

"To do?" I have worked rather hard,
    And my present position is cosy;
But I haven't done much as a Bard,
    And my prose—well, of course, it is prosy!
The schemes and the aims of my youth
    Have long from old Time had a floorer,
And I doubt—shall I tell you the truth?
    If the world be a penny the poorer!
      If you cannot your vanity curb,
        You must either, my friend, be a duffer,
      Or you haven't yet learnt that a verb
        Is "To Be, or to Do, or to Suffer!"

"To suffer?" I took my degrees
    Long ago in that branch of our knowledge,
Where our hearts and our hopes are the fees,
    And the universe serves as a college.
I have had, as it is, rather more
    Than the usual share of affliction;
And that much is remaining in store
    Is my very decided conviction.
      But I find myself growing with years,
        Insensibly tougher and tougher;
      I can manage, I think, without tears,
        "To Be, and to Do, and to Suffer!"

I have stated the facts of the case,
    But heaven forbid I should grumble;
And I need not complain of a place
    That suits my capacities humble.
I have learnt how "to be"—well, a man:
    How "to do"—well, a part of my duty:
And in "suffering," own that the Plan
    Of the world is all goodness and beauty!
      Still at times from the path I may stray,
        And thus make the journeying rougher;
      But, at least, I am learning the way
        "To Be, and to Do, and to Suffer!"

W. JEFFERY PROWSE.

Thou art, O God.

Air—Unknown.

"The day is Thine, the night also is Thine: Thou hast prepared the light and the sun. Thou hast set all the borders of the earth: Thou hast made summer and winter."—PSALM lxxiv. 16, 17.

Thou art, O God, the life and light
  Of all this wondrous world we see;
Its glow by day, its smile by night,
  Are but reflections caught from Thee.
Where'er we turn, Thy glories shine,
And all things fair and bright are Thine!

When day, with farewell beam, delays
  Among the op'ning clouds of even,
And we can almost think we gaze
  Through golden vistas into heaven—
Those hues that make the sun's decline
So soft, so radiant, Lord! are Thine.

When night, with wings of starry gloom,
  O'ershadows all the earth and skies,
Like some dark, beauteous bird, whose plume
  Is sparkling with unnumber'd eyes—
That sacred gloom, those fires divine,
So grand, so countless, Lord! are Thine.

When youthful spring around us breathes,
  Thy Spirit warms her fragrant sigh;
And every flower the summer wreathes
  Is born beneath that kindling eye.
Where'er we turn, Thy glories shine,
And all things fair and bright are Thine.

                        MOORE.

The Village Preacher.

NEAR yonder copse, where once the garden smiled,
And still where many a garden flower grows wild,
There, where a few torn shrubs the place disclose,
The village preacher's modest mansion rose.
A man he was to all the country dear,
And passing rich with forty pounds a-year.
Remote from towns he ran his godly race,
Nor e'er had chang'd, nor wished to change, his place.
Unskilful he to fawn, or seek for power,
By doctrines fashioned to the varying hour ;
For other aims his heart had learned to prize—
More bent to raise the wretched than to rise.
His house was known to all the vagrant train :
He chid their wanderings, but relieved their pain.
The long-remember'd beggar was his guest,
Whose beard, descending, swept his aged breast ;
The ruined spendthrift, now no longer proud,
Claim'd kindred there, and had his claims allow'd ;
The broken soldier, kindly bid to stay,
Sat by his fire, and talk'd the night away,
Wept o'er his wounds, or, tales of sorrow done,
Shoulder'd his crutch, and show'd how fields were won.
Pleas'd with his guests, the good man learned to glow,
And quite forgot their vices in their woe :
Careless their merits or their faults to scan,
His pity gave ere charity began.

Thus to relieve the wretched was his pride,
And ev'n his failings lean'd to virtue's side ;
But in his duty prompt at every call,
He watch'd and wept, he pray'd and felt for all ;

And, as a bird each fond endearment tries,
To tempt its new-fledg'd offspring to the skies,
He tried each art, reprov'd each dull delay,
Allur'd to brighter worlds, and led the way.

Beside the bed where parting life was laid,
And sorrow, guilt, and pains, by turns dismay'd,
The reverend champion stood. At his control,
Despair and anguish fled the struggling soul ;
Comfort came down the trembling wretch to raise,
And his last falt'ring accents whisper'd praise.

At church, with meek and unaffected grace,
His looks adorn'd the venerable place ;
Truth from his lips prevail'd with double sway,
And fools who came to scoff remain'd to pray.
The service past, around the pious man,
With steady zeal, each honest rustic ran :
Even children followed, with endearing wile,
And pluck'd his gown, to share the good man's smile—
His ready smile a parent's warmth exprest ;
Their welfare pleased him, and their cares distrest :
To them his heart, his love, his griefs, were given,
But all his serious thoughts had rest in heaven :
As some tall cliff that lifts its awful form,
Swells from the vale, and midway leaves the storm,
Though round its breast the rolling clouds are spread,
Eternal sunshine settles on its head.

OLIVER GOLDSMITH.

TAKE noble care of the works that are handed down to you and the voices that come to you from the silent world. We look too carelessly on that store and its riches. It is so large, and they are so various, tha we treat them like things too common : and great books and great deeds become like wayside flowers which men glance at and pass by. But we get no good of a thing until we study it, and honour it, and love it. The wealth of the past thought reveals itself, like the beauty of the daisy, to him who kneels down to see it.

STOPFORD A. BROOKE.

Whom have I in Heaven but Thee?

I LOVE, and have some cause to love, the Earth:
    She is my Maker's creature, therefore good;
She is my mother, for she gave me birth;
    She is my tender nurse, she gives me food.
But what's a creature, Lord, compared with Thee?
Or what's my mother or my nurse to me?

I love the air: her dainty sweets refresh
    My drooping soul, and to new sweets invite me;
Her shrill-mouthed choir sustain me with their flesh,
    And with their polyphonian notes delight me.
But what's the air, or all the sweets that she
Can bless my soul withal, compared with Thee?

I love the sea: she is my fellow-creature;
    My careful purveyor—she provides me store;
She walls me round, she makes my diet greater,
    She wafts my treasure from a foreign shore.
But, Lord of oceans, when compared with Thee,
What is the ocean or her wealth to me?

To heaven's high city I direct my journey,
    Whose spangled suburbs entertain mine eye;
Mine eye, my contemplation's great attorney,
    Transcends the crystal pavement of the sky.
But what is heaven, great God, compared with Thee?
Without Thy presence, heaven's no heaven to me!

                        FRANCIS QUARLES (1635).

Perpetual Force.

WE cannot afford to miss any advantage. Never was any man too strong for his proper work. Art is long and life short, and he must supply this disproportion by borrowing and applying to his task the energies of Nature. Reinforce his self-respect, show him his means, his arsenal of forces, physical, metaphysical, immortal:

> "More servants wait on man
> Than he'll take notice of."

Show him the riches of the poor, show him what mighty allies and helpers he has. And though King David had no good from making his census out of vainglory, yet I find it wholesome and invigorating to enumerate the resources we can command; to look a little into this arsenal, and see how many rounds of ammunition, what muskets, and how many arms better than Springfield muskets we can bring to bear.

The hero in the fairy tales has a servant who can eat granite rocks, another who can see the grass grow, and a third who can run a hundred leagues in half an hour; so man in nature is surrounded by a gang of friendly giants who can accept harder stints than these, and help him in every kind. Each by itself has a certain omnipotence; but all, like contending kings and emperors, in the presence of each other, are antagonized and kept polite, and own the balance of power.

There is no porter like gravitation, who will bring down any weight you cannot carry, and if he wants aid, knows how to find his fellow-labourers. Water works in masses, sets his irresistible shoulder to your mill or to your ships, or transports vast boulders of rock, neatly packed in his iceberg, a thousand miles. But its far greater power depends on its talent of becoming little, and entering the smallest holes and pores. By this agency, carrying in solution elements needful to every point, the vegetable world exists.

Who are the farmer's servants? Who but geology, chemistry, the quarry of the air, the water of the brook, the lightning of the cloud, the plough of the frost? Before he was born into the field the sun of ages soaked it with light and heat, mellowed his land, decomposed the rocks, covered it with vegetable film, then with forests, and accumulated cubic acres of sphagnum whose decays make the peat of his meadow. The rocks crack like glass by inequality of contraction in heat and cold, and flakes fall constantly into the soil. The tree can draw on the whole air, the whole earth, on all the rolling main. The plant, the tree, is all suction-pipe, imbibing from the ground by its roots, from the air by its twigs, with all its might. Take up a spadeful or a buck-load of loam; who can guess what it holds? But a gardener knows that it is full of peaches, full of oranges, and he drops in a few seeds by way of keys to unlock and combine its virtues: let it lie in sun and rain, and, by and by, it has lifted into the air its full weight in golden fruit.

What agencies of electricity, gravity, light, affinity, combine to make every plant what it is, and in a manner so quiet, that the presence of these tremendous powers is not ordinarily suspected! Faraday said that "a grain of water is known to have electric relations equivalent to a very powerful flash of lightning." The ripe fruit is dropped at last without violence; but the lightning fell and the storm raged, and strata were deposited and uptorn and bent back, and chaos moved from beneath, to create and flavour the fruit on your table to-day.

Go out of doors and get the air. Ah, if you knew what was in the air! See what your robust neighbour, who never feared to live in it, has got from it; strength, cheerfulness, power to convince, heartiness and equality to each event. As the sea is the receptacle of all rivers, so the air is the receptacle from which all things spring, and into which they all return; an immense distillery, a sharp solvent, drinking the oxygen from plants, carbon from animals, the essence and spirit of every solid on the globe; a menstruum which melts the mountains into it. All the earths are burnt metals. One half the avoirdupois of the rocks which compose the solid crust of the globe consists of oxygen. The adamant is always passing into smoke, Nature turns her capital day by day. All things are flowing, even those that seem immovable. The earth burns, the mountains burn; slower, but as incessantly as wood in the fire. The marble column, the brazen statue, burn under the daylight, and would soon decompose, if their molecular structure, disturbed by the raging sunlight, were not restored by the darkness of night. Plants and animals burn, or perpetually exhale their own bodies, into the air and earth again.

While all thus burns, the universe in a blaze, kindled from the torch of the sun, it needs a perpetual tempering, a phlegm, a sleep, atmospheres of azote, deluges of water to check the fury of the conflagration—a hoarding to check the spending, a centripetence to the centrifugence. And this is uniformly supplied. Nature is as subtle as she is strong, and, like a cautious testator, ties up her estate so as not to bestow it all on one generation, but has a forelooking tenderness and equal regard to the next and the next and the fourth and the fortieth. The winds and the rains come back a thousand and a thousand times. The coal on your grate gives out in decomposing to-day, exactly the same amount of light and heat which was taken from the sunshine in its formation in the leaves and boughs of the antediluvian tree.

The earliest hymns of the world were hymns to these natural forces. The Vedas of India, which have a date older than Homer, are hymns to the winds, to the clouds, and to fire.

They all have certain properties which adhere to them, such as conservation, persisting to be themselves, impossibility of being warped. The sun has lost no beams, the earth no elements; gravity is as adhesive, heat as expansive, light as joyful, air as virtuous, water as medicinal, as on the first day. There is no loss, only transference. When the heat is less here it is not lost, but more heat is there. When the rain exceeds on the coast, there is drought on the prairie. When the continent sinks, the opposite continent, that is to say, the opposite shore of the ocean, rises. When life is less here, it spawns there.

These forces are in an ascending series, but seem to leave no room for the individual; man or atom, he only shares them; he sails the way these irresistible winds blow. But behind all these are finer elements, the sources of them, and much more rapid and strong; a new style and series, the spiritual Intellect and morals appear only the material forces on a higher plane. The laws of material nature run up into the invisible world of the mind, and hereby we acquire a key to those sublimities which skulk and hide in the caverns of human consciousness. And in the impenetrable mystery which hides—and hides through absolute transparency—the mental nature, I await the insight which our advancing knowledge of material laws shall furnish.

RALPH WALDO EMERSON.

THERE are times when the mind, like the body, had best feed, gorge if you will, and leave the digestion of its food to the unconscious alchemy of nature. It is as unwise to be always saying to oneself, "Into what pigeonhole of my brain ought I to put this fact, and what conclusion ought I to draw from it?" as to ask your teeth how they intend to chew, and your gastric juice how it intends to convert your three courses and dessert into chyle. Whether on a Scotch moor or a tropic forest, it is well at times to have full faith in Nature; to resign yourself to her as a child upon a holiday, and to lie still and let her speak. She knows best what to say.—"*At Last*," *Charles Kingsley*.

The Turf shall be my Fragrant Shrine.

THE turf shall be my fragrant shrine;
My temple, Lord! that arch of thine;
My censer's breath the mountain airs,
And silent thoughts my only prayers.

My choir shall be the moonlight waves,
When murm'ring homeward to their cave,
Or when the stillness of the sea,
Even more than music, breathes of Thee.

I'll seek by day some glade unknown,
All light and silence, like Thy throne!
And the pale stars shall be, at night,
The only eyes that watch my rite.

Thy heaven, on which 'tis bliss to look,
Shall be my pure and shining book,
Where I shall read, in words of flame,
The glories of Thy wondrous name.

I'll read Thy anger in the rack
That clouds a while the day-beam's track;
Thy mercy in the azure hue
Of sunny brightness breaking through.

There's nothing bright above, below,
From flowers that bloom to stars that glow,
But in its light my soul can see
Some features of Thy Deity.

There's nothing dark below, above,
But in its gloom I trace Thy love,
And meekly wait that moment when
Thy touch shall turn all bright again!

MOORE.

Character of Charles I.

The news that Charles had taken his father's place was received with general satisfaction. "The joy of the people," as a contemporary expressed it, "devoured their mourning." Of the character of the new king, silent and reserved as he was, little was known, and still less had reached the public ear of his questionable proceedings in the negotiation of the marriage treaty. It was enough that, ever since his return from Madrid, he had been the consistent advocate of war with Spain.

When Ville-aux-Clercs went back to France with the marriage treaty, Richelieu asked him what he thought of Charles. "He is either an extraordinary man," was the shrewd reply, "or his talents are very mean. If his reticence is affected in order not to give jealousy to his father, it is a sign of consummate prudence. If it is natural and unassumed, the contrary inference may be drawn."

The extreme reserve of the young king was doubtless closely connected with that want of imaginative power which lay at the root of his faults. With all his confidence in his own thoughts, he failed to give to his ideas an expression which was satisfactory to others or even to himself. He did not like to be contradicted, and his father's rapid utterance had swept away his slow conceptions as with a torrent before he could find out what he really meant to say. The man who is too vain to bear contradiction, and not sufficiently brilliant or wise to overpower it, must of necessity take refuge in silence.

Unfortunately, the defect which hindered Charles from being a good talker hindered him also from being a good ruler. The firm convictions of his mind were alike proof against arguments which he was unable to understand, and unalterable by the impression of passing events, which slipped by him unnoticed. The wisest of men, the most decisive of facts, were no more to him than the whistling of the storm is to the man who is seated by a warm fireside. They passed him by, or, if he heeded them at all, it was only to wonder that they did not conform to his own beneficent intentions. "I cannot," he said on one occasion, "defend a bad, nor yield in a good cause." Conscious of the purity of his own motives, he never ceased to divide mankind into two simple classes,—into those who agreed with him, and those who did not; into sheep to be cherished, and goats to be rejected. Such narrowness of view was no guarantee for fixity of purpose. When the moment came at last for the realities of life to break through the artificial atmosphere in which he had been living, when forms unknown and unimagined before crowded on his bewildered

King Charles I.

vision, it was too late to gain knowledge the acquisition of which had been so long deferred, or to exercise that strength of will which is only to be found where there is intelligent perception of the danger to be faced.

The same explanation will probably in a great measure account for the special fault which has, more than any other, cost Charles the respect of posterity. The truthful man must be able to image forth in his own mind the impression his engagements leave upon those with whom they were made; and must either keep them in the sense in which they are understood by others, or must openly and candidly show cause why it is wrong or impossible so to keep them. The way in which Charles gave and broke his promises was the very reverse of this. He looked too much into his own mind, too little into the minds of those with whom he was bargaining. When he entered into an engagement he either formed no clear conception of the circumstances under which he would be called upon to fulfil it, or he remembered too clearly this or that consideration which would render his promise illusory, or would at least, if it had been spoken out, have prevented those with whom he was dealing from accepting his word. When the time came for him to fulfil an engagement, he could think of nothing but the limitations with which he had surrounded it, or with which he fancied that he had surrounded it, when his word had been given. Sometimes he went still farther, apparently thinking that it was lawful to use deception as a weapon against those who had no right to know the truth.

GARDINER.

Anecdote concerning the Execution of Charles I.

RICHARD BRANDON, common executioner or hangman at that time, died upon Wednesday, June 20th, 1649 (within five months after the King's martyrdom). The Sunday before Brandon died, a young man of his acquaintance, being to visit him, asked him how he did, and whether he was not troubled in conscience for cutting off the king's head. Brandon replied Yes, because he was at the king's trial, and heard the sentence pronounced against him, which caused Brandon to make this solemn vow or protestation—viz., wishing God might perish his body and soul if ever he appeared on the scaffold to do the act or lift up his hand against him. And he further declared that he was no sooner entered upon the scaffold (to do that wicked act), but immediately he fell a trembling, and hath (ever since) to his death continued in the like agony. He likewise confessed that he had thirty pounds for his pains, all paid him in half-crowns, within one hour after the blow was struck; and that he had an orange stuck full of cloves, and a handkerchief, out of the king's pocket. As soon as he was carried off from the scaffold, he was proffered twenty shillings for that orange by a gentleman in Whitehall, but refused the same. He afterwards sold it for ten shillings in Rosemary-lane. About six o'clock that night he returned home to his wife, living in Rosemary-lane, and gave her the money, saying it was the dearest money that ever he earned in his life, which prophetical words were soon made manifest. About three days before he died, he lay speechless, uttering many a sigh and heavy groan, and in a most deplorable manner departed from his bed of sorrow. For his burial great store of wine was sent in by the Sheriff of London, and a great multitude of people stood waiting to see his corpse carried to the churchyard, some crying out, "Hang him, rogue; bury him in a dunghill!" others pressing upon him, saying they would quarter him for executing the king, insomuch that the churchwardens and masters of the parish were obliged to come for the suppressing of them; and with great difficulty he was at last carried to Whitechapel Churchyard, having a bunch of rosemary at each end of the coffin, and on the top thereof, with a rope tied across from one end to the other.

The man that waited upon this executioner when he gave the fatal blow, and appeared in the same dress, was a ragman in Rosemary-lane.

The Universal Entertainer, August 1750.

Posies for thine own Bed-chamber.

WHAT wisdome more, what better life, than pleaseth God to send?
What worldly goods, what longer use, than pleaseth God to lend?
What better fare than well content, agreeing with thy wealth?
What better ghest than trusty friend in sickness and in health?
What better bed than concience good to passe the night in sleepe?
What better work than daily care, from sin thy selfe to keepe?
What better thought than think on God, and daily Him to serve?
What better gift than to the poore, that ready be to sterve?
What greater praise of God and man than mercy for to shew?
Who mercilesse, shall mercy find, that mercy shews to few?
What worse despaire than loth to dye, for feare to go to hell?
What greater faith than trust in God, through Christ in heaven to dwell?

THOMAS TUSSER (1560).

Fainting by the Way.

SWARTHY wastelands, wide and woodless, glittering miles and miles away,
Where the south wind seldom wanders, and the winters will not stay—
Lurid wastelands, pent in silence, thick with hot and thirsty sighs,
Where the scanty thorn-leaves twinkle, with their haggard, hopeless eyes—
Furnaced wastelands, hunched with hillocks, like to stony billows rolled,
Where the naked flats lie swirling, like a sea of darkened gold—
Burning wastelands, glancing upward with a weird and vacant stare,
Where the languid heavens quiver o'er red depths of stirless air.

"Oh, my brother, I am weary of this wildering waste of sand;
In the noontide we can never travel to the promised land!
Lo! the desert broadens round us, glaring wildly in my face,
With long leagues of sun-flame on it—O the barren, barren place!
See, behind us gleams a green plot: shall we thither turn and rest,
Till a cool wind flutters over—till the day is down the west?
I would follow, but I cannot! Brother, let me here remain,
For the heart is dead within me, and I may not rise again."

"Wherefore stay to talk of fainting? rouse thee for a while, my friend;
Evening hurries on our footsteps, and this journey soon will end;
Wherefore stay to talk of fainting, when the sun, with sinking fire,
Smites the blocks of broken thunder, blackening yonder craggy spire?
Even now the far-off landscape broods and fills with coming change,
And a withered moon grows brighter, bending o'er that shadowed range;
At the feet of grassy summits sleeps a water calm and clear;
There is surely rest beyond it! comrade, wherefore tarry here?

"Yet a little longer struggle; we have walked a wilder plain,
And have met more troubles, trust me, than we e'er shall meet again.
Can you think of all the dangers you and I are living through,
With a soul so weak and fearful—with the doubts I never knew?
Dost thou not remember that the thorns are clustered with the rose,
And that every Zin-like border may a pleasant land enclose?

FAINTING BY THE WAY.

Oh, across these sultry deserts many a fruitful scene we'll find ;
And the blooms we gather shall be worth the wounds they leave behind!"

"Ah! my brother, it is useless! see, o'erburdened with their load,
All the friends who went before us fall or falter by the road.
We have come a weary distance, seeking what we may not get ;
And I think we are but children chasing rainbows through the wet.
Tell me not of vernal valleys! Is it well to hold a reed
Out for drowning men to clutch at in the moments of their need?
Go thy journey—on without me! it is better I should stay,
Since my life is like an evening—fading, swooning fast away.

"Where are all the springs you talked of? Have I not with pleading mouth
Looked to heaven through a silence stifled in the crimson drouth?
Have I not, with lips unsated, watched to see the fountains burst,
Where I searched the rocks for cisterns, and they only mocked my thirst?
Oh! I dreamt of countries fertile, bright with lakes and flashing rills
Leaping from their shady caverns, streaming round a thousand hills!
Leave me, brother! all is fruitless, barren, measureless, and dry ;
And my God will *never* help me, though I pray, and faint, and die."

"Up! I tell thee this is idle! Oh, thou man of little faith ;
Doubting on the verge of Aidenn—turning now to covet death?
By the fervent hopes within me, by the strength which nerves my soul,
By the heart that yearns to help thee, we shall live and reach the goal!
Rise, and lean thy weight upon me! Life is fair and God is just ;
And He yet will show us fountains, if we only look and trust!
Oh, I know it; and He leads us to the glens of stream and shade,
Where the low, sweet waters gurgle round the banks which cannot fade."

Thus he spake, my friend and brother, and he took me by the hand,
And I think we walked the desert till the night was on the land,
Then we came to flowery hollows, where we heard a far-off stream
Singing in the moony twilight, like the rivers of my dream ;
And the balmy winds came tripping softly through the pleasant trees,
And I thought they bore a murmur like a voice from sleeping seas.
So we travelled—so we reached it ; and I never more will part
With the peace as calm as sunset, folded round my weary heart.

HENRY KENDALL
(AN AUSTRALIAN POET.)

Abou Ben Adhem.

Abou Ben Adhem (may his tribe increase!)
Awoke one night from a deep dream of peace,
And saw within the moonlight in his room,
Making it rich, and like a lily in bloom,
An Angel writing in a book of gold :—
Exceeding peace had made Ben Adhem bold,
And to the Presence in the room, he said,
" What writest thou ? "—The Vision raised its head,
And with a look made of all sweet accord,
Answered, " The names of those who love the Lord."
" And is mine one ? " said Abou. " Nay, not so,"
Replied the Angel. Abou spoke more low,
But cheerily still ; and said, " I pray thee then,
Write me as one that loves his fellowmen."

The Angel wrote and vanished. The next night
It came again with a great wakening light,
And showed the names whom love of God had blessed,
And lo ! Ben Adhem's name led all the rest.

LEIGH HUNT.

"Sometimes," John Newton says, " I compare the troubles we have to undergo in the course of a year to a great bundle of fagots, far too large for us to lift. But God does not require us to carry the whole at once. He mercifully unties the bundle, and gives us first one stick, which we are to carry to-day, and then another, which we are to carry to-morrow, and so on. This we might easily manage if we would only take the burden appointed for us each day ; but we choose to increase our trouble by carrying yesterday's stick over again to-day, and adding to-morrow's burden to our load before we are required to bear it."

The Hour of Prayer.

A Journey across the American Plains.

AND now, as we again set out on our journey westward, the beautiful prairie country seemed more beautiful than ever, and we caught glimpses of the fertile valley of the Platte, in which our imaginary freehold estates lay awaiting us. On and on we went, with the never-ending undulations of grass and flowers glowing all around us in the sunlight—the world below a plain of gold, the world above a vault of the palest blue. The space, and light, and colour were altogether most cheerful; and as the train went at a very gentle trot along the single line, we sat outside, for the most part, in the cool breeze. Occasionally we passed a small hamlet, and that had invariably an oddly extemporized look. The wooden houses were stuck down anyhow on the grassy plain, without any trace of the old-fashioned orchards, and walled gardens, and hedges that bind, as it were, an English village together. Here there was but the satisfaction of the most immediate needs. One wooden building labelled "Drug Store," another wooden building labelled "Grocery Store," and a blacksmith's shop, were ordinarily the chief features of the community. All day we passed in this quiet gliding onwards; and when the sun began to sink towards the horizon, we found ourselves in the midst of a grassy plain, apparently quite uninhabited, and of boundless extent. As the western sky deepened in its gold and green, and as the sun actually touched the horizon, the level light hit across this vast plain in long shafts of dull fire, just catching the tops of the taller rushes near us, and touching some distant sandy slopes into a pale crimson. Lower and lower the sun sank, until it seemed to eat a bit out of the horizon, so blinding was the light; while far above, in a sea of luminous green, lay one long narrow cloud—an island of blood-red.

In a second, when the sun sank, the world seemed to grow quite dark. All around us the prairie land had become of a cold, heavy, opaque green; and the only objects which our bewildered eyes could distinguish were some pale white flowers—like the tufts of canna on a Scotch moor. But presently, and to our intense surprise, the world seemed to leap up again into light and colour. This after-glow was most extraordinary. The immeasurable plains of grass became suffused with a rich olive green; the western sky was all a radiance of lemon-yellow and silvery grey; while along the eastern horizon—the most inexplicable thing of all—there stretched a great band of smoke-like purple and pink. We soon became familiar with this phenomenon out in the West—this appearance of a vast range of roseate Alps along the eastern horizon where there was neither mountain nor cloud. It was merely the shadow of the earth projected by the sunken sun into the earth's atmosphere. But it was an unforgettable thing; this mystic belt of colour far away in the east over the dark earth, and under the pale and neutral hues of the sky.

WILLIAM BLACK.

The Birth of Freedom.

SCHOLARS have said that the old Greeks were the fathers of Freedom; and there have been other peoples in the world's history who have made glorious and successful struggles to throw off their tyrants and be free. And they have said: "We are the fathers of Freedom; Liberty was born with us." Not so, my friends! Liberty is of a far older, and far nobler house; Liberty was born, if you will receive it, on the first Easter night—on the night to be much remembered among the children of Israel—ay, among all mankind—when God Himself stooped from heaven to set the oppressed free. Then was Freedom born. Not in the counsels of men, however wise; or in the battles of men, however brave: but in the counsels of God, and the battle of God—amid human agony and terror, and the shaking of heaven and the earth; amid the great cry throughout Egypt, when a first-born son lay dead in every house; and the tempest which swept aside the Red Sea waves; and pillar of cloud by day, and the pillar of fire by night; and the Red Sea shore covered with the corpses of the Egyptians; and the thunderings, and earthquakes, and lightnings of Sinai; and the sound of a trumpet waxing loud and long; and the voice, most human and most divine, which spake from off the lonely mountain-peak to that vast horde of coward and degenerate slaves, and said:

"I am the Lord thy God, who brought thee out of the land of Egypt. Thou shalt obey My laws, and keep My commandments to do them."

Oh, the man who would rob his suffering fellow-creatures of that story—he knows not how deep and bitter are the needs of men!

Then was Freedom born; but not of man; not of the will of the flesh, nor of the will of man, but of the will of God, from whom all good things come; and of Christ, who is the life and the light of men and of nations, and of the whole world, and all worlds—past, present, and to come.

CANON KINGSLEY.

Right-Hand Gloves.

NOT only literally, but metaphorically, we often have to endure the annoyance of being thrown into contact with two right-hand gloves. Believers in the possibility of discerning character by the handwriting, the shape of the nose, or the colour of the hair, generally place great faith in the test of asking a person suddenly to clasp his hands; when, if the right thumb is uppermost, it is said that he has a strong will, and is made to govern, but if the left, that he has a submissive will, and is made to be governed. As the rule applies to both sexes, it follows that when the "clasping thumb of both husband and wife happens to be that of the right hand, complications are apt to ensue. Before marriage, a couple may appear, both to themselves and to the world, as admirably suited to each other as two right-hand gloves lying in waiting for some unsuspecting victim. Their tastes are similar, their ages are suitable, and they are both clever. Each of them is fond of hunting, both of them are good talkers, and it is hard to say which is the better dressed. All promises well, but a few months after marriage the prognostications which we have above described are wonderfully verified. They prove to have an equal love of their own way, they are equally young and inexperienced, and they are so clever at repartee that tiffs are their daily bread. Each is so fond of hunting that more horses are required than their income will allow; both being good talkers, but bad listeners, domestic conversation becomes blocked; and it is hard to say which is the more extravagant in the matter of dress. The common possession of some special talent is singularly conducive to conjugal hot water. A famous French author once married a still more famous French authoress. But, on an unlucky day, the wife stumbled upon a copy of one of her works in which the husband had drawn the point of his pencil through all the "superfluous adjectives." An agony scene followed, and their bliss was blighted. We have heard it said of two excellent persons that they ought to marry each other because they are both "so religious;" but a male and female divine are more likely to quarrel than an author and an authoress; two cats tied together by their tails and hung over a tight-rope would probably pass a more peaceful time. It may be urged that, at any rate, the marriage of two persons having excellent tempers and similar views must be conducive to happiness; but it must be allowed that the exquisite harmony of their married life, although highly admirable, may prove somewhat dull.—*Saturday Review.*

Benny.

I HAD told him Christmas morning,
   As he sat upon my knee,
Holding fast his little stockings,
   Stuffed as full as full could be,
And attentive listening to me,
   With a face demure and mild,
That good Santa Claus, who filled them,
   Does not love a naughty child.

" But we'll be good, won't we, moder ? "
   And from off my lap he slid,
Digging deep among the goodies
   In his crimson stockings hid :
While I turned me to my table,
   Where a tempting goblet stood,
Brimming high with dainty egg-nog,
   Sent me by a neighbour good.

But the kitten there before me,
   With his white paw, nothing loth,
Sat by way of entertainment,
   Slapping off the shing froth :
And in not the gentlest humour
   At the loss of such a treat,
I confess I rather rudely
   Thrust him out into the street.

Then how Benny's blue eyes kindled !
   Gathering up his precious store
He had busily been pouring
   In his tiny pinafore,

With a generous look that shamed me,
   Sprang he from the carpet bright,
Showing, by his mien indignant,
   All a baby's sense of right.

" Come back, Harney ! " called he, loudly,
   As he held his apron white,
" You sall have my candy wabbit ! "
   But the door was fastened tight.
So he stood, abashed and silent,
   In the centre of the floor,
With defeated look alternate
   Bent on me and on the door.

Then, as by some sudden impulse,
   Quickly ran he to the fire ;
And while eagerly his bright eyes
   Watched the flames go high and higher,
In a brave, clear key he shouted,
   Like some lordly little elf,
" Santa Caus ! Come down de chimney,
   Make my moder 'have herself ! "

" I will be a good girl, Benny,"
   Said I, feeling the reproof ;
And straightway recalled poor Harney
   Mewing on the gallery-roof.
Soon the anger was forgotten,
   Laughter chased away the frown,
And they played beneath the live-oaks
   Till the dusky night came down.

In my dim, fire-lighted chamber,
   Harney purred beneath my chair,
And my play-worn boy beside me
   Knelt to say his evening prayer :
" God bess fader—God bess moder—
   God bess sister "—— Then a pause,
And the sweet young lips devoutly
   Murmured, " God bess Santa Caus ! "

> He is sleeping. Brown and silken
> Lie the lashes, long and meek,
> Like caressing, clinging shadows,
> On his plump and peachy cheek;
> And I bend above him, weeping
> Thankful tears, O Undefiled!
> For a woman's crown of glory—
> For the blessing of a child!
>
> From "*Lotos Flowers.*"

Kissing the Baby.

THE following interesting anecdote is related by a writer in *Appleton's Journal*:—

"It was once the lot of the writer to dwell in the white tents of Camp Harrison, in Georgia, in that lower part of the State where families are always far between, and much more so in war times. For long weeks we had not seen a woman or a child. At last the railroad to the camp was repaired, and in the first train there was a lady, with a wide-awake kicking baby.

"Some hundreds of rough soldiers were around the cars, and Captain Story, of the 57th Infantry, was the biggest and roughest among them, if we judge of the tree by its bark. The lady, with the baby in her arms, was looking from a window, and he took off his hat, and said,—

"'Madam, I will give you five dollars if you will let me kiss that baby.'

"One look at his bearded face told her that there was nothing bad in it, and saying, with a pleased laugh, 'I do not charge anything for kissing my baby,' it was handed over.

"The little one was not afraid, and the bushy whiskers, an eighth of an ell long, was just the playhouse it had been looking for. More than one kiss did the captain get from the little red lips, and there was energy in the hug of the little arms.

"Then other voices said, 'Pass him over here, cap;' and before the train was ready to move, half a hundred men had kissed the baby. He was on his best behaviour, and kicked, crowed, and tugged at whiskers as only a happy baby can.

"It was an event of the campaign; and one giant of a mountaineer, as he strode past us with tread like a mammoth, but with tear-dimmed eyes and quivering lips, said,—

"'By George! it makes me feel and act like a fool; but I've got one just like it at home.'"

Flowers and Snow.

I.

It was the pleasing summer time,
When winds were soft as rose or rhyme,
And, in the soothing evenglome,
The windows of an English home,
Open at dusk, let odours in
Of lily and early jessamine,
And mignonette, and linden flowers,
Late-lingering in their leafy bowers:
There father grave and mother mild
Sat gossiping of friend and child;
And, favoured by the deepening shade,
Thoughts that, in daylight half-afraid,
Sank in a tremor or a blush,
Found utterance in the twilight hush
All unabashed. And thus they spoke:

HE. Well, well, my dear, I meant no joke,
Although it seems and sounds so wild,
To ask to keep a child a child
For ever. Yes; they must grow up,
These mites. But if some chemic Cup
Of Babyhood were in my skill,
I almost think I have the will—
I think—I don't think—ah, my dear,
Mysterious is this mortal sphere;
I only wish——

 [*And here they laugh.*]

SHE. Ah, now you are too wise by half;
Original too. How new the thought
That life with mystery is fraught!
But, dearest love, I understand:
 [*And here she gently touched his hand.*]

We want, we two, impossible things :
To see the flight, yet clip the wings ;
To keep the bud, yet find the flower ;
Live on, yet pause upon the hour.
You dread the day, and so do I——
[*Here in the dusk he heard her sigh ;
Speech made a pause, sad but unvext,
The sermon stopped beside the text,
And it was his to rebegin it.*]

HE.   A house without a baby in it—
Yes, dear, that is the thing we dread !
How we shall miss the pattering tread !
The lisping tongue, the fearless eye,
That keeps its memory of the sky ;
The wit that has not learned to think,
Yet takes our wisdom to the brink,
At one touch of the infinite ;
The simpleness of child-delight ;
The unabashed, unwondering hope,
That, ignorant yet of mortal scope,
Asks for the sun, the moon, the air,
And sweets, with equal lack of care—
(Oh for a trust so much divine !
" Behold, all this is mine and thine ! ")
But, after all, what can we do ?
The children must grow up, dear.

SHE.   True.
[*Here an old friend looked in, to say
His daughter was betrothed that day.
Going to be married within the year,
But likely to live always near,
And when the young birds leave the nest,
To have them near at hand was best :
His eldest son was coining gold
Out in New Zealand.   This all told,
Our couple went to sleep that night
Leaving their problem open quite.*]

FLOWERS AND SNOW.

II.

It was mid-winter, and the snow
Fell on a grave shut long ago
Over the coffin of a child;
And father grave and mother mild
Sat in the firelit evenglome
And talked.

HE.   How quiet is our home!
But in our neighbour's, I can catch,
At moments when they lift the latch,
The noise of pattering baby feet,
And baby crying, scarce less sweet
Than baby laughter.

SHE.   Even so;
And how, John Anderson my jo,
Wise as you are—how would you have it?
You cannot eat your cake and save it.
[*We boast, we men, but after all,*
'Tis women who are practical;
And when we prune our waxen wings,
They find the heaven of common things.]

HE. Well, Jane is hearty: Jess is wed:
And Tom is prospering: so is Ned:
And——
    [*Here the fuffing of the fire*
Fills up a pause. Their hands draw nigher;
A sound of bells is in the air
And turns the silence into prayer;
Then softly speaks that mother mild.]

SHE. And yet, my dear, we have a child:
I see her now, I hear her voice
(Shall we have out the hoarded toys?)
I hear her little trampling feet—
She climbs your knee, she takes her seat—

HE. She croons a song. She droops her eyes;
  She sleeps. Dead darling! Yes, she dies.

SHE. She is the only child we have:
  Soft falls the snow upon her grave:
  Dead darling! Though the tears must fall.
  We keep our child, dear, after all.

HE. How strange that she should go that night
  I never understood it quite.
  Gone, gone! But to this very day,
  Can you not see the child at play
  As I do? Yes, I know you can.
  Lord, Lord, how poor a thing is man!

SHE. But after all we keep our child—
  [*Thou incoherent mother mild!*
  My tale grows weak—nay, more, 'tis false;
  For even by love, within four walls,
  Such things are never said right out,
  But speech goes faltering round about,
  In dread lest rough words break the locks
  Threefold of heavenly paradox.
  But, father grave!—but, mother mild!
  Oh, did you ever lose a child,—
  To weep, and ask what God could mean
  When the Spring put on its silent green,
  As if no change, no change had come;
  To weep and call, and then sit dumb;
  To weep, and think that Life was gone,
  And death would ne'er be clothed upon;
  And then, to see her, young and bright,
  In many a vision of the night—
  And then, to see your child at play
  In every sparkle of the day,
  And feel in every conquered smart
  The beating of her glad young heart,
  And find that, losing, you had won
  More than an empire in the sun?

AUTHOR OF "LILLIPUT LEVEE."

A real Christmas Gift.

It was true Christmas weather. So cold that the snow had lain on the ground for nearly a week, and the Ratzwald village looked rather bleak and dreary till you came to the belt of dark green pines and the bright shrubs that decked the wood beyond the Ratzbach, which was the name of the broad stream (here quite shallow, but lying in deep dark pools towards the open rocky country) which flowed through the fields and went winding and bubbling round one corner of the great wood. Not that it was flowing much now, for it was covered with great lumps of ice that had been welded together by the frost; so that there was no use for Karl's ferry-boat even to carry the few passengers who wanted to cross, and those who were afraid to go over the ice itself were obliged to walk a mile further up the stream to the wooden bridge, close to the old chateau belonging to the Graf Rabensfeder, one of the great mansions of the country, and the only fine house for a dozen miles of the Ratzwald district. The fact of the stream being frozen over made Christmas all the harder for Father Karl, as he was called by his neighbours; and he was a poor man even at the best of times, though he worked hard enough all the year through. He was a shoemaker by trade; but in the summer time not many shoes were wanted in the village, and in the winter people liked such thick strong soles that they lasted too long to give Karl much work; so that if it hadn't been for the ferry-boat in spring and summer, and fagot-chopping in autumn, and shoemaking and bellows-mending, and even a little coopering, all the year round, he would have found it still more difficult to keep a wife and four children, though the eldest, Fritz, who was nicknamed Kochapfel, because his round face was like a codlin, had been taken as a learner by Master Schwartz, the clockmaker, who lived at the top of the village, and played the church organ on Sundays. No doubt things would have been a little better in Ratzwald village if the Graf and Grafin Rabensfeder had lived at the old chateau; but they had not visited it for more than a year, and for three years had only spent a week there occasionally. It was said that the Grafin had no heart for the house ever since the loss of her dear little daughter three years before. Especially at the Christmas season was the place distasteful to her; for it was during a grand assembly at Christmas-tide that this great sorrow had befallen her. Four ladies, intimate friends of the Grafin, had asked to see the little darling asleep in her white and rose-coloured bed in the nursery, and they all crept softly up to the room, the fond mother leading the way. When they reached the room, the fire burned low in the stove; there was no light in the room, and, behold, the bed was empty! There was a terrible scene. The Grafin fell fainting on the ground when she heard that the nurse, whose duty it was to be in the room, had left the little creature fast asleep in the bed, and had only run downstairs to speak to her cousin, who was servant to one of the guests. Everybody in the chateau was summoned, horses were saddled, and men rode all about the country inquiring for the missing child; but the snow was on the ground, and people were all indoors keeping Christmas, so that no tidings could be heard even from the charcoal-burners, who seldom answer questions, and many of whom would have stolen the child themselves if they could have got anything by it, or would have tried to find her on the same terms. Only one person was suspected, and that was a laundress who had been discharged a week before, and had threatened to be revenged; but nobody knew where she lived or who were her relations, though it was believed that she came from the great mining district. So it happened that the chateau was now empty at Christmas-tide, and things were dull in the village.

Nobody could tell how it was that Kochapfel felt so moody and discontented the night before Christmas Eve when he went home. Perhaps it was because he would have liked to make his sisters Katie and Lisa a nice present, and was afraid that they would be disappointed to find nothing in their stockings in the morning except two little pewter brooches that he had bought from a pedlar with the money that he gained for working overtime. If there had been more business, so that he could have made watches instead of blowing the bellows to Master Schwartz's organ, he might have bought his father a handsome fur cap instead of a woollen one, and his mother a whole workbox instead of only a thimble and scissors; but as it was—— Well, he felt so moody that he gave his little brother Franz only one out of the two groschen that were left after his dealings with the pedlar.

It happened, then, that there was a cloud on his brow when he came down the morning of Christmas Eve, though he had found one stocking full of a great worsted comforter, a pair of knitted hand-mittens, and a smart necktie, all the work of his mother and sisters, a lucky stone threaded on to a horsehair watch-guard, plaited by little Franz, and a little Bible and psalter, the gift of his father. He felt so ill at ease and in such a moody humour that he didn't like to keep his gloomy face at the family table, and went out directly after breakfast, saying that he should take a long walk, and not come back till dusk. Somehow, the black bread and fried potatoes and porridge were not quite to his taste either; not that he had been used to anything much better, but there was no Christmas smile in his heart, and he was for the time impatient and under the dark cloud of discontent. It was true that at two or three houses which he passed in the village the people seemed happy enough; and at one place, where they were putting up great green fir boughs and making ready for the next day's merriment, his sullen looks attracted the notice of an old man who was playing with a dozen children at some Christmas game. "What's the matter with thee, Kochapfel?" he cried. "There's nothing wrong at home, is there? Neighbour Karl is well, I hope, and the good mother, and the little ones? What art thou looking so dark for?" And when Kochapfel told him—"Tut!" he cried, slapping the lad on the back, "go and find out somebody that has a bit of real trouble, and see if thou canst do them any good. That's the way to cure the megrims. Let the Christmas sunlight of good deeds and loving words shine on thy heart, my boy."

Kochapfel felt a little ashamed of himself, but he couldn't well shake off the shadow that had fallen on him; and even when the daylight began to fade, and he thought of turning his steps homeward, he was still muttering to himself, "If I could only take home a nice Christmas present for the good father or my dear mother—a gift that would make them all happy just for once in the year—I should be satisfied." He had scarcely noticed what road he had taken, with his eyes cast on the ground that lay all white with snow before him, but, looking up, he saw that he was before a great house, in the windows of which lights were shining and flitting to and fro. For a moment he did not recognise the chateau of the Graf Rabensfeder, for it was a rare occurrence indeed to see that great glaring place lighted up; but presently he noted the carved griffins that supported the gateway, and the quaint gables and peaks of the building grew familiar to him, standing out white and red against the wintry sky. He saw, too, that a poorly-clad woman—a beggar, he thought, by her rough dress—had crept up to the iron gate with a little girl, as though they were hesitating whether they should go and ask for alms at the grand house. They stood there so silently or spoke so low that he could not hear a word, even in the frozen stillness of the place; but presently they turned to go, and had no sooner passed out of sight than Kochapfel remembered that he had in his pocket a groschen for which he had no need, and felt a sting of conscience that he should not have offered it to the woman. Old Father Schmidt's words had stuck in his mind, and he set off to overtake the beggars, who had turned aside into the wood. He walked a good way, and began to think they must have disappeared under the ground, when he heard a pattering of feet and a child's voice crying just behind him; and, turning round, saw a little girl—the same girl who had been with the woman—running as hard as she could, crying out for her mother, and begging him to stop.

"Why, what has become of thy mother, little one?" said he.

"She told me that, if I stirred a step till she came back, she would beat me, and then she ran away. See, there she goes!"

It was true that the woman was at that moment going swiftly in the opposite direction, and Kochapfel gave chase, and called to her to stop; but she kept on, and only shouted back derisively. So, fearing that the poor little girl would either fall down and hurt herself, or get lost in the wood, he gave up the pursuit. What was to be done? Night was coming on, and the child, a pretty little thing of about five years old, was crying bitterly. Her mother would beat her, she said, as she had often beaten her before, ever since she lived in the black houses with the black men, and when they went begging about the country. Kochapfel could not tell what to make of it; but as the little creature was trembling with cold, he took off his coat and wrapped it round her, urging her to step along quickly. It was evident that she was already tired out; and when they were within two miles of the village he was obliged to take her on his back, where her head fell over his shoulder and her little cold cheek rested against his own face, for the smooth look of which he had got the name of Kochapfel. It is strange, but his heart felt as warm as his face by the time he reached his father's door.

"See here, father, what I have brought thee for a Christmas gift!" he said, as he let the little one slip down and unwound her from his coat.

Little Katie and Lisa and the good mother were soon busy about the child, while the lad told his story. The good old shoemaker scratched his head, with a puzzled look, for a moment; but at last a smile broke over his face.

"It's only one more to eat a little of our soup and share our bread, mother," he said; "and we dare not refuse this offering. Let us take it as a Christ-gift for this holy season. My son, thou must share thy dinner with the little one."

"That I will, heartily," said Kochapfel; and just at that moment in came the children, with the little beggar maiden, washed and dressed in some warm old clothes. She was so delicately fair, now that her skin was clean, and had such fine silken hair, that old Karl started.

"We must call thee Lili, my child," he said, kissing her on the cheek, "and thou must eat part of my son's dinner. We call him Kochapfel; but he will not, perhaps, like thee to call him so."

"She may call me what she likes," said Kochapfel stoutly, as he ladled half his soup into her little basin, and divided his hunch of bread between them.

The next day Karl and all the family, except the good mother and Katie, went to the church, and Kochapfel, who had to blow the organ, took the little stranger with him into the gallery, where she kept hold of his coat all the time of the service, and looked over with a scared face. There was great excitement when, a minute before the service began, the Graf and Grafin Rabensfeder, with two or three friends, walked into their great carved pew, and folk noticed the Grafin start in the midst of the service and cover her eyes with her hand. It was whispered outside afterwards that she had fancied an apparition of her dead child looked down on her, and so she had felt her worst fears confirmed; but this was contradicted by others, who knew from the servants that the old chateau was to be opened, and that the Grafin intended living there again all the winter. Even while this was being gossiped about a messenger was going through the village, bidding the poorer folk go up to the chateau, where they would be provided with good Christmas fare to take home with them. They and their families and quite a large crowd had already started in answer to this hospitable appeal. "We may as well go with the rest," said old Karl to his wife, "so put on thy cloak, and we will walk together; and, Kochapfel, thou shalt take charge of thy little Lili, just as though thou wert the Knecht Rupert taking a gift to the Grafin; perhaps she will do something for the poor little one, and if not, we will still keep her, never fear."

So they went up; and there, in the great backyard of the kitchen, were vast jars of soup, and pieces of cooked meat, and bread, sausages, and beer, and wine, and pies, and all sorts of jolly Christmas fare being distributed to the poor villagers, with the Grafin herself superintending it all. "For," said her husband in a loud voice, "we have determined to mourn no longer for our child, but to make other children happy in memory of what she might have been to us."

Now, it happened that Karl and his family had come quite close to the

Grafin as this was said, and when the noble lady looked down she saw—a fair child's face looking up at her with great eager blue eyes. "Who is this?" she cried, and in another moment she was on her knees before Lili, pressing her in her arms and calling her all sorts of endearing names. But, for all that, Lili would not at first leave go of Kochapfel's coat, to which she clung so tight that they all had to go into the chateau together, and there the whole story came out. Of course you can guess who Lili was? She was actually the little lost one for whom the lady had mourned so long; and I think it was no more than fair that in return for such a Christmas gift as that Kochapfel should now be a thriving watchmaker in Berlin, and that old Karl should have ended his days as general overlooker of the outdoor-work at the chateau, where Katie and her sister were the Grafin's own maids.

THOMAS ARCHER.

His Pilgrimage.

GIVE me my scallop-shell of quiet,
My staff of faith to walk upon;
My scrip of joy, immortal diet;
My bottle of salvation;
My gown of glory (hope's true gage),
And thus I'll take my pilgrimage.
Blood must be my body's balmer—
No other balm will there be given;
Whilst my soul like quiet palmer,
Travelleth towards the land of heaven:
Over the silver mountains,
Where spring the nectar fountains.
 There will I kiss
 The bowl of bliss
And drink mine everlasting fill
Upon every milken hill.
My soul will be a-dry before;
But after, it will thirst no more.
 I'll take them first
 To quench my thirst
And taste of nectar suckets,
 At those clear wells
 Where sweetness dwells,
Drawn up by saints in crystal buckets.

Then by that happy, blissful day,
More peaceful pilgrims I shall see,
That have cast off their rags of clay,
And walk apparelled fresh like me;
And when our bodies and all we
Are filled with immortality,
Then the blessed parts we'll travel
Strewed with rubies thick as gravel;
Ceilings of diamonds, sapphire flowers,
High walls of coral, and pearly bowers.
From thence to heaven's bribeless hall,
Where no corrupted voices brawl,
No conscience molten into gold,
No forged accuser bought or sold,
No cause deferred, no vain-spent journey;
For there Christ is the King's attorney,
Who pleads for all without degrees,
And he hath angels, but no fees.
And when the grand twelve-million jury
Of our sins, with direful fury,
'Gainst our souls black verdicts give,
Christ pleads His death, and then we live.
Be thou my Speaker, taintless Pleader,
Unblotted Lawyer, true Proceeder,
Thou wouldst salvation even for alms,
Not with a bribèd Lawyer palms.
This is mine eternal plea
To Him that made heaven, earth, and sea,
That since my flesh must die so soon,
And want a head to dine next noon,
Just at the stroke, when my veins start and spread,
Set on my soul an everlasting head;
Then am I ready, like a palmer fit,
To tread those blessed paths which before I writ!
Of death and judgement, heaven and hell,
Who oft doth think, must needs die well!

SIR WALTER RALEIGH.

Sir Roger at Church.

I AM always very well pleased with a country Sunday; and think, if keeping holy the seventh day were only a human institution, it would be the best method that could have been thought of for the polishing and civilising of mankind. It is certain the country people would soon degenerate into a kind of savages and barbarians were there not such frequent returns of a stated time, in which the whole village meet together, with their best faces and in their cleanliest habits, to converse with one another upon indifferent subjects, hear their duties explained to them, and join together in adoration of the Supreme Being. Sunday clears away the rust of the whole week, not only as it refreshes in their minds the notion of religion, but as it puts both the sexes upon appearing in their most agreeable forms, and exerting all such qualities as are apt to give them a figure in the eye of the village. A country fellow distinguishes himself as much in the churchyard as a citizen does upon the 'Change, the whole parish politics being generally discussed in that place either after sermon or before the bell rings.

My friend Sir Roger being a good churchman, has beautified the inside of this church with several texts of his own choosing; he has likewise given a handsome pulpit-cloth, and railed in the communion-table at his own expense. He has often told me, that at his coming to his estate he found his parishioners very irregular; and that, in order to make them kneel and join in the responses, he gave every one of them a hassock and a Common Prayer-Book; and at the same time employed an itinerant singing-master, who goes about the country for that purpose, to instruct them rightly in the tunes of the psalms; upon which they now very much value themselves, and indeed outdo most of the country churches that I have ever heard.

As Sir Roger is landlord to the whole congregation, he keeps them in very good order, and will suffer nobody to sleep in it besides himself; for if by chance he has been surprised into a short nap at sermon, upon recovering out of it he stands up and looks about him, and if he sees anybody else nodding, either wakes them himself, or sends his servant to them. Several other of the old knight's peculiarities break out upon these occasions: sometimes he will be lengthening out a verse in the singing psalms half a minute after the rest of the congregation have done with it; sometimes, when he is pleased with the matter of his devotion, he pronounces Amen three or four times to the same prayer; and sometimes stands up when everybody else is upon their knees, to count the congregation, or see if any of his tenants are missing.

I was yesterday very much surprised to hear my old friend, in the midst of the service, calling out to one John Matthews to mind what he was about, and not disturb the congregation. This John Matthews, it seems, is remarkable for being an idle fellow, and at that time was kicking his heels for his diversion.

This authority of the knight, though exerted in that odd manner which accompanies him in all circumstances of life, has a very good effect upon the parish, who are not polite enough to see anything ridiculous in his behaviour; besides that, the general good sense and worthiness of his character make his friends observe these little singularities as foils that rather set off than blemish his good qualities.

As soon as the sermon is finished, nobody presumes to stir till Sir Roger is gone out of the church. The knight walks down from his seat in the chancel between a double row of his tenants, that stand bowing to him on each side; and every now and then he inquires how such an one's wife, or mother, or son, or father do, whom he does not see at church; which is understood as a secret reprimand to the person that is absent.

The chaplain has often told me that upon a catechising day, when Sir Roger has been pleased with a boy that answers well, he has ordered a Bible to be given him next day for his encouragement; and sometimes accompanies it with a flitch of bacon to his mother. Sir Roger has likewise added five pounds a year to the clerk's place: and that he may encourage the young fellows to make themselves perfect in the church-service, has promised, upon the death of the present incumbent, who is very old, to bestow it according to merit.

ADDISON.

Above and Below.

I.

O DWELLERS in the valley-land,
  Who in deep twilight grope and cower
Till the slow mountain's dial-hand
  Shortens to noon's triumphal hour,—
While ye sit idle, do ye think
  The Lord's great work sits idle too?
That light dare not o'erleap the brink
  Of morn, because 'tis dark with you?

Though yet your valleys skulk in night,
  In God's ripe fields the day is cried,
And reapers with their sickles bright,
  Troop, singing, down the mountain-side:
Come up and feel what health there is
  In the frank Dawn's delighted eyes,
As, bending with a pitying kiss,
  The night-shed tears of Earth she dries!

Ararat.

ABOVE AND BELOW.

The Lord wants reapers: oh, mount up,
  Before night comes and says,—"Too late!"
Stay not for taking scrip or cup,
  The Master hungers while ye wait;
'Tis from these heights alone your eyes
  The advancing spears of day can see,
Which o'er the eastern hill-tops rise,
  To break your long captivity.

II.

Lone watcher on the mountain-height!
  It is right precious to behold
The first long surf of climbing light
  Flood all the thirsty east with gold;
But we, who in the shadow sit,
  Know also when the day is nigh,
Seeing thy shining forehead lit
  With his inspiring prophecy.

Thou hast thine office; we have ours:
  God lacks not early service here,
For what are thine eleventh hours
  He counts with us for morning cheer;
Our day, for Him, is long enough,
  And when He giveth work to do,
The bruisèd reed is amply tough
  To pierce the shield of error through.

But not the less do thou aspire
  Light's earlier messages to preach;
Keep back no syllable of fire,—
  Plunge deep the rowels of thy speech.
Yet God deems not thy aeried sight
  More worthy than our twilight dim,—
For meek Obedience, too, is Light,
  And following that is finding Him

J. R. LOWELL.

Not many Things, but one Thing well.

We cannot well doubt, indeed, that even the Lord Jesus, little as He cared for what we call "the good things of this life," approved of thrift, industry, skill, good sense, and good taste; or that, though He was content with simple fare, He preferred to have it properly cooked, and delicately served. We cannot doubt that He who, because He would suffer no waste, commanded the apostles to gather up the fragments of the loaves and fishes with which He had fed the five thousand, approves of you when you prevent waste, by making the most and best of the gifts of His Father's bounty. You can never please Him by wasting good food, or by suffering it to be wasted and spoiled. You cannot fail to please Him when you do the best you can with it, and serve it, or have it served, with a grace and a refinement which turns the simplest of meals into a feast. You may be quite sure that if Martha, when she had done her best in the kitchen and at the table, instead of pressing new dainties upon the Master, or passing about her dishes and flasks, had felt that there were higher things than eating and drinking, things for which He cared infinitely more; if she had thought to enter into His thoughts, and sympathise with His aims, and learn some new lesson or take some new gift of Him, He would have been just as pleased with her as He was with Mary. Why, even we ourselves are distressed if, when a friend asks us to her house, she lets us see that she is thinking of nothing but the dinner or the supper; if she fritters away the ease and pleasure of social intercourse by her anxiety as to what we shall eat and drink, by her fears lest she should not have got what we like, or lest the servants should make some stupid mistake. Even we feel that simple fare, carefully prepared and served, with a hearty welcome and pleasant unembarrassed intercourse, is far better, far more refreshing, than the most sumptuous feast with nothing to stimulate the mind and gratify the heart. How much more vexing and disappointing, then, must it have been to the pure and lofty spirit of Jesus to see that Martha could think of nothing but the dinner; and that, cumbered with many cares, she was losing a rare opportunity of friendly intercourse and spiritual communion!

None of you girls, I hope, will ever think yourselves too fine, or too cultured, to attend to your domestic duties, or even, if need be, to turn up your sleeves and pin on an apron, and toss off some dainty little dish which may stimulate the appetite of the weary or the sick ; for even in such humble services as these you may be pleasing and serving the Lord as truly and devoutly as in any act of public worship. But I also hope that you will not forget there are still

higher duties than these ; that in ministering to the spirit, you do more and better than in ministering to the body. For if there is one creature more pitiable than the fine lady who cannot condescend to the cares of the table or the house, it is the woman who degrades herself into a mere kitchen drudge, and whose soul seems never to get out of the pepper-box and salt-cellar.— *Dr. Cox's Sermons to Children.*

The Day is done.

THE day is done, and the darkness
    Falls from the wings of Night,
As a feather is wafted downward
    From an eagle in his flight.

I see the lights of the village
    Gleam through the rain and the mist,
And a feeling of sadness comes o'er me,
    That my soul cannot resist:

A feeling of sadness and longing,
    That is not akin to pain,
And resembles sorrow only,
    As the mist resembles the rain.

Come read to me some poem,
    Some simple and heartfelt lay,
That shall soothe this restless feeling,
    And banish the thoughts of day.

Not from the grand old masters,
    Not from the bard sublime,
Whose distant footsteps echo
    Through the corridors of Time.

For, like strains of martial music,
    Their mighty thoughts suggest
Life's endless toil and endeavour;
    And to-night I long for rest.

Read from some humbler poet,
    Whose songs gushed from his heart,
As showers from the clouds of summer
    Or tears from the eyelids start;

Who, through long days of labour,
   And nights devoid of ease,
Still heard in his soul the music
   Of wonderful melodies.

Such songs have power to quiet
   The restless pulse of care,
And come like the benediction
   That follows after prayer.

Then read from the treasured volume
  The poem of thy choice,
And lend to the rhyme of the poet
  The beauty of thy voice.

And the night shall be filled with music,
  And the cares that infest the day
Shall fold their tents, like the Arabs,
  And as silently steal away.

LONGFELLOW.

The Battle of Blenheim.

It was a summer evening,
  Old Kaspar's work was done,
And he, before his cottage door,
  Was sitting in the sun;
And by him sported on the green
His little grandchild Wilhelmine.

She saw her brother Peterkin
  Roll something large and round,
That he, beside the rivulet,
  In playing there had found;
She ran to ask what he had found,
That was so large, and smooth, and round.

Old Kaspar took it from the boy,
  Who stood expectant by;
And then the old man shook his head,
  And with a natural sigh,
" 'Tis some poor fellow's skull," said he,
" Who fell in the great victory.

THE BATTLE OF BLENHEIM.

"I find them in my garden, for
    There's many hereabout;
And often when I go to plough,
    The ploughshare turns them out;
For many thousand men," said he,
"Were slain in that great victory."

"Now tell us what 'twas all about,"
    Young Peterkin he cries;
And little Wilhelmine looks up
    With wonder-waiting eyes;—
"Now tell us all about the war,
And what they killed each other for?"

"It was the English," Kaspar cried,
    "Who put the French to rout;
But what they killed each other for,
    I could not well make out.

But everybody said," quoth he,
" That 'twas a famous victory.

" My father lived at Blenheim then,
    Yon little stream hard by ;
They burned his dwelling to the ground,
    And he was forced to fly :
So with his wife and child he fled,
Nor had he where to rest his head.

" With fire and sword the country round
    Was wasted far and wide ;
And many a wretched mother then
    And new-born baby died ;—
But things like that, you know, must be
At every famous victory.

" They say, it was a shocking sight
    After the field was won :
For many thousand bodies here
    Lay rotting in the sun !—
But things like that, you know, must be
After a famous victory.

" Great praise the Duke of Marlborough won
    And our good Prince Eugene."
" Why, 'twas a very wicked thing !"
    Said little Wilhelmine.
" Nay—nay—my little girl," quoth he,
" It was a famous victory !

" And everybody praised the Duke,
    Who this great fight did win :"
" But what good came of it at last ?"
    Quoth little Peterkin :
" Why, that I cannot tell,' said he ;
" But 'twas a famous victory."

SOUTHEY.

The Battle of Blenheim.

The Pilgrims and Giant Despair.

Now there was, not far from the place where they lay, a castle, called Doubting Castle, the owner whereof was Giant Despair, and it was in his grounds they now were sleeping; wherefore he, getting up in the morning early, and walking up and down in his fields, caught Christian and Hopeful asleep in his grounds. Then with a grim and surly voice he bid them awake, and asked them whence they were, and what they did in his grounds. They told him that they were pilgrims, and that they had lost their way. Then said the giant, "You have this night trespassed on me by trampling in and lying on my grounds, and therefore you must go along with me." So they were forced to go, because he was stronger than they. They also had but little to say, for they knew themselves in a fault. The giant, therefore, drove them before him, and put them into his castle, into a very dark dungeon, nasty and loathsome to the spirits of these two men. Here, then, they lay from Wednesday morning till Saturday night, without one bit of bread or drop of drink, or light, or any to ask how they did; they were therefore here in evil case, and were far from friends and acquaintance. Now, in this place Christian had double sorrow, because it was through his unadvised haste that they were brought into this distress.

Now Giant Despair had a wife, and her name was Diffidence; so when he was gone to bed, he told his wife what he had done, to wit, that he had taken a couple of prisoners, and cast them into his dungeon for trespassing on his grounds. Then he asked her also what he had best to do further to them. So she asked him what they were, whence they came, and whither they were bound, and he told her. Then she counselled him, that when he arose in the morning he should beat them without mercy. So when he arose, he getteth him a grievous crab-tree cudgel, and goes down into the dungeon to them, and there first falls to rating of them as if they were dogs, although they never gave him a word of distaste. Then he falls upon them, and beats them fearfully in such sort that they were not able to help themselves, or to turn them upon the floor. This done, he withdraws, and leaves them there to condole their misery, and to mourn under their distress: so all that day they spent their time in nothing but sighs and bitter lamentations. The next night, she, talking with her husband further about them, and understanding that they were yet alive, did advise him to counsel them to make away with themselves. So, when morning was come, he goes to them in a surly manner, as before, and perceiving them to be very sore with the stripes that he had given them the day before, he told them that since they were never like to come out of that place, their only way would be forthwith to make an end of themselves, either with knife, halter, or poison; for why, said he, should you choose to live, seeing it is attended with so much bitterness? But they desired him to let them go. With that he looked ugly upon them, and, rushing to them, had doubtless made an end of them himself, but that he fell into one of his fits (for he sometimes in sunshiny weather fell into fits), and lost for a time the use of his hands; wherefore he withdrew, and left them as before to consider what to do.

Well, towards evening, the giant goes down into the dungeon again, to see if his prisoners had taken his counsel. But when he came there, he found them alive, and, truly, alive was all; for now, what for want of bread and water, and by reason of the wounds they received when he beat them, they could do little but breathe. But, I say, he found them alive; at which he fell into a grievous rage, and told them, that seeing they had disobeyed his counsel, it should be worse with them than if they had never been born.

At this they trembled greatly, and I think that Christian fell into a swoon: but coming a little to himself again, they renewed their discourse about the giant's counsel, and whether yet they had best take it or no.

Now night being come again, and the giant and his wife being in bed, she asked him concerning the prisoners, and if they had taken his counsel; to which he replied, "They are sturdy rogues; they choose rather to bear all hardships than to make away with themselves." Then said she, "Take them into the castle-yard to-morrow, and show them the bones and skulls of those thou hast already despatched, and make them believe, ere a week comes to an end, thou wilt tear them in pieces, as thou hast done their fellows before them."

So when the morning was come, the giant goes to them again, and takes them into the castle-yard, and shows them as his wife had bidden him. "These," said he, "were pilgrims as you are, once, and they trespassed on my grounds as you have done; and when I thought fit, I tore them in pieces; and so within ten days will I do you. Go, get you down to your den again," and with that he beat them all the way thither. They lay therefore all day on Saturday in lamentable case as before. Now when night was come, and when Mrs. Diffidence and her husband the giant were got to bed, they began to renew their discourse of the prisoners; and withal the old giant wondered that he could neither by his blows nor counsel bring them to an end. And with that his wife replied, "I fear," said she, "that they live in hopes that some will come to relieve them, or that they have picklocks about them, by the means of which they hope to escape." "And sayest thou so, my dear?" said the giant; "I will therefore search them in the morning."

Well, on Saturday about midnight, they began to pray, and continued in prayer till almost break of day.

Now, a little before it was day, good Christian, as one half amazed, broke out into this passionate speech: "What a fool," quoth he, "am I, to lie in a dungeon, when I may as well walk at liberty! I have a key in my bosom called Promise, that will, I am persuaded, open any lock in Doubting Castle." Then said Hopeful, "That's good news; good brother, pluck it out of thy bosom and try."

Then Christian pulled it out of his bosom, and began to try at the dungeon-door, whose bolt, as he turned the key, gave back, and the door flew open with ease, and Christian and Hopeful both came out. Then he went to the outward door that leads into the castle-yard, and with his key opened that door also. After that he went to the iron gate, for that must be opened too, but that lock went desperately hard, yet the key did open it. Then they thrust open the gate to make their escape with speed; but that gate, as it opened, made such a creaking, that it waked Giant Despair, who, hastily rising to pursue his victims, felt his limbs to fail; for his fits took him again, so that he could by no means go after them. Then they went on, and came to the king's highway again, and so were safe, because they were out of his jurisdiction.

JOHN BUNYAN.

YOU are a modest man; you love quiet and independence, and have a delicacy and reserve in your temper which renders it impossible for you to elbow your way in the world and be the herald of your own merits. Be content, then, with a modest retirement—with the esteem of your intimate friends, with the praises of a blameless heart, and a delicate ingenuous spirit; but resign the splendid distinctions of the world to those who can better scramble for them.

DR. THOMAS BROWN.

INFINITE toil would not enable you to sweep away a mist; but by ascending a little, you may often look over it altogether; so it is with our moral improvement; we wrestle fiercely with a vicious habit, which could have no hold upon us if we ascended into a higher moral atmosphere.

A. HELPS.

Turn the Carpet.

As at their work two weavers sat,
Beguiling time with friendly chat,
They pick'd upon the price of meat,
So high, a weaver scarce could eat.

"What with my brats and sickly wife,"
Quoth Dick, "I'm almost tired of life;
So hard my work, so poor my fare,
'Tis more than mortal man can bear.

"How glorious is the rich man's state!
His house so fine, his wealth so great!
Heaven is unjust, you must agree;
Why all to him, and none to me?

"In spite of what the Scripture teaches,
In spite of all the parson preaches,
This world (indeed, I've thought so long)
Is ruled, methinks, extremely wrong.

"Where'er I look, howe'er I range,
'Tis all confused, and hard, and strange;
The good are troubled and oppress'd,
And all the wicked are the bless'd."

Quoth John, "Our ignorance is the cause
Why thus we blame our Maker's laws;
Parts of His way alone we know;
'Tis all that man can see below.

"Seest thou that carpet, not half done,
Which thou, dear Dick, hast well begun?
Behold the wild confusion there,
So rude the mass it makes one stare.

TURN THE CARPET.

"A stranger, ignorant of the trade,
Would say no meaning's there conveyed;
For where's the middle, where's the border?
Thy carpet now is all disorder."

Quoth Dick, "My work is yet in bits,
But still in every part it fits.
Besides, you reason like a lout:
Why, man, that carpet's inside out."

Says John, "Thou say'st the thing I mean,
And now I hope to cure thy spleen:
This world that clouds thy soul with doubt,
Is but a carpet inside out.

"As when we view these shreds and ends,
We know not what the whole intends;
So when on earth things look but odd,
They're working still some scheme of God.

"No plan, no pattern, can we trace,
All wants proportion, truth, and grace;
The motley mixture we deride,
Nor see the beauteous upper side.

"But when we reach the world of light,
And view these works of God aright,
Then shall we see the whole design,
And own the workman is Divine.

"What now seem random strokes will there
All order and design appear;
Then shall we praise what here we spurned,
For then the carpet shall be turned."

"Thou'rt right," quoth Dick; "no more I'll grumble,
That this sad world's so strange a jumble;
My impious thoughts are put to flight,
For my own carpet sets me right."

HANNAH MOORE.

Home should be First.

"LET home stand first before all other things! No matter how high your ambition may transcend its duties, no matter how far your talents or your influence may reach beyond its doors, before everything else build up a true home! Be not its slave; be its minister! Let it not be enough that it is swept and garnished, that its silver is brilliant, that its food is delicious; but feed the love in it, feed the truth in it, feed thought and aspiration, feed all charity and gentleness in it. Then from its walls shall come forth the true woman and the true man, who shall together rule and bless the land."

Is this an over-wrought picture? We think not. What honour can be greater than to found such a home? What dignity higher than to reign its undisputed honoured mistress? What is the ability to speak from a public platform to large intelligent audiences, or the wisdom that may command a seat on the judge's bench, compared to that which can ensure and preside over a true home, that husband and children "rise and call her blessed"? To be the guiding star, the ruling spirit in such a position is higher honour than to rule an empire. HARRIET BEECHER STOWE.

Carlyle on a Future State.

THE following letter was written in 1848, by Thomas Carlyle, in reply to an inquiry put before him by a young lady, who had given her mind much to the moral problems involved in the question of a future state:—" The Grange, Arlesford, September 27, 1848.—My dear Madam,—The question that perplexes you is one that no man can answer. You may console yourself by reflecting that it is by its nature insoluble to human creatures—that what human creatures mainly have to do with such a question is to get it well put to rest, suppressed if not answered, that so their life and its duties may be attended to without impediment from it. Such questions in this our earthly existence are many. 'There are two things,' says the German philosopher, 'that strike me dumb—the starry firnament (palpably infinite), and the sense of right and wrong in man.' Whoever follows out that 'dumb' thought will come upon the origin of our conception of heaven and hell—of an infinitude of merited happiness, and an infinitude of merited woe—and have much to reflect upon under an aspect considerably changed. Consequences, good and evil, blessed and accursed, it is very clear, do follow from all our actions here below, and prolong and propagate and spread themselves into the infinite, or beyond our calculation and conception; but whether the notion of reward and penalty be not, on the whole, rather a human one, transferred to that immense divine fact, has been doubtful to many. Add this consideration, which the best philosophy teaches us, 'that the very consequences (not to speak of the penalties at all) of evil actions die away, and become abolished long before eternity ends; and it is only the consequences of good actions that are eternal—for these are in harmony with the laws of this universe, and add themselves to it, and co-operate with it for ever; while all that is in disharmony with it must necessarily be without continuance, and soon fall dead.' As perhaps you have heard in the sound of a Scottish psalm amid the mountains, the true notes alone support one another, and the psalm which was discordant enough near at hand, is a perfect melody when heard from afar. On the whole, I must account it but a morbid, weak imagination that shudders over this wondrous divine universe as a place of despair to any creature; and contrariwise, a most degraded human sense, sunk down to the region of the brutal (however common it be), that in any case remains blind to the infinite difference there ever is between right and wrong for a human creature—or God's law and the devil's law.—Yours very truly,

"THOMAS CARLYLE."

My Playmate.

The pines were dark on Ramoth hill,
  Their song was soft and low;
The blossoms in the sweet May wind
  Were falling like the snow.

The blossoms drifted at our feet,
  The orchard birds sang clear;
The sweetest and the saddest day
  It seemed of all the year.

For, more to me than birds or flowers,
  My playmate left her home,
And took with her the laughing spring,
  The music and the bloom.

She kissed the lips of kith and kin,
  She laid her hand in mine;
What more could ask the bashful boy
  Who fed her father's kine?

She left us in the bloom of May;
  The constant years told o'er
Their seasons with as sweet May morns,
  But she came back no more.

I walk, with noiseless feet, the round
  Of uneventful years;
Still o'er and o'er I sow the spring
  And reap the autumn ears.

MY PLAYMATE.

She lives where all the golden year
  Her summer roses blow;
The dusky children of the sun
  Before her come and go.

There haply with her jewelled hands
  She smooths her silken gown,
No more the homespun-lap wherein
  I shook the walnuts down.

The wild grapes wait us by the brook,
  The brown nuts on the hill,
And still the May-day flowers make sweet
  The woods of Follymill.

The lilies blossom in the pond,
  The bird builds in the tree,
The dark pines sing on Ramoth hill
  The slow song of the sea.

I wonder if she thinks of them,
  And how the old time seems,
If ever the pines of Ramoth wood
  Are sounding in her dreams?

I see her face, I hear her voice;
  Does she remember mine?
And what to her is now the boy
  Who fed her father's kine?

What cares she that the orioles build
  For other eyes than ours,
That other hands with nuts are filled,
  And other laps with flowers?

O playmate in the golden time!
  Our mossy seat is green,
Its fringing violets blossom yet,
  The old trees o'er it lean.

The winds so sweet with birch and fern
    A sweeter memory blow;
And there in spring the veeries sing
    The song of long ago.

And still the pines of Ramoth wood
    Are moaning like the sea,
The moaning of the sea of change
    Between myself and thee!

J. G. WHITTIER.

Universal Beauty.

THE ancient Greeks called the world Beauty. Such is the constitution of all things, or such the plastic power of the human eye, that the primary forms—as the sky, the mountain, the tree, the animal—give us a delight *in and for themselves*; a pleasure arising from outline, colour, motion, grouping. This seems partly owing to the eye itself. The eye is the best of artists. By the mutual action of its structure and of the laws of light, perspective is produced, which integrates every mass of objects, of what character soever, into a well-coloured and shaded globe, so that where the particular objects are mean and unaffecting, the landscape which they compose is round and symmetrical. And as the eye is the best composer, so light is the first of painters. There is no object so foul that intense light will not make it beautiful. And the stimulus it affords to the sense, and a sort of infinitude which it hath, like space and time, make all matters gay. Even the corpse has its own beauty. But besides this general grace diffused over Nature, almost all the individual forms are agreeable to the eye, as is proved by our endless imitations of some of them—as the acorn, the grape, the pinecone, the wheat-ear, the egg, the wings and forms of most birds, the lion's claw, the serpent, the butterfly, sea-shells, flames, clouds, buds, leaves, and the forms of many trees, as the palm.

The simple perception of natural forms is a delight. The influence of the forms and actions in Nature is so needful to man, that in its lowest functions it seems to lie on the confines of commodity and beauty. To the body and mind which have been cramped by noxious work or company, Nature is medicinal, and restores their tone. The tradesman, the attorney, comes out of the din and craft of the street, and sees the sky and the woods, and is a man again. In their eternal calm he finds himself. The health of the eye seems to demand a horizon. We are never tired, so long as we can see far enough.

But in other hours, Nature satisfies by its loveliness, and without any mixture of corporeal benefit. I see the spectacle of morning from the hilltop over against my house, from daybreak to sunrise, with emotions which an angel might share. The long, slender bars of cloud float like fishes in the sea of crimson light. From the earth, as a shore, I look out into that silent sea. I seem to partake its rapid

transformations; the active enchantment reaches my dust, and I dilate and conspire with the morning wind. How does Nature deify us with a few cheap elements! Give me health and a day, and I will make the pomp of emperors ridiculous. The dawn is my Assyria, the sunset and moonrise my Paphos, and unimaginable realms of faerie; broad noon shall be my England of the senses and the understanding; the night shall be my Germany of mystic philosophy and dreams.

R. W. EMERSON.

The Efficacy of Prayer.

"CHELSEA, June 9, 1870.—Dear Sir,—You need no apology for addressing me; your letter itself is of amiable ingenuous character, pleasant and interesting to me in no common degree. I am sorry only that I cannot set at rest, or settle into clearness, your doubts on that important subject. What I myself practically, in a half-articulate way, believe on it, I will try to express for you. First, then, as to your objection of setting up *our* poor wish or will in opposition to the will of the Eternal, I have not the least word to say in contradiction of it. And this seems to close, and does in a sense, though not perhaps in all senses, close the question of our prayers being *granted*, or what is called 'heard;' but that is not the whole question. For, on the other hand, prayer is, and remains always, a native and deepest impulse of the soul of man; and, correctly gone about, is of the very highest benefit—nay, one might say, indispensability—to every man aiming morally high in this world. No prayer, no *religion*, or at least only a dumb or lamed one! Prayer is a turning of one's soul, in heroic reverence, in infinite desire and *endeavour* towards the highest, the All-Excellent, Omnipotent, Supreme. The modern hero, therefore, ought *not* to give up praying, as he has latterly all but done. *Words* of prayer in this epoch I know hardly any. But the act of prayer in great moments I believe to be still possible, and that one should gratefully accept such moments, and count them blest when they come, if come they do—which latter is a most rigorous preliminary question with us in all cases. '*Can I pray* in this moment,' much as I may *wish* to do so? If not, then, no! I can at least stand silent, inquiring, and *not* blasphemously *lie* in this Presence. On the whole, silence is one safe form of prayer known to me in this poor sordid era—though there are ejaculatory words, too, which occasionally rise on one with a felt propriety and veracity, words very welcome in such case. Prayer is the aspiration of our poor, struggling, heavy-laden soul towards its eternal Father; and with or without words ought not to become impossible, nor, I persuade myself, need it ever. Loyal sons and subjects *can* approach the King's throne who have no 'request' to make there, except that they may continue loyal. Cannot they?

"THOMAS CARLYLE."

The Old "Discipline" for the Child.

THE whisper of mortality was ever audible to him, was ever destroying, with its still small voice, his peace of spirit. He was taught to note the fall of the

leaf, and not its budding growth. He was bidden to fix his attention rather upon the decay of autumn than the hopeful lessons of spring. The summer suns might be bright, and the summer skies one wide overarching vault of unfathomable cloudless blue, but there were clouds which were sure to rise, and pitiless rains were ever being drawn up from the seas into heaven.

Thus it was that, imperceptibly, the entire life of the child became overhung by the shadow of some coming eclipse. A vague presentiment of calamity, of total darkness that might at any moment descend upon the earth and cover all, a chronic state of mute, mournful, passive acquiescence in a grim and tyrannical dispensation, were the outcome of the influences by which he was surrounded. The future never suggested itself as an infinite succession of glad possibilities. It seemed rather to shape itself to the childish and most fearful imagination as a narrow sunless path, never once turning to right or left, stretching on, on, on, for weary mile after weary mile, till it became lost in blinded mists and rain, beyond which were fiery terrors and the torture-house of implacable Fate.

T. H. S. ESCOTT.

The Lie; or, the Soul's Errand.

Go, Soul, the body's guest,
  Upon a thankless arrant;
Fear not to touch the best,
  The truth shall be thy warrant:
    Go, since I needs must die,
    And give the world the lie.

Say to the Court, it glows,
  And shines like rotten wood;
Say to the Church, it shows
  What's good, and doth no good:
    If Church and Court reply,
    Then give them both the lie.

Tell Potentates they live,
  Acting by other's actions;
Not 'oved, unless they give,
  Not strong but by their factions:
    If Potentates reply,
    Give Potentates the lie.

THE LIE.

Tell men of high condition,
  That in affairs of state,
Their purpose is ambition,
  Their practice only hate:
    And if they once reply,
    Then give them all the lie.

Tell them that brave it most,
  They beg for more by spending,
Who in their greatest cost
  Seek nothing but commending:
    And if they make reply,
    Give them likewise the lie.

Tell Zeal it lacks devotion;
  Tell Love it is but lust;
Tell Time it is but motion;
  Tell Flesh it is but dust:
    And wish them not reply,
    For thou must give the lie.

Tell Age it daily wasteth;
  Tell Honour how it alters;
Tell Beauty how she blasteth;
  Tell Favour how it falters:
    And as they shall reply,
    Give every one the lie.

Tell Wit how much she wrangles
  In tickle points of niceness;
Tell Wisdom she entangles
  Herself by much preciseness:
    And when they do reply,
    Straight give them both the lie.

Tell Physic of her boldness;
  Tell Skill it is pretension;

Tell Charity of coldness;
  Tell Law it is contention:
    And as they do reply,
    So give them still the lie.

Tell Fortune of her blindness;
  Tell Nature of decay;
Tell Friendship of unkindness;
  Tell Justice of delay:
    And if they will reply,
    Then give them all the lie.

Tell Arts they have no soundness,
  And vary by esteeming;
Tell Schools they want profoundness,
  And stand too much on seeming:
    If Arts and Schools reply,
    Give Arts and Schools the lie.

Tell Faith it's fled the city;
  Tell how the Country erreth;
Tell, Manhood shakes off pity;
  Tell, Virtue least preferreth:
    And if they do reply,
    Spare not to give the lie.

So when thou hast, as I
  Commanded thee, done blabbing,
Although to give the lie
  Deserves no less than stabbing;
    Stab at thee who what will,
    No stab the soul can kill!

(ATTRIBUTED TO SIR WALTER RALEIGH.)

"PERHAPS the very best idea of prayer is, what He will think back to us, and do; not just thinking toward God and waiting for trying to tell Him anything."

New-Born.

A SINGLE gentle rain makes the grass many shades greener. So our prospects brighten on the influx of better thoughts. We should be blessed if we lived in the present always, and took advantage of every accident that befell us, like the grass which confesses the influence of the slightest dew that falls on it ; and

did not spend our time in atoning for the neglect of past opportunities, which we call doing our duty. We loiter in winter while it is already spring. In a pleasant spring morning all men's sins are forgiven. Such a day is a truce to vice. While such a sun holds out to burn, the vilest sinner may return. Through our own recovered innocence we discern the innocence of our neighbours. You may have known your neighbour yesterday for a thief, a drunkard, or a sensualist, and merely pitied or despised him, and despaired of the world; but the sun shines bright and warm this first spring morning, re-creating the world, and you meet him at some serene work, and see how his exhausted and debauched veins expand with still joy and bless the new day, feel the spring influence with the innocence of infancy, and all his faults are forgotten. There is not only an atmosphere of goodwill about him, but even a savour of holiness groping for expression, blindly and ineffectually, perhaps, like a new-born instinct, and for a short hour the south hillside echoes to no vulgar jest. You see some innocent, fair shoots preparing to burst from his gnarled rind and try another year's life, tender and fresh as the youngest plant. Even he has entered into the joy of his Lord. Why the gaoler does not leave open his prison-doors, why the judge does not dismiss his case, why the preacher does not dismiss his congregation. It is because they do not obey the hint God gives them, nor accept the pardon which He freely offers to all.

A return to goodness produced each day in the tranquil and beneficent breath of the morning, causes that, in respect to the love of virtue and the hatred of vice, one approaches a little the primitive nature of man, as the sprouts of the forest which has been felled. In like manner the evil which one does in the interval of a day prevents the germs of virtues which began to spring up again from developing themselves and destroys them.

After the germs of virtue have been prevented many times from developing themselves, then the beneficent breath of evening does not suffice to preserve them. As soon as the breath of evening does not suffice longer to preserve them, then the nature of man does not differ much from that of the brute. Men seeing the nature of this man like that of the brute, think that he has never possessed the innate faculty of reason. Are these the true and natural sentiments of man?

H. D. THOREAU.

An old Highland clergyman, who had received several calls to parishes, asked his servant where he should go.

His servant said:

"Go where there is most sin, sir."

The preacher concluded that was good advice, and went where there was most money.

The Rose.

Press me not to take more pleasure
    In this world of sugared lies,
And to use a larger measure
    Than my strict yet welcome size.

First, there is no pleasure here:
    Colour'd griefs indeed there are;
Blushing woes that look as clear,
    As if they could beauty spare.

Or if such deceits there be,
    Such delights I meant to say;
There are no such things to me,
    Who have passed my right away.

But I will not much oppose
    Unto what you now advise;
Only take this gentle rose,
    And therein my answer lies.

What is fairer than a rose?
    What is sweeter? Yet it purgeth.
Purgings enmity disclose,
    Enmity forbearance urgeth.

If, then, all that worldlings prize
    Be contracted to a rose;
Sweetly there indeed it lies,
    But it biteth in the close.

> So this flower doth judge and sentence
>   Worldly joys to be a scourge:
> For they all produce repentance,
>   And repentance is a purge.
>
> But I health, not physic, choose:
>   Only though I you oppose,
> Say that fairly I refuse,
>   For my answer is a rose.

GEORGE HERBERT.

Mere "Duty."

THERE are minds in which the idea of duty stands immovably as the only assertion of man's spiritual being. In such men it resembles a rock unclothed of all verdure, from which all life-sustaining soil has been washed away, and with nothing near it but a dreary tossing sea of passions and strivings.

Duty is thus felt as the great painful burden of existence, but which it is nobler to bear than escape from, as the mind assures itself of its own strength only by the effort of upholding its load. But the exertion is so painful that it often disturbs all clear, calm views of the world around. The suffering and the sense of contradiction embody themselves in the belief, that the whole universe is equally jarring, perilous, and tortured.

Hence a reckless ferocity of opposition to whatever claims a quiet and stable dominion. Hence, too, a fretful, bitter scorn for the convictions and sympathies of those who maintain that, either for their own minds or for mankind as a race, escape is provided from the bondage of law into the freedom of life and love. From the feeling of perpetual struggle, in which victory promises no reward but the dreary pride of victory, arises a sympathy with all struggle, however mad and blind, against any restraining force, and a cruel and disdainful spite against the attempts, in a progressive system necessarily inadequate and imperfect, at introducing order amid the world's confusions.

Unless, in truth, these should happen to be chiefly remarkable as fierce and plundering revolts against the previous and more lasting endeavours, the uppermost feeling in the mind being that of resistance, that of holding fast one's ground against hostility, the tendency will always be to look with favour on all kindred efforts, however desperate and insane, and to scout as lies, hypocrisy, vanity, pedantry, and so forth, the notion that there can be any good in the traditional maxims, symbols, and institutions of society.

It is a dreary picture; but, though insufficiently transferred to language, its originals have an undeniable existence. However horrid the thought of their Cain-like isolation and ulcerated feelings, their inextricable clinging to a strong and deep principle, under the heavy pressure of anguish and despair, makes them objects of true and brotherly sympathy to every believer in spiritual realities. The great error seems to be, the substitution of a law for a personal being, a God. A law must be obeyed at whatever cost of reluctance, and has no tendency to make obedience easy.

It is only a person that can be loved; and with love comes life and hope.

JOHN STERLING.

MIND AND BODY.—By too much sitting still the body becomes unhealthy, and soon the mind. This is Nature's law. She will never see her children wronged. If the mind, which rules the body, ever forgets itself so far as to trample upon its slave, the slave is never generous enough to forgive the injury, but will rise and smite its oppressor. Thus has many a monarch-mind been dethroned.
LONGFELLOW.

JOHNSON once said: "A man's mind grows narrow in a narrow place, whose mind is enlarged only because he has lived in a large place; but what is got by books and thinking is preserved in a narrow place as well as in a large place. A man cannot know modes of life as well in Minorca as in London; but he may study mathematics as well in Minorca."

IF you want to spoil *all* that God gives you, if you want to be miserable yourself and a maker of misery to others, the way is easy enough. Only be selfish, and it is done at once. Think about yourself, what respect people ought to pay to you, what people think of you, and then to you nothing will go well.
CHARLES KINGSLEY.

AN old judge is credited with the remark: "I don't know which does the most harm, enemies with the worst intentions or friends with the best."

INNOVATIONS.—It were good that men in their innovations would follow the example of time itself, which, indeed, innovateth greatly but quietly, and by degrees scarce to be perceived.
LORD BACON.

SYDNEY SMITH once gave a lady two-and-twenty recipes against melancholy. One was a bright fire; another, to remember all the pleasant things said to her; another, to keep a box of sugar-plums on the chimney-piece, and a kettle simmering on the hob.

"I thought this mere trifling at the moment," continues he, "but have in after-life discovered how true it is that these little pleasures often drive melancholy away better than higher and more exalted objects; and that no means ought to be thought too trifling which can oppose it either in ourselves or in others."

REMEMBER that one gives no other answer to the rose for its precious fragrance than to inhale it with delight.

Love's Supremacy.

AT first it surprises one that love should be made the principal staple of all the best kinds of fiction ; and, perhaps, it is to be regretted that it is only one kind of love that is chiefly depicted in works of fiction. But that love itself is the most remarkable thing in human life there cannot be the slightest doubt. For see what it will conquer. It is not only that it prevails over selfishness, but it has the victory over weariness, tiresomeness, and familiarity.

When you are with a person loved, you have no sense of being bored. This humble and trivial circumstance is the great test, the only sure and abiding test of love. With the persons you do not love you are never supremely at your ease. You have some of the sensation of walking upon stilts. In conversation with them, however much you admire them and are interested in them, the horrid idea will cross your mind of "What shall I say next?" Converse with them is not perfect association. But with those you love, the satisfaction in their presence is not unlike that of the relation of heavenly bodies one to another, which, in their silent revolutions, lose none of their attractive power. The sun does not talk to the world, but it does attract it.

GEORGE ELIOT.

Instruments or Exercises to Procure Contentedness.

WHEN anything happens to our displeasure, let us endeavour to take off its trouble by turning it into spiritual or artificial advantage, and handle it on that side in which it may be useful to the designs of reason. For there is nothing but hath a double handle, or at least we have two hands to apprehend it. When an enemy reproaches us, let us look on him as an impartial relater of our faults, for he will tell thee truer than thy fondest friend will; and thou mayest call them precious balms though they break thy head, and forgive his anger while thou makest use of the plainness of his declamation. *The ox when he is weary treads surest;* and if there be nothing else in the disgrace but that it makes us to walk warily, and tread sure for fear of our enemies, that is better than to be flattered into pride and carelessness. This is the charity of Christian philosophy, which expounds the sense of the divine providence fairly, and reconciles us to it by a charitable construction: and we may as well refuse all physic, if we consider it only as unpleasant in the taste; and we may find fault with the rich valleys of Thasus because they are circled by sharp mountains; but so also we may be in charity with every unpleasant accident, because, though it taste bitter, it is intended for health and medicine.

If, therefore, thou fallest from thy employment in public, take sanctuary in an honest retirement, being indifferent to thy gain abroad or thy safety at home. If thou art out of favour with thy prince, secure the favour of the King of kings, and then there is no harm come to thee. And when Zeno Citiensis lost all his goods in a storm, he retired to the studies of philosophy, to his short cloak, and a severe life, and gave thanks to Fortune for his prosperous mischance. When the north wind blows hard and it rains sadly, none but fools sit down in it and cry; wise people defend themselves against it with a warm garment, or a good fire, and a dry roof. When a storm of a sad mischance beats upon our spirits, turn it into some advantage by observing where it can serve another end, either of religion or prudence, or more safety or less envy: it will turn into something that is good, if we list to make it so; at least it may make us weary of the world's vanity, and take off our confidence from uncertain riches, and make our spirits to dwell in those regions where content dwells essentially. If it does any good to our souls, it hath made more than sufficient recompense for all the temporal affliction. He that threw a stone at a dog, and hit his cruel stepmother, said, that although he intended it otherwise, yet the stone was not quite lost: and if we fail in the first design, if we bring it home to another equally to content us, or more to profit us, then we have put our conditions past the power of chance; and this was called in the old Greek comedy "a being revenged on fortune by becoming philosophers," and turning the chance into reason or religion: for so wise a man shall overrule his stars, and have a greater influence upon his own content than all the constellations and planets of the firmament.

Never compare thy condition with those above thee; but, to secure thy content, look upon those thousands with whom thou wouldst not for any interest change thy fortune and condition. A soldier must not think himself unprosperous, if he be not successful as the son of Philip, or cannot grasp a fortune as big as the Roman empire. Be content that thou art not lessened as was Pyrrhus; or if thou beest, that thou are not routed like Crassus; and when that comes to thee, it is a great prosperity that thou art not caged and made a spectacle like Bajazet, or thy eyes were not pulled out like Zedekiah's, or that thou wert not flayed alive like Valentinian. If thou admirest the greatness of Xerxes, look also on those that digged the mountain Atho, or whose ears and noses were cut off because the Hellespont carried away the bridge. It is a fine thing (thou thinkest) to be carried on men's shoulders; but give God thanks that thou art not forced to carry a rich fool upon thy shoulders, as those poor men do whom thou beholdest. There are but a few kings in mankind, but many thousands who are very miserable, if compared to thee. However, it is a huge folly rather to grieve for the good of others, than to rejoice for that good which God hath given us of our own.

And yet there is no wise or good man that would change persons or conditions entirely with any man in the world. It may be he would have one man's wealth added to himself, or the power of a second, or the learning of a third; but still he would receive these into his own person, because he loves that best, and therefore esteems it best, and therefore overvalues all that which he is, before all that which any other man in the world can be. Would any man be Dives to have his wealth, or Judas for his office, or Saul for his kingdom, or Absalom for his beauty, or Ahithophel for his policy? It is likely he would wish all these, and yet he would be the same person still. For every man hath desires of his own and objects just fitted to them, without which he cannot be, unless he were not himself. And let every man that loves himself so well as to love himself before all the world, consider if he have not something for which, in the whole, he values himself far more than he can value any man else. There is therefore no reason to take the finest feathers from all the winged nation to deck that bird that thinks already she is more valuable than any of the inhabitants of the air. Either change all or none. Cease to love yourself best, or be content with that portion of being and blessing for which you love yourself so well.

It conduces much to our content, if we pass by those things which happen to our trouble, and consider that which is pleasing and prosperous, that by the representation of the better, the worse may be blotted out; and at the worst you have enough to keep you alive, and to keep up and to improve your hopes of heaven. If I be overthrown in my suit at law, yet my house is left me still and my land; or I have a virtuous wife, or hopeful children, or kind friends, or good hopes. If I have lost one child, it may be I have two or three still left me. Or else reckon the blessings which already you have received, and therefore be pleased in the change and variety of affairs to receive "evil from the hand of God as well as good." Antipater of Tarsus used this art to support his sorrows on his death-bed, and reckoned the good things of his past life, not forgetting to recount it as a blessing, an argument that God took care of him, that he had a prosperous journey from Cilicia to Athens. Or else please thyself with hopes of the future; for we were not born with this sadness upon us; and it was a change that brought us into it, and a change may bring us out again. Harvest will come, and then every farmer is rich, at least for a month or two. It may be thou art entered into the cloud which will bring a gentle shower to refresh thy sorrows.

Now suppose thyself in as great a sadness as ever did load thy spirit, wouldst thou not bear it cheerfully and nobly, if thou wert sure that within a certain space some strange excellent fortune would relieve thee, and enrich thee, and recompense thee, so as to overflow all thy hopes and thy desires and capacities? Now then, when a sadness lies heavy upon thee, remember that thou art a Christian, designed to the inheritance of Jesus; and what dost thou think concerning thy great fortune, thy lot and portion of eternity? Dost thou think thou shalt be saved or damned? Indeed, if thou thinkest thou shalt perish, I cannot blame thee to be sad,—sad till thy heart-strings crack; but then why art thou troubled at the loss of thy money? What should a damned man do with money, which in so great a sadness it is impossible for him to enjoy? Did ever any man upon the rack afflict himself because he had received a cross answer from his mistress? or call for the particulars of a purchase upon the gallows? If thou dost really believe thou shalt be damned, I do not say it will cure the sadness of thy poverty, but it will swallow it up. But if thou believest thou shalt be saved, consider how great is that joy, how infinite is that change, how unspeakable is the glory, how excellent is the recompense for all the sufferings in the world, if they were all laden upon thy spirit! So that, let thy condition be what it will, if thou considerest thy own present condition, and comparest it to thy future possibility, thou canst not feel the present smart of a cross fortune to any great degree, either because thou hast a far bigger sorrow or a far bigger joy. Here thou art but a stranger travelling to thy country, where the glories of a kindgom are prepared for thee: it is therefore a huge folly to be much afflicted because thou hast a less convenient inn to lodge in by the way.

JEREMY TAYLOR.

The Forsaken Farmhouse.

AGAINST the wooded hills it stands,
    Ghost of a dead home, staring through
Its broken lights on wasted lands
    Where old-time harvests grew.

Unploughed, unsown, by scythe unshorn,
    The poor forsaken farm-fields lie,
Once rich and rife with golden corn
    And pale-green breadths of rye.

Of healthful herb and flower bereft,
    The garden-plot no housewife keeps;
Through weeds and tangle only left
    The snake, its tenant, creeps.

A lilac spray, once blossom-clad,
    Sways bare before the empty rooms;
Beside the roofless porch, a sad
    Pathetic red rose blooms.

His track, in mould and dust of drought,
    On floor and hearth the squirrel leaves;
And in the fireless chimney's mouth,
    His web the spider weaves.

THE FORSAKEN FARMHOUSE.

The leaning barn, about to fall,
   Resounds no more on husking eves;
No cattle low in yard or stall,
   No thresher beats his sheaves.

So sad, so drear! It seem almost
   Some haunting Presence makes its sign;
That down yon shadowy lane some ghost
   Might drive his spectral kine!

J. G. WHITTIER.

The great Colliery Accident at Hartley, 1862.

THE main features of the calamity at Hartley Colliery may be soon indicated. Closely adjoining the shaft of the mine on the east side, was a substantial stone structure containing the machinery employed for keeping the pit clear of water. The pumping-engine was one of the largest to be met with in the coal trade, with a power equal to 400 horses.

The accident occurred about half-past ten in the morning. The greater body of the miners in the pit had gone in at one o'clock in the morning, and were just about being relieved to come to bank by the back shift, which went in at nine o'clock. In fact, two sets of men of the first shift had got to bank, and the third shift was "riding" or coming up the shaft in the cage, and had got hauled halfway up when the beam of the pumping-engine overhanging the shaft at the bank suddenly and without any warning snapped in two, the projecting outer half, weighing upwards of twenty tons, falling with a tremendous crash right down the centre of the shaft. It struck the top of the brattice, and carried the wood work and timber, which extended from the top to the bottom of the shaft, with it down the shaft. It encountered the ascending cage, bringing up eight miners, halfway. The survivors of the party stated that they first observed something shoot past them with the velocity of a thunderbolt, and presently found themselves overwhelmed by a perfect hail of broken beams and planks. The iron cage in which they were ascending was shattered to pieces by the shock, and two of the unfortunate men were killed on the spot, and carried far down among the ruins. Of the remaining six, three survived for some time, and the others were ultimately rescued.

Of course, as soon as the accident was known, help arrived from the neighbouring collieries, and every effort was made to reach the number of men and boys imprisoned below; but only two men at a time could work at removing the obstruction, and they had to be slung by ropes in the narrow space. Meanwhile the scene around the pit's mouth and in the neighbourhood was sad and touching. The police had some difficulty in keeping the space about the bank top sufficiently clear for the work to be carried on. Crowds of people came from the adjoining mining villages, and even from distant places. Numbers of women remained all day in sad foreboding groups, after having stood near the mine in the chill air of the November night. The wives and families of the men who were imprisoned below passed hither and thither with sorrow-stricken faces. There were plenty of experienced men, with brave hearts and strong hands, but the work could only be effected slowly; and though it was said that at one time on the Saturday (the third day of their imprisonment) the men for whom they were labouring were heard working and signalling in the shaft, the obstructions had been found to be more solid and closely wedged together as the explorers worked to the lower part of the shaft. Signals were made and not answered, and the sounds which had been

heard ceased. It was supposed that the men had retired more into the workings. The managers of the pit felt confident that there was not the least cause for alarm, unless the men should suffer from the effects of foul air; and this apprehension, as the event proved, was unhappily too well founded. The work of clearing away the obstructions in the shaft was continued night and day with unremitting vigour; but the men engaged in this praiseworthy, but difficult and dangerous, task felt the effects of the gases which had been generated below, and were compelled to suspend operations till a ventilating apparatus, composed of cloth, and called a cloth bratticing, could be arranged. This was completed on Wednesday afternoon; and the shaft being cleared to some extent of gas, the terrible tragedy was revealed in all its horrors. Three pitmen (volunteers) went down, penetrated the obstruction, got into the yard seam by the engine-drift, and found men lying dead at the furnace. They pushed their way through. The air was bad. Within the door they found a large body of men sleeping the sleep of death. They retreated and came to bank with the appalling intelligence.

Those who went all through the works found no living man, but a hecatomb of dead bodies. The bulk of the bodies were lying in the gallery near the shaft. Families were lying in groups; children in the arms of their fathers; brothers with brothers. Most of them looked placid as if asleep; but higher up, near the furnace, some tall stout men seemed to have died hard. The corn-bins were all cleared. Some few of the men had a little corn in their pockets. A pony was lying dead among the men, but untouched.

To the usual danger of foul air was added the inroad of water into the workings. The "yard seam," where most of the men had taken refuge, was not reached till the 22nd, and those lying there bore the appearance of having been suffocated two or three days before.

Indications of piety and of courage were not wanting from the first. Two of the men who were knocked out of the cage were partly buried in the ruins which choked the shaft. The elder Sharp could be heard praying among the rubbish where he was buried. Thomas Watson, who was hanging by the broken cage, heard the moans and prayers of his unfortunate companion, and though much bruised by the wood that had struck him, he dropped himself down the pump on to the rubbish in which poor Sharp was buried, and prayed with him until he expired, though every moment Watson himself expected to be engulfed where he stood. After Sharp's death, Watson scrambled back to the cage, where he hung for many hours, till he and his other two companions were rescued.

Amos, the "overman," and one of his deputies named Tennant, a fine fellow who had been to the Australian gold mines but had returned, would, it was believed, lead the men out of the pit and to a place secure from the water. This they succeeded in doing, and, like true captains of industry, they died at their post. They had struggled up through the furnace drift after the accident, and had hacked and hewn at the obstruction in the shaft until the Sunday afternoon, when a fall of stone took place in the shaft which drove them away, and they were found lying at the post of danger, but the post of duty—the furnace—having died in mortal agony, the men and boys "in by" having subsequently slept quietly away.

The Hartley colliers had the character of being steady and thoughtful men. There was no public-house within a mile of the village; many of the miners were abstainers from intoxicating drinks, and several of them were local preachers and class leaders among the Methodist communities. A number of the dead were lying in rows on each side, all quiet and placid as if in a deep sleep after a heavy day's work. In a book taken from the pocket of the overman was a memorandum dated "Friday afternoon (17), half-past two o'clock. Edward Armstrong, Thomas Gledson, John Hardie, Thomas Bell, and others, took extremely ill. We had also a prayer-meeting at a quarter to two, when Tibbs, H. Sharp, J. Campbell, H. Gibson, and William Palmer—(here the sentence was incomplete). Tibbs exhorted to us again, and Sharp also."

Messages to families were found scratched on flasks and boxes: there appeared to have been no little calm and peace at meeting death.

The scene as the bodies were slowly rescued and brought to the bank was very painful. About five thousand people had assembled by that time, and the widows and orphans knew the worst. Occasionally a stifled groan or a hysteric cry would be heard from the crowd as some well-known face slowly rose up out of the dark chasm, but for the most part a reverent silence was kept throughout. With the shaft in its present condition it was found impossible to lower a cage of the usual character, and the bodies were brought up in slings passed under the armpits. As each came to earth it was unslung, wrapped in a winding-sheet, and placed in a coffin which stood by on a truck. As each was identified his name was chalked on the coffin, and it was wheeled away from the platform and delivered over to the friends who stood waiting outside the barrier. The bodies of those men who lived in the village hard by were carried there at once, and for others who came from a distance there were hearses and carts in waiting. Still, this process was slow, and in leaving the colliery to get to the railway station the path lay through long lines of piled-up coffins, some of which had already received their ghastly burden, and others were standing ready for it. The coffins were made in a peculiar fashion, the head part opening out on a hinge, so that it might be readily turned back for the relatives to cast a last look on the features of the dead. Almost every cottage had a coffin, some two, one five; and one poor woman had lost a husband, five sons, and a boy whom they had brought up and educated. Most of the funerals took place on Sunday at Earsdon Church, in a piece of ground given by the Duke of Northumberland. The scene was solemn and deeply touching as the relations followed the coffins to the graves, singing the hymn commencing,

"O God, our help in ages past."

Deep sympathy was everywhere manifested on behalf of the bereaved sufferers, and by no one more than by the bereaved Queen at Osborne, who directed that intelligence should be constantly conveyed to her, and whose first message said she was "most anxious to hear that there are hopes of saving the poor people in the colliery, for whom her heart bleeds."

On the sad Sunday of the funerals a letter, addressed to Mr. Carr, the head-viewer of the colliery, by command of Her Majesty, was read by the incumbent of Earsdon at a large religious meeting held on the pit-head.

"OSBORNE, *Jan.* 23, 1862.

"The Queen, in the midst of her own overwhelming grief, has taken the deepest interest in the mournful accident at Hartley, and up to the last had hoped that at least a considerable number of the poor people might have been recovered alive. The appalling news since received has afflicted the Queen very much. Her Majesty commands me to say that her tenderest sympathy is with the poor widows and mothers, and that her own misery only makes her feel the more for them. Her Majesty hopes that everything will be done as far as possible to alleviate their distress, and Her Majesty will have a sad satisfaction in assisting in such a measure."

There were 103 widows and 257 children left destitute, while the number of sisters, parents, and other relatives who had relied for support on those who had perished, made the total 407. Her Majesty had readily sent £200 towards their relief, and other subscriptions quickly followed. The large sum of £81,000 was ultimately subscribed, a fourth part of which was contributed to a fund opened by the Lord Mayor at the Mansion-House. Of course the large coal-owners, many of the mining engineers, the Earl of Durham, the Duke of Northumberland, and others, contributed largely; and the London Stock Exchange subscribed nearly £1000 in a single day.—"*Fifty Years of Social and Political Progress.*"

THOMAS ARCHER.

THERE are some persons who, from a mistaken view of consequences, are always chary of praise. They fancy it will puff up with conceit the one thus favoured, or lead him to think that he needs no further improvements in that particular direction. So their children or their dependents go on from day to day, unconscious of any pleasure their efforts may afford, uncheered by any kindly encouragement, uninspired by the thought or hope of giving satisfaction. No greater mistake could be made.

To Autumn.

SEASON of mists and mellow fruitfulness!
    Close bosom-friend of the maturing sun ;
Conspiring with him how to load and bless
    With fruit the vines that round the thatch-eaves run ;

To bend with apples the moss'd cottage-trees,
    And fill all fruit with ripeness to the core ;
      To swell the gourd, and plump the hazel shells
With a sweet kernel ; to set budding more,

And still more, later flowers for the bees,
Until they think warm days will never cease,
  For summer has o'er-brimm'd their clammy cells.

Who hath not seen thee oft amid thy store?
 Sometimes whoever seeks abroad may find
Thee sitting careless on a granary floor,
 Thy hair soft-lifted by the winnowing wind;
Or on a half-reap'd furrow sound asleep,
 Drowsed with the fume of poppies, while thy hook
  Spares the next swath and all its twined flowers;
And sometimes like a gleaner thou dost keep
 Steady thy laden head across a brook;
Or by a cider-press, with patient look,
 Thou watchest the last oozings, hours by hours.

Where are the songs of spring? Ay, where are they?
 Think not of them, thou hast thy music too,
While barrèd clouds bloom the soft-dying day,
 And touch the stubble-plains with rosy hue;
Then in a wailful choir the small gnats mourn
 Among the river sallows, borne aloft
  Or sinking as the light wind lives or dies;
And full-grown lambs loud bleat from hilly bourn;
 Hedge-crickets sing; and now with treble soft
The red-breast whistles from a garden-croft,
 And gathering swallows twitter in the skies.

JOHN KEATS.

WHOLESOME ENJOYMENTS.—All real and wholesome enjoyments possible to man have been just as possible to him since first he was made of the earth as they are now; and they are possible to him chiefly in peace. To watch the corn grow and the blossom set; to draw hard breath over ploughshare and spade; to read, to think, to love, to hope, to pray—these are the things to make man happy; they have always had the power of doing these—they never will have power to do more.
RUSKIN.

A CERTAIN minister believes n the efficacy of prayer, but he does not appear to believe in praying to heaven for things which will be furnished in the natural course of events without being prayed for. Speaking to a number of his parishioners, he indicated his feelings by stating:

"I have often prayed that I might be kept humble; I never prayed that I might be poor. I could trust Buttonwood Street Church for that."

The Young Couple.

A WEDDING FIFTY YEARS AGO.

THERE is to be a wedding this morning at the corner-house in the terrace. The pastry-cook's people have been there half-a-dozen times already. All day yesterday there was a great stir and bustle, and they were up this morning as soon as it was light. Miss Emma Fielding is going to be married to young Mr. Harvey.

Heaven alone can tell in what bright colours this marriage is painted upon the mind of the little housemaid at number six, who has hardly slept a wink all night with thinking of it, and now stands on the unswept doorsteps, leaning upon her broom and looking wistfully towards the enchanted house.

Nothing short of omniscience can divine what visions of the baker, or the greengrocer, or the smart and most insinuating butterman, are flitting across her mind—what thoughts of how she would dress on such an occasion if she were a lady, of how she would dress if she were only a bride, of how cook would dress, being bridesmaid conjointly with her sister "in place" at Fulham, and how the clergyman, deeming them so many ladies, would be quite humble and respectful. What day-dreams of hope and happiness,—of life being one perpetual holiday, with no master and no mistress to grant or withhold it, of every Sunday being a Sunday out, of pure freedom as to curls and ringlets, and no obligation to hide fine heads of hair in caps,—what pictures of happiness, vast and immense to her, but utterly ridiculous to us, bewilder the brain of the little housemaid at number six, all called into existence by the wedding at the corner!

We smile at such things, and so we should, though perhaps for a better reason than commonly presents itself. It should be pleasant to us to know that there are notions of happiness so moderate and limited, since upon those who entertain them happiness and lightness of heart are very easily bestowed.

But the little housemaid is awakened from her reverie, for forth from the door of the magical corner-house there runs towards her, all fluttering in smart new dress and streaming ribands, her friend Jane Adams, who comes all out of breath to redeem a solemn promise of taking her in, under cover of the confusion, to see the breakfast-table set forth in state, and—sight of sights!—her young mistress ready dressed for church.

And there, in good truth, when they have stolen upstairs on tiptoe and edged themselves in at the chamber door—there is Miss Emma "looking like the sweetest picter," in a white chip bonnet and orange-flower, and all other elegances becoming a bride (with the make, shape, and quality of every article of which the girl is perfectly familiar in one moment, and never forgets to her

dying day); and there is Miss Emma's mamma in tears, and Miss Emma's papa comforting her, and saying how that of course she has been long looking forward to this, and how happy she ought to be; and there, too, is Miss Emma's sister with her arms round her neck, and the other bridesmaid, all smiles and tears, quieting the children, who would cry more but that they are so finely dressed, and yet sob for fear sister Emma should be taken away—and it is all so affecting, that the two servant-girls cry more than anybody; and Jane Adams, sitting down upon the stairs, when they have crept away, declares that her legs tremble so that she don't know what to do, and that she will say for Miss Emma, that she never had a hasty word from her, and that she does hope and pray she may be happy.

But Jane soon comes round again, and then surely there never was anything like the breakfast-table, glittering with plate and china, and set out with flowers and sweets, and long-necked bottles, in the most sumptuous and dazzling manner. In the centre, too, is the mighty charm, the cake, glistening with frosted sugar, and garnished beautiful. They agree that there ought to be a little Cupid under one of the barley-sugar temples, or at least two hearts and an arrow; but, with this exception, there is nothing to wish for, and a table could not be handsomer. As they arrive at this conclusion, who should come in but Mr. John, to whom Jane says that its only Anne, from number six; and John says *he* knows, for he's often winked his eye down the area, which causes Anne to blush and look confused. She is going away, indeed; when Mr. John will have it that she must drink a glass of wine, and he says,—

"Never mind it's being early in the morning, it won't hurt her;" so they shut the door and pour out the wine; and Anne, drinking Jane's health, and adding,—

"And here's wishing you yours, Mr. John," drinks it in a great many sips— Mr. John all the time making jokes appropriate to the occasion.

At last Mr. John, who has waxed bolder by degrees, pleads the usage at weddings, and claims the privilege of a kiss, which he obtains after a great scuffle; and footsteps being now heard on the stairs, they disperse suddenly.

By this time a carriage has driven up to convey the bride to church, and Anne of number six, prolonging the process of "cleaning her door," has the satisfaction of beholding the bride and bridesmaids, and the papa and mamma hurry into the same and drive rapidly off. Nor is this all, for soon other carriages begin to arrive with a posse of company all beautifully dressed, at whom she could stand and gaze for ever; but having something else to do, is compelled to take one last long look and shut the street door.

And now the company have gone down to breakfast, and tears have given place to smiles, for all the corks are out of the long-necked bottles, and their contents are disappearing rapidly.

Miss Emma's papa is at the top of the table; Miss Emma's mamma at the bottom; and beside the latter are Miss Emma herself and her husband— admitted on all hands to be the handsomest and most interesting young couple ever known. All down both sides of the table, too, are various young ladies, beautiful to see, and various young gentlemen who seem to think so; and there, in a post of honour, is an unmarried aunt of Miss Emma's, reported to possess unheard of riches, and to have expressed vast testamentary intentions respecting her favourite niece and new nephew.

This lady has been very liberal and generous already, as the jewels worn by the bride abundantly testify, but that is nothing to what she means to do, or even to what she has done, for she put herself in close communication with the dressmaker three months ago, and prepared a wardrobe (with some articles worked by her own hands) fit for a princess. People may call her an old maid, and so she may be, but she is neither gross nor ugly for all that; on the contrary, she is very cheerful and pleasant-looking, and very kind and tender-hearted; which is no matter of surprise except to those who yield to popular prejudices without thinking why, and will never grow wiser and never know better.

Of all the company, though, none are more pleasant to behold or better pleased with themselves than two young children, who, in honour of the day, have seats among the guests. Of these, one is a little fellow of six or eight years old, brother to the bride, and the other a girl of the same age, or something younger, whom he calls "his wife." The real bride and bridegroom are not more devoted than they: he all love and attention, and she all blushes and fondness, toying with a little bouquet which he gave her this morning, and placing the scattered rose-leaves in her bosom with nature's own coquettishness. They have dreamt of each other in their quiet dreams, these children, and their little hearts have been nearly broken when the absent one has been dispraised in jest. When will there come in after-life a passion so earnest, generous, and true as theirs! What, even in its gentlest realities, can have the grace and charm that hover round such fairy lovers!

By this time the merriment and happiness of the feast have gained their height; certain ominous looks begin to be exchanged between the bridesmaids, and somehow it gets whispered about that the carriage which is to take the young couple into the country has arrived. Such members of the party as are most disposed to prolong its enjoyments affect to consider this a false alarm, but it turns out too true, being speedily confirmed, first by the retirement of the bride and a select file of intimates who are to prepare her for the journey, and secondly by the withdrawal of the ladies generally. To this there ensues a particularly awkward pause, in which everybody essays to be facetious, and nobody succeeds; at length the bridegroom makes a mysterious disappearance in obedience to some equally mysterious signal, and the table is deserted.

Now, for at least six weeks past it has been solemnly devised and settled that the young people should go away in secret; but they no sooner appear without the door than the drawing-room windows are blocked up with ladies waving their handkerchiefs and kissing their hands, and the dining-room panes with gentleman's faces beaming farewell in every queer variety of its expression. The hall and steps are crowded with servants in white favours, mixed up with particular friends and relations who have darted out to say good-bye; and foremost in the group are the tiny lovers, arm-and-arm, thinking, with fluttering hearts, what happiness it would be to dash away together in that gallant coach, and never part again.

The bride has barely time for one hurried glance at her old home, when the steps rattle, the door slams, the horses clatter on the pavement, and they have left it far away.

A knot of women-servants still remain clustered in the hall, whispering among themselves, and there of course is Anne from number six, who has made another escape on some plea or other, and been an admiring witness of the departure. There are two points on which Anne expatiates over and over again, without the smallest appearance of fatigue, or intending to leave off; one is, that she "never see in all her life such a—oh, such a angel of a gentleman as Mr. Harvey!"—and the other, that she "can't tell how it is, but it don't seem a bit like work-a-day, or a Sunday neither—it's all so unsettled and unregular."

CHARLES DICKENS.

How to preserve Youth.

A HITHERTO unpublished letter of Longfellow's has appeared in the *Pall Mall Gazette*. It was written to the mistress of a girls' school in Chicago a year or two before his death, and runs as follows:—"To those who ask how I can write 'so many things that sound as if I were as happy as a boy,' please say that there is in this neighbourhood or neighbouring town a pear tree planted by Governor Endicott two hundred years ago, and that this tree still bears fruit which it is impossible to distinguish from the young tree in flavour. I suppose that the tree makes new wood every year, so that some part of it is always young. Perhaps that is the way with some men when they grow old. I hope it is so with me. I am glad to hear that your boys and girls continue to take so great an interest in poetry. That is a very good sign, for poetry may be said to be the flower and perfume of thought, and a perpetual delight, clothing all the mere commonplaces of life 'with golden exhalations of the dawn.'"

The Comic Literature of the Japanese.

THERE are few foreigners who have, as yet, acquired a sufficient knowledge not only of the language, but also of the daily life, of these people, so as to be able to understand their irrepressible love of the grotesque, the humorous, and witticisms; but those who have succeeded in mastering the first difficulties have been amply repaid for their trouble and encouraged to continue their studies.

The proverbial and epigrammatic phrases of daily life, even of the least educated classes, are worthy of the student's attention; and their caricatures and other sketches are interesting, even to our artists, for a few apparently offhand dashes with the pencil give a most graphic and complete sketch.

A word-picture on this topic is no easy task to be completed, but it may be reasonably hoped that ere long the pictures themselves will be given to the world; for hitherto, beyond a few conventional designs of frequent recurrence, such as Jarvis gives from the Hoku Sai series, nothing has as yet been published of this inexhaustible store.

During the change of government, and the consequent breaking up of the feudal system, political enmity found vent, to some extent through the pencil of the caricaturist, as well as the pen of the satirist, but was of necessity somewhat cloaked, officials being despotic, private individuals revengeful, and assassination not uncommon.

The numerous clans, the leading princes and officials, were usually depicted as children, the scanty clothing being printed in colours and in patterns so like the cognisance (each clan having a distinct badge) as to be unmistakable, or in some cases alluding to some *sobriquet*.

For instance, the Prince of Aidza was represented with candles crossed, his province being celebrated for this article, and he having set fire to the imperial palace, when it was his duty to guard it; others show leaves of plants, vegetables, etc. (as we would give a leek to a Welshman).

One of these coloured sketches, in seven or eight colours, represents an apothecary's shop. The bald-pated and learned-looking doctor is seated on a patch of carpet, with the rows of drawers and curious bottles and jars as a background; he is feeling the pulse of a truculent-looking warrior, a gentleman (?) with long arms and two huge swords, evidently a free lance, ready to fight for what he can seize. The peculiar cut of his clothes, and the mode of wearing his hair, denote that he affects the style of the class who having nothing to lose, and hoping to gain much, have become the "self-appointed regenerators of their country." Others are waiting their turn. One seems all eyes; he is meant to represent one of the princes who, with his followers, waited and watched. Next to him is one all mouth; that is the great talker who does nothing else. Then comes one without arms; one clan who refused to take part, the excuse being they had no weapons or money. There is one without legs; a far-off clan could not march to the scene of strife in time. All came to

be cured—that is, after the government had been once more established, to receive a share of the confiscated property of their active opponents. In the background sits a little boy, crying, and evidently blind and helpless; this is the young emperor, ignored, and merely an excuse and blind for usurped authority.

Another picture represents the months of the year, the twelve signs of the Zodiac in costume.

A battle between the articles of native production and old-time pattern, and foreign articles, is most amusing. Paper lanterns opposed to kerosine lamps;

a native with a bag of Japanese rice conquers a Chinese with a sack of Saigon rice; a newsvendor demolishes the stand of a fortune-teller; a native ship is in collision with a foreign steamship; a sharp encounter between a gingham umbrella and a paper one, and so on.

Two groups of boys bespattering each other with mud depicts the quarrels of the clans who were victorious, and fight amongst themselves for the plunder.

A sharp hit at effete Buddhism is one sketch depicting the most popular divinities and their votaries. A dancing and singing girl is praying for additional charms wherewith to draw money from her admirers; the artisan for increased wages and shorter hours; the actor for public applause; the bankrupt for restoration to fortune; the student for a royal road to learning, especially for knowledge of the learning of the bearded foreigners; a servant-girl wishes a celebrated actor may fall in love with her and reciprocate her love for him; the deities, meanwhile, with a smirk on their faces, await contributions; in the background the priests are devouring the offerings in kind of the faithful.

Spiritualism is represented by little sprites, agents of good and of evil, who by invisible strings lead the weak-minded, and there is often a struggle between the two for possession of a mortal. A series of sketches by some Japanese Hogarth, where the Rake's Progress, the Two Apprentices, and kindred subjects are depicted, gives a very true picture of native life in many phases, good and bad.

The revival of the ancient cults, the disestablishment of the Buddhist church, and the decline of the priesthood, are represented in a cartoon, where the temple's idols and other religious paraphernalia, also the instruments of torture in the numerous purgatories, are being broken up and sold to dealers in old building materials, old metal, etc. Meanwhile, the divinities are having their hair cropped, and are robing themselves in garments of foreign fashion and material, some reading "News of the World" and studying sketches of foreign ships, machinery, etc.

This is the more modern adaptation of the old-fashioned humour.

Illustrated proverbs. One of these is of a jealous woman, at dead of night, trying to bewitch her lover and rival, but she drops down dead with fright, with the legend, "Witchcraft may dig a grave for both." Again, an ox runs off with some garment on his horns, followed by women, and takes refuge in a temple— "Only to church when driven or dragged."

Wasted energy is shown by a warrior in armour shooting at a rock thinking it a tiger. Blind men face dangers they see not—three blind beggars stepping over a sleeping dragon.

A group of blind men discussing works of art might be reproduced here at home, and the hint taken with advantage.

The robber, with gory sword, frightened by suddenly approaching a stone idol, of some wayside shrine, shows the guilty conscience.

A man smashing jelly with a huge sledge-hammer—great efforts to produce little effect.

Pride and poverty shown by a princess in robes of state greedily devouring a mean potato.

A man holding an angry controversy with an ape — suggestive of Darwinism.

The oft-seen ghouls with long noses have been ever misunderstood. This is in allusion to the pride of those conscious of their own attainments; thus professors of literature or experts are depicted sparring with huge, long nasal appendages.

A man of learning and theories, literary called in Japan, "a book insect," is pictured writing "Take care of fire" on a house already in flames, to the intense amusement of the fire-fiend who is fanning the conflagration.

The intense love of fun of this light-hearted and single-minded race is ever rising to the surface, like sparkling wine. A broad grin will be easily produced on slight pretext, and the sweet method of clinching an argument, calming the rising temper, subduing impatience, or settling a knotty point, is to cap it with a sprightly joke, a well-timed epigram, or a clever play upon words.—*From Notes of a Lecture by C. Pfoundes, F.R.G.S., Author of "Fu Se Mimi Bukino," etc.*

"WITH respect to duels, indeed, I have my own ideas. Few things in this so surprising world strike me with more surprise. Two little visual spectra of men, hovering with insecure enough cohesion in the midst of the UNFATHOMABLE, and to dissolve therein, at any rate, very soon, make pause at a distance of twelve paces asunder, whirl round, and, simultaneously, by the cunningest mechanism explode one another into dissolution, and offhand become air, and non-extant! Deuce on it (*ver-damut*), the little spitfires! Nay, I think, with old Hugo von Trimberg: 'God must needs laugh outright, could such a thing be, to see His wondrous mannikins here below.'" CARLYLE.

HE that has not religion to govern his morality is not a dram better than my mastiff dog,—so long as you stroke him and please him, and do not pinch him, he will play with you as finely as may be; he is a very good *moral* mastiff—but, if you hurt him, he will fly in your face, and tear out your throat.

THE HYPOCRITE.—He is the stranger's saint, the neighbour's disease, the blot of goodness, a rotten stick on a dark night; the poppy in a cornfield; an ill-tempered candle with a great snuff, that in going out smells ill; an angel abroad, a devil at home; and worse when an angel than when a devil.—*From Bishop Hall's "Delineations of Character."*

The Widow of Naples.

THERE dwelt in Naples a matron named Corsina, wife of a worthy cavalier known as Roamondo del Balzo. Now, it pleased Heaven to take the husband of Corsina, leaving her an only child, named Carlo, who was in every way the counterpart of his father. Thus the mother resolved that he should inherit all her fortune, and determined to send him to study at Bologna, in order that he might learn all the accomplishments of his age. With this view she secured a master for her son, furnished him with books and every other necessary, and, in the name of Heaven, sent him to Bologna. There the youth made rapid progress,

and in a brief time became a ripe scholar; and all the students admired him for his genius, and loved him for the excellence of his life. In course of time the boy became a young man, and, having finished his studies, prepared himself to return home to Naples, when he suddenly fell into a sickness which defeated the skill of all the physicians of Bologna. When Carlo found that death was inevitable, he thus ruminated with himself:—

"I am not afflicted for my own sake, but for my disconsolate mother, who has no child save me, in whom she has garnered all her earthly hopes, and from whom she looks for future support and for the regeneration of our house. And when she knows that I am dead, and that, too, without her even seeing me, sure I am she herself will suffer a thousand deaths."

Thus did he lament more for his mother than for himself. Now, dwelling on these thoughts, he conceived a plan by which he hoped to lessen the bitterness of his death to his parent ; to which end he wrote a letter in the following words :—

"MY DEAREST MOTHER,—I entreat you that you will be pleased to send me a shirt made by the hands of the most cheerful woman in Naples,—a woman who shall be free from every sorrow—every care."

This letter was despatched to his mother, who instantly disposed herself to fulfil the desires of her son. She searched throughout Naples, and where, from outward appearance, she hoped to meet the woman free from sorrow, there she learnt a story of some lurking grief—some deep, though well-disguised affliction.

At this, Corsina said,—

"I see there is no one free from misery—there is no one who hath not her tribulation ; and they, too, who seem the happiest, have the greatest cause for wretchedness."

With this conviction she answered the letter of her son, excusing herself for the non-fulfilment of her commission, assuring him that, with all her search, she could not discover the person whom he desired might make the garment.

In a few days she received the tidings of her son's death. It was then that she felt the full wisdom of the lesson he had taught her, and with meekness and resignation bowed to the will of God.

THE "SONG OF SIXPENCE."—Mr. Tyler thus applies to this nursery rhyme the way in which myths, or old-world stories, are explained. The four-and-twenty blackbirds, he supposes, are the four-and-twenty hours, and the pie which holds them is the underlying earth, covered with the overarching sky. How true a touch of Nature it is, when the day breaks the birds begin to sing !

The king is the sun, and his counting out his money is pouring out the sunshine, like showers of gold. The queen is the moon, and the transparent honey the moonlight. The maid is the rosy-fingered dawn, who rises before the sun (her master), and hangs out the clouds (his clothes) across the sky. The blackbird who ends the tale in so tragic a way by snipping off her nose, is the hour of sunset.

THE DAY'S WORK.— Every day in this world has its work ; and every day as it rises fresh out of eternity keeps putting to each of us the question afresh : What will you do before to-day has sunk into eternity and nothingness again?

Yesterday, last week, last year—they are gone. Yesterday, for example, was such a day as never was before, and never can be again. Out of darkness and eternity it was born a new, fresh day ; into darkness and eternity it sank again for ever. It had a voice of its own calling to us, its own work, its own duties. What were we doing yesterday?

There is a past which is gone for ever. But there is a future which is still our own.

REV. F. W. ROBERTSON.

Every Moment's Duty.

No man can order his life, for it comes flowing over him from behind. But if it lay before us, and we could watch its current approaching from a long distance, what would we do with it before it had reached the flow? In likewise a man thinks foolishly who imagines he could have done this and that with his own character and development, if he had but known this and that in time. Were he as good as he thinks himself wise, he could but at best have produced a fine cameo in very low relief; with a work in the round, which he is meant to be, he could have done nothing.

The one secret of life and development is not to devise and plan, but to fall in with the forces at work—to do every moment's duty aright—that being the part in the process allotted to us; and let come—not what will, for there is no such thing—but what the Eternal Thought wills for each of us, has intended in each of us from the first.

If men would but believe that they are in process of creation, and consent to be made—let the Maker handle them as the potter his clay, yielding themselves in respondent motion and submissive hopeful action with the turning of His wheel—they would ere long find themselves able to welcome every pressure of that hand upon them, even when it was felt in pain, and sometimes not only to believe but to recognise the divine end in view, the bringing of a son into glory; whereas, behaving like children who struggle and scream while their mother washes and dresses them, they find they have to be washed and dressed notwithstanding, and with the more discomfort; they may even have to find themselves set half naked and but half dried in a corner, to come to their right minds, and ask to be finished.

GEORGE MAC DONALD.

FASHION.—Fashion is a poor vocation. Its creed, that idleness is a privilege and work a disgrace, is among the deadliest errors. Without depth of thought, or earnestness of feeling, or strength of purpose, living an unreal life, sacrificing substance to show, substituting the factitious for the natural, mistaking a crowd for society, finding its chief pleasure in ridicule, and exhausting its ingenuity in killing time—fashion is amongst the last influences under which a human being who respects himself or comprehends the great end of life would desire to be placed.

CHANNING.

How to keep Christmas.

Do not those among us who have been seared by the great branding-iron of worldliness feel a kind of shame when we talk the common cant of "Christmas" being "all very well for children"? Isn't there something in the large-eyed, serious, wistful look of the little ones, when they hear such a remark, which is wonderfully akin to the sad deprecating smile of the old folks, who feel somehow that there is a deep meaning in the Christmas observances, which makes it profanity to speak of them with contempt, or even with a self-satisfied depreciation? The old and the young meet very close together on the Holy Eve—the threshold, as it were, of the byre of Bethlehem. Both may fancy they hear the angels sing—the children of seven and of seventy alike seeming to have a certain solemn familiarity with the heavenly song, in which, to the latter, some voices once known on earth will blend—some forms once loved appear in guise of heavenly light; while often, the former, ponder mysteriously, as though they were yet not quite out of the faint border-land of glory, whence they may have come.

There is something very wonderful to us, who are perpetually wondering at something, in the imperturbable acceptance of mysteries by a child. What is a puzzle to us seems, in a fashion which we have forgotten, to be clear as food and air and light to many an infant. We find this out partly when we contrive all kinds of surprises for the little ones, and are disappointed that they so often fail, the truth being that children are too ready to accept the infinite possibilities of the universe to be in ecstasies over a tricky toy. Why, even a new live animal will but just set a baby pleasantly reflecting and establishing proper relations—where we should be trying to construct our own theories on the science of things as they ought to be if nobody knew any more than we do.

Here again the child-likeness in young and old comes close together—the circumference of experience touches the centre of experiment, and the circles blend, and radiate love and mutual trust. Therein, if we can indeed become as little children, we shall inherit a blessing—inherit the earth—inherit the kingdom of heaven—where the power is service, the glory love and self-sacrifice—the kingdom itself, grand and immeasurable self-forgetfulness.

One dare scarcely—at the commencement of our round of Christmas feasts, and before joining in our games—say all that might be said of the *very* meaning with which the season should come to us, and all the fulness of suggestion which it imparts to our highest as well as to our commonest pleasures.

Commonest! No pleasure would or could be common, in any low sense, in the light of the child-likeness, and is it not this manifestation of the divine child-likeness which makes the true interpretation of the holy day?

Amidst the gleam of lights, and holly, and winter wreaths—with the sound of music and sweet honest laughter—at the well-filled board or round the blazing fire—in the house of feasting and of song, the thought of this should keep our pleasures pure, and make them all the heartier.

Yes, and in the house of mourning the same divine light may break with the dawn of a new heaven and a new earth—a gleam of glory from the land where there is neither age nor youth, but the same blessed child-likeness upon all.

It is when we come to realize this meaning in the day which we all need to keep right joyously that we shall be able, in spirit and in truth, to cry to each other: "A MERRY CHRISTMAS, AND A HAPPY NEW YEAR."

THOMAS ARCHER.

www.ingramcontent.com/pod-product-compliance
Lightning Source LLC
Chambersburg PA
CBHW031338230426
43670CB00006B/369